Praise for *Powering Up*

Powering Up Your School deliberately and proudly conceptualises schools as centres of learning, rejecting all the distracting paraphernalia of narrow metrics and crushing accountability. It's about how we empower young people as learners ready to take their place in a complex world, and provides a powerful and practical mandate for teachers and leaders to make it happen. The ambition of the book, combined with the credibility of its team of authors, makes it a compelling read.

Geoff Barton, General Secretary, Association of School and College Leaders, UK

Energising and refreshing in equal measure, *Powering Up Your School* is a down-to-earth and practical book for all those school leaders and teachers who want to help their students to become more powerful learners. The insights into how leaders can help to develop an improvement culture among both staff and students are particularly valuable.

Steve Munby, Visiting Professor, University College London, UK

Guy Claxton and his co-authors have written a remarkable book. Drawing on decades of rich learning from approaches such as Building Learning Power, the authors have created a powerful framework within which to think about how create a school culture that promotes what they call "results plus".

This open, honest, and very personal book is not a one-size-fits-all blueprint of what leaders should do. Nor is it another set of generic leadership attributes or processes. *Powering Up Your School* is a book firmly rooted in the belief that a culture that enables every adult and child to develop powerful personal habits, can unleash huge potential in our next generation of leaders, teachers, and their students.

Using powerful practical examples that don't gloss over how hard change can be, the authors set out what an effective change process could look like: developing clarity about the "why"; building buy-in through wide discussion; and creating long-term change that leads to deep, sustainable benefits. But this book is far from being a prescriptive manual. As the authors suggest, think "garden" rather than "model aeroplane kit". It's about creating the conditions within which children and adults can all thrive and grow.

Written by highly respected and successful school leaders, *Powering Up Your School* is a must-read for anyone who believes our role as educators is to enable each and every pupil to achieve more than just a great set of exam results.

Andy Buck, founder, Leadership Matters, UK

For those seeking to move beyond the paradigm of judging a good education by academic outcomes – and in Australia that would be inclusive of all independent schools that offer a liberal, holistic educational experience – this book provides practical, honest, and realistic insights into the journeys that school leaders have taken to transform their school's provision and equip students with the dispositions, skills, and knowledge that they will need in order to live fulfilling and satisfying lives.

The authors understand that one size does not fit all, and so while driven by similar educational visions, each leader's pathway is different – thereby opening up a range of possibilities, approaches, challenges, and solutions for readers. As a result, the book abounds with collective wisdom that is very readable and accessible, and inviting of a collaborative and distributive style of leadership.

I have no doubt that *Powering Up Your School* will resonate with all school leaders and provide inspiration for determined, resilient, and visionary leadership.

Beth Blackwood, CEO, Association of Heads of Independent Schools of Australia (AHISA Ltd)

Educators in many countries and regions buy in to the philosophy of the Learning Power Approach, and the essential message in *Powering Up Your School* is that school reform is a kind of culture change that should be pursued by all educators who wish for the all-round growth of their students.

From this book, school leaders will obtain detailed ideas about how to achieve sustainable development of their schools for generations to come. Readers will be convinced of the potential of the LPA and, via the various case studies, gain invaluable tips on how to accomplish it. They will also learn how best to cultivate the approach in their own school setting by responding to the invitations to reflect that are scattered throughout.

School leaders worldwide will learn a lot from this book.

Toshiyuki Kihara, Professor of the Graduate School of Professional Teacher Education,
Osaka Kyoiku University, Japan

Grounded in research, rooted in practice, and oriented to the future, *Powering Up Your School* is an excellent guide to help school leaders bring about much-needed changes in education. In particular, it offers a combination of professional guidance and personal reflections to leaders interested in implementing powerful approaches to learning.

Yong Zhao, Foundation Distinguished Professor, University of Kansas, USA, and Professor in Educational Leadership, Melbourne Graduate School of Education, Australia

Powering Up Your School is filled with insights, ideas, wonderings, honest reflections, and useful tools and resources. It is an inspiring read and a valuable practical contribution to current thinking about schools as learning organisations.

Louise Stoll, Professor of Professional Learning, University College London Institute of Education, UK

When it comes to growing as a professional, the light-bulb moments and the most telling advancements often occur when research collides with practice. *Powering Up Your School* illustrates the benefits of such a combination, and the fruits of Guy Claxton's lifelong work are there for all to see in the real-life experiences of a range of school leaders driving their schools onwards and upwards.

The stories which feature throughout the book are strong and are presented in a succinct and targeted way which is easily accessible. Furthermore, readers are given the opportunity to get to know the leaders and their stories over time and in context: the gradual reveal of their full stories is engaging.

Best of all, the book doesn't simply paint a rosy picture where the world is entirely wonderful; instead, the authors communicate the real work that is involved in changing school cultures, practices, and, ultimately, student learning. It is real work that has its challenges, but we see in *Powering Up Your School* that it is very possible, in different ways and in different contexts, and exceptionally rewarding.

Darryl Buchanan, education leader in New South Wales, Australia

POWERING UP YOUR SCHOOL

The Learning Power Approach to School Leadership

Guy Claxton, Jann Robinson, Rachel Macfarlane, Graham Powell, Gemma Goldenberg, and Robert Cleary

Foreword by Michael Fullan

Crown House Publishing Limited
www.crownhouse.co.uk

First published by

Crown House Publishing

Crown Buildings, Bancyfelin, Carmarthen, Wales, SA33 5ND, UK

www.crownhouse.co.uk

and

Crown House Publishing Company LLC

PO Box 2223, Williston, VT 05495, USA

www.crownhousepublishing.com

© Guy Claxton, Jann Robinson, Rachel Macfarlane, Graham Powell, Gemma Goldenberg, Robert Cleary, and Crown House Publishing, 2020

The rights of Guy Claxton, Jann Robinson, Rachel Macfarlane, Graham Powell, Gemma Goldenberg, and Robert Cleary to be identified as the authors of this work have been asserted by them in accordance with the Copyright, Designs and Patents Act 1988.

First published 2020.

All rights reserved. Except as permitted under current legislation no part of this work may be photocopied, stored in a retrieval system, published, performed in public, adapted, broadcast, transmitted, recorded or reproduced in any form or by any means, without the prior permission of the copyright owners. Enquiries should be addressed to Crown House Publishing Limited.

Cover image © Svyatoslav Lypynskyy – stock.adobe.com. Page i: "The Leader" from *Sky in the Pie* by Roger McGough reprinted by permission of Peters Fraser & Dunlop (www.petersfraserdunlop.com) on behalf of Roger McGough. Page 52: Figure 2.1 © Juan and Becky Carlzon. Page 94: illustration © Karolina Varvarovska. Page 129: Figure 5.1 is used with kind permission of Neil Tetley. Page 132: Figure 5.4 used with kind permission of Surbiton High School and Hannah Horwood. Page 133: Figure 5.5 used with kind permission of Louise Blondell. Page 134: Figure 5.6 used with kind permission of Neil Tetley. Page 142: Figures 5.7 and 5.8 used with kind permission of Sue Plant. Page 144: Figure 5.9 used with kind permission of Sue Plant. Page 145: Figure 5.10 used with kind permission of The Arthur Terry School (https://www.arthurterry.bham.sch.uk/). Page 162: Figure 6.1, the Learning Pit is © James Nottingham and used with kind permission. Page 163: Figure 6.3, the Blob Tree is © Pip Wilson and Ian Long and used with kind permission. Page 176: Figure 6.4 is taken from Powell, Chambers, and Baxter, *Pathways to Classroom Observation* © TLO Limited and used with kind permission. Page 195: Figure 7.1 used with kind permission of Wren Academy and Gavin Smith. Page 222: the photograph is used with kind permission of Woolenwich Infant and Nursery School and Usha Dhorajiwala. Page 253: Figure 9.6 is © TLO Limited and used with kind permission. Page 254: Figure 9.7 is © TLO Limited and used with kind permission. Page 266: Figure 10.2 is © Expansive Education Network and used with kind permission of Bill Lucas.

Quotes from Ofsted and Department for Education documents used in this publication have been approved under an Open Government Licence. Please see: http://www.nationalarchives.gov.uk/doc/open-government-licence/version/3/.

Crown House Publishing has no responsibility for the persistence or accuracy of URLs for external or third-party websites referred to in this publication, and does not guarantee that any content on such websites is, or will remain, accurate or appropriate.

British Library Cataloguing-in-Publication Data

A catalogue entry for this book is available from the British Library.

Print ISBN: 978-178583456-1
Mobi ISBN: 978-178583488-2
ePub ISBN: 978-178583489-9
ePDF ISBN: 978-178583490-5

LCCN 2020934543

Printed and bound in the UK by
TJ International, Padstow, Cornwall

To all the brave school principals we know, and the many more we don't, who are forging 21st century education every day in their schools

The Leader

I wanna be the leader
I wanna be the leader
Can I be the leader?
Can I? I can?
Promise? Promise?
Yippee I'm the leader
I'm the leader

OK what shall we do?

                                      Roger McGough

Foreword by Michael Fullan

The Learning Power Approach (LPA) is a highly beneficial and effective educational idea: one that transforms teaching and learning in schools. And *Powering Up Your School* shows school leaders exactly what it takes to turn that idea into a living reality that pervades the whole culture of the school. This remarkable, and oh so grounded, book is for those who know that something is wrong with the learning system in their schools but can't quite put their finger on the problem. *Powering Up Your School* enables readers not only to identify the problem, but also to use both hands – and their minds – to pursue and eventually grasp the solution.

This book is in my wheelhouse[1] because it is rooted in personal, practical experience. Guy Claxton's co-authors are all doers: school leaders who are already well on their way with the LPA. They take us on a reflective journey that reveals their own commitment in action – a journey that gets deeper and wider – both inside and outside their schools. From the beginning of the book we have the sense that these leaders want to be better than the systems which they inhabit. They are conscious that the big wide world is changing in ways that far outstrip the traditional practices of schools.

Early in the book the authors spell out the challenge they faced: how to design, research, pursue, establish, and evaluate powerful new approaches to learning in their schools. They knew that their model had to be coherent and comprehensive. And they also knew the most important change principle: getting buy-in from all concerned by creating an enterprise of excitement, exploration, and collaborative problem-solving. They knew that their job was to build a team of leader-developers. In my terms, they were working out how to use internal and external pressure to generate the widespread internal commitment that would produce both the solution and the means to get there.

Powering Up Your School poses key questions in every chapter, and offers prompts and suggestions, born of the authors' own experience, that encourage readers to find

---

1 A North American idiom meaning "very close to one's own area of interest or expertise".

and formulate their own ways forward. Early on, for example, they focus on how to create a staff culture of learning. The questions they pose are challenging; they get below the surface and stimulate you to understand your own setting more deeply, and to see how to change direction. But the authors also reveal how they grappled with and responded to these questions in their own situations. In so doing they not only leave the reader with some great ideas and insights, but also with the responsibility to address their own situations. Time and again the reader is taken to the key areas of powerful learning, shown the problems and types of solutions, and left with the insight and motivation to create initiatives for themselves that seem both urgent and doable.

What I especially like about this book is that it covers all the bases. For example, there is a strong chapter on how leaders might use external pressures to stimulate growth and change in internal cultures. This discussion is combined with eight powerful strategies for developing those cultures – all of which serve to strengthen teachers' daily habits and get them interacting in productive ways. The discussions always pinpoint practical strategies to foster focused, specific learning cultures – such as establishing a common shared language, targeting pedagogy, involving students, and much more.

Everything in the school becomes grist to the LPA mill. I could find no key aspect of the culture change process about which the authors didn't have something useful to say. There is a chapter on making learning stick, with four great ideas on how to use students as carriers of the new culture. The chapter on evidencing progress includes practical suggestions about how to determine impact, and use that information to embed the LPA ever more deeply. Many more specific ideas for charting and reflecting on the journey are presented in the appendix in a detailed self-assessment grid. There is a useful list of "wonderings" at the end of every chapter. Everything in this book resonates strongly with my, and my colleagues', own ideas about deep learning, and with our experience working to embed them in over 2,000 schools in eight countries so far.[2]

Throughout the book, we are taken on the authors' personal "odysseys" – warts and all. We hear them reflecting on the things they tried – their successes, failures, and lessons learned along the way – and constantly witness both their honesty and their

---

2   See www.michaelfullan.ca.

determination. When all is said and done, this is a book that shouts out with deep, practical, all-embracing analyses and suggestions, yet always wisely leaves readers – both school leaders and those who might manage clusters of schools or local systems – to make up their own minds in the light of their own unique conditions. In *Powering Up Your School* we have the information, the personal messages, and, above all, the guided wisdom for making our schools bedrocks of transformation. Guy Claxton and his friends demonstrate convincingly that schools and systems are already capable of transforming themselves into places not just of achievement but of empowerment. And they invite and encourage us to join them on the journey which they have so carefully mapped out. The trip is not without its challenges, but with such strong and experienced guides to lead us, it is surely hard to resist. Time to power up learning in all our schools!

Michael Fullan, Professor Emeritus, Ontario Institute for
Studies in Education, University of Toronto

Acknowledgements

First and foremost, we owe a huge debt of gratitude to all those school leaders who participated in our research for this book by agreeing to fill in our survey, take part in interviews, and comment on and correct our transcripts and interpretations. They are: Hugh Bellamy, former head, George Pindar School, former executive principal, South Dartmoor Community College; Jane Bellamy, former head teacher, Leigham Primary School and former CEO of Connect Academy Trust; Gavin Smith, executive principal, John Keohane, deputy principal, Michael Whitworth, former principal, and Will Ponsonby, student voice lead, Wren Academy; Mark Fenton, former head, and Mark Sturgeon, former deputy head, Dr Challoner's Grammar School; Neil Tetley, former head of Woodbridge School, now principal of Hastings International School, Madrid; Tessa Hodgson, head teacher, Oaklands Primary School; Jonny Spowart, Lee Beskeen, and Rebecca Archer, Heath Mount School; Paul Jensen, head teacher, and Andrea Jensen, head of English and whole-school literacy, Sunnydown School, Hannah Trickett, head teacher, Maple Cross Junior Mixed Infant and Nursery School; Malcolm White, head teacher, Leventhorpe School; Usha Dhorajiwala, head teacher, Christina Anderson, inclusion teacher, Laura Pezeshkpour, deputy head teacher, and Ben Reader, assistant head teacher, Woolenwick Infant and Nursery School; and Jackie Egan, head teacher, Icknield Infant and Nursery School. In addition to the hundreds of innovative and insightful teachers with whom we have worked:

Jann would especially like to thank: Dr James Pietsch, dean of professional development and learning, 2014–2017; Alma Loreaux, current dean of professional development and learning; the other original members of the working group: Jennifer Pollock, Adam Lear, and Jodie Bennett; and Maria Caristo, debating teacher – all at St Luke's Grammar School; Lorrae Sampson, principal, Nowra Anglican College; Felicity Marlow, principal, Norwest Christian College; Dr Simon Breakspear of Agile Schools; and all the teachers at these schools who have come on this journey.

Rachel would like to thank: Janet Cassford, Laura Fearon, and Sue Milligan from Walthamstow School for Girls; Jo Spencer, head teacher, Tam Broadway, primary head teacher, and Farhana Ali, primary teacher, Isaac Newton Academy; Hannah

Trickett, head teacher, Maple Cross Junior Mixed Infant and Nursery School; and Malcolm White, head teacher, Leventhorpe School.

Graham would like to thank: Elizabeth Coffey, former principal of Landau Forte College, now executive head teacher, States of Guernsey; Sue Plant, principal, John Taylor Free School; Barry O'Callaghan of the National Association of Principals and Deputies (Ireland); Tony Barnes, former head teacher of Park High School (now retired); and Keir Smith, principal, William Perkin High School.

Gemma and Robert would like to thank: the governing board of Sandringham Primary School, especially David Hall and the chair of governors, David Curtin; their leadership team colleagues: deputy head teachers Louise Bridge and Becky Reuben, and assistant head teachers Sharon Bridgeman, Tanya Roberts, Katie Bowles, Claire Botterill, and Kate Brennan; the LPA champions: Mariyam Seedat, Bimla Singh, Frazana Shahid, Satty Kudhail, Mark Gunthorp, and K'dee Bernard; and teachers Emma O'Regan and Amy Fisher. Thanks also to Killian Moyles and Alex Handiman from Whole Education; Latifa Akay and Fabiolla Lorusso from Maslaha; Brigitte Boylan, Ben Sperring, and Jo Franklin from the London East Teacher Training Alliance (LETTA); and Owen O'Regan, former Sandringham deputy, now head teacher of Lansbury Lawrence Primary School.

And – in addition to his hard-working and inspiring co-authors – Guy would like to thank Bill Lucas for information about the Expansive Education Network; Dr Judith Mortell, for robust and helpful conversations; TLO Limited for permission to use their materials; and Michael Fullan for his brilliant foreword.

Contents

Foreword by Michael Fullan iii

Acknowledgements vii

Introduction 1
    Results Plus 1
    Values Precede Style 3
    Culture Eats Strategy 5
    Stability and Morale 7
    Principals for the Future 8
    Not a Recipe 11
    About This Book 12

Chapter 1. Getting the Bug 15
    Jann's Story 16
    Robert and Gemma's Story 19
    Gavin and John's Story 24
    Concerns Over Existing Ways of Doing Things 27
    Dissatisfactions with Existing Ways of Doing Things 31
    Critical Events and Encounters 33
    Summary 34

Chapter 2. Learning Power: The Facts at Your Fingertips 37
    What Are the Values Behind the LPA? 42
    What Exactly Is the LPA? 43
    Why Is the LPA Needed? 44
    What Is the Research Evidence Behind the LPA? 47
    Where Does the LPA Come From and Who Is Behind It? 50
    How Does the LPA Look at the Classroom? 51

What Practical Resources Does the LPA Offer Teachers? 53
Getting Her Head Around the LPA: Jann's Story 60
What Should We Be Reading and Watching? 62
Summary 69

Chapter 3. Getting Buy-In: Onboarding All the Stakeholders 71
What Leader Behaviours Are Most Effective for Engaging Others with the LPA? 72
How Might You Get Staff on Board? 74
Is It Important to Have a Strategic Plan or Can the LPA Grow Organically? 79
Who Should Lead the LPA At Your School? 85
How Should You Deal with Any Sceptics, Cynics, and Blockers? 91
How Might You Introduce the LPA to Students? 97
How Can You Ensure That Everyone Is on Board? 100
Summary 102

Chapter 4. Creating a Staff Culture of Learning 103
How Do School Leaders Cope with Balancing "Tight" and "Loose" in Building the Learning Culture? 104
What Are the Characteristics of Teacher Learning Communities (TLCs)? 105
How Is A Staffroom Culture of Openness, Experimentation, and Support Built? 107
How Might the Traditional Walls That Isolate Practice Be Broken Down? 113
How Can Teachers Share Their Practice? 115
How Might Leaders Use External Pressures to Build Culture? 118
Summary 122

Chapter 5. A Language for Learning 125
Why Is Having a Common Language for Learning Important? 126
How Can You Open Up a Debate About Students' Learning Habits? 127

How Can the Vocabulary and Concepts of Learning Power Be Introduced to Students? 135
How Do You Keep the LPA Language Alive and Fresh? 139
How Do You Talk About Learning with Parents? 146
How Do You Weave Learning Power Language into Everyday Talk? 148
Summary 153

Chapter 6. Targeting Pedagogy: The Design Principles of Learning Power Teaching **157**
What, Exactly, Should You Ask Teachers to Do, Change, and Adapt? 158
How Do You Share Practice to Support Change, without It Feeling Like a High-Stakes Monitoring Exercise? 175
How Can You Distil Your Collective Experience and Pass It On? 183
Summary 184

Chapter 7. Beyond the Classroom: Changing Structures and Practices on a Wider Scale **187**
Which of the School's Structural Features Might Leaders Need to Reconsider? 189
How Can You Involve Students More Directly in the Leadership of Learning? 192
Are Your Methods of Reporting, Record-Keeping, and Nurturing Relationships with Parents Fit for LPA Purpose? 196
Can Leaders Design or Modify School Buildings to Enhance Learning Opportunities? 200
Summary 202

Chapter 8. Making It Stick: Sustainability **205**
What Might Leaders Do to Ensure That the LPA Persists After They Leave? 205
How Do Leaders Keep the LPA Fresh and Sustain It Over Time? 211
How Can You Develop and Distribute Leadership Capacity in Other Members of Staff? 219

    How Can Students Become the Carriers of the LPA Culture? 221
    Summary 223

Chapter 9. Evidencing Progress and Progression **225**
    What Is It Appropriate to "Assess" and Which Methods of "Measurement" Are Valid? 227
    How Can Learning Power Be Evidenced in Learners? 229
    How Can You Engage the Learners Themselves in Assessing the Development of Their Learning Power? 236
    How Can You Measure the Impact on Staff? 246
    How Can You Evidence the Impact on Parents? 248
    How Can You Know That Your School Has a Well-Embedded LPA Culture? 250
    Summary 255

Chapter 10. Connecting with the Wider World **257**
    How Can You Make Best Use of LPA-Minded Professional Development Organisations? 260
    How Should You Go About Building Your Own LPA-Focused Network? 273
    How Can You Build an LPA Alliance with Parents? 277
    Summary 283

Chapter 11. Some Tentative Conclusions **285**

Appendix: A Self-Assessment Grid for School Leaders 289
    Where Am I Heading? 290
    How Are Things Going So Far? 295

Further Reading 301

About the Authors 307

Introduction

Welcome to *Powering Up Your School*. We hope that you will enjoy it and find it useful. But it is worth saying up front who this book is for and what it contains – so, if you are just browsing at the moment, you can save your time and money if it is not for you. Because it isn't for every school leader, and it is not like the shelf-fuls of other books on educational leadership with which you might be familiar.

Results Plus

This book is about how to develop the culture of your school in a particular direction. It is for leaders who know in their hearts that 21st century education has to be about more than good examination results, good inspection reports, the trophies displayed in the foyer, and tidy, polite youngsters. It is for people who are not satisfied with a few vague platitudes on the website about "helping all our students fulfil their potential", or with earnest but empty protestations that "we are not an exam factory, you know". It is for school principals and head teachers who know that the "examination game" is rigged to produce losers as well as winners, and who lose sleep wondering how to provide a genuinely useful education for the inevitable "losers". It is for leaders who are actively searching for a way to tee all their students up for a fulfilling and satisfying life, not just for the next stage of formal education – *as well as* (not instead of) helping them learn to read, write, calculate, and get the grades. It is for those who have as much concern for the "far horizon" of a successful life as they do for the "near horizon" of exams.[1]

---

[1] By the way, this book is for anyone who wants to take a lead on bringing this approach to life in their school. We will use terms like "head teacher", "principal", "school leader", and "member of the senior leadership team (SLT)", but if none of those describes your role accurately, just insert a different form of words in your own head as you read. We do, however, frequently refer to features within the English system, such as: SATs, GCSEs, and A levels (all high-stakes exams, taken at ages 11, 16, and 18 respectively); Ofsted (the body that inspects and judges schools); and Years and Key Stages (into which high school education is divided). The UK primary school system runs from "Reception" (which

This book is for those who have come to suspect that the key to a fulfilling life lies in the attitudes that people develop while they are young: principally, their attitudes to other people, and to difficulty and uncertainty. Put bluntly, you have a better chance of feeling good about your life if you are resilient, adventurous, and self-aware, and if you are a good partner, parent, friend, and neighbour. This book is for those who believe that school has the potential to influence the development of these attitudes – that education is about growing dispositions as well as knowledge and expertise.

So the Learning Power Approach (LPA) aims to develop a culture in which a clear and collective understanding of the valued, sought-after outcomes of education – of character strengths developed *as well as* academic successes achieved, what we call *results plus* – drive everything in the school: the curriculum content, the structure of the timetable, the forms of assessment and record-keeping, the degree to which students are involved in the running of the school, communication with parents,[2] and – most important of all – the pedagogical style of every member of staff. It is the LPA leader's job to orchestrate change in all these different aspects of school life, so that they become ever more aligned around the core vision. The LPA is a way of facilitating *culture change* throughout the school and *habit change* in the style and focus of individual teachers.

The LPA is a school of thought about teaching and learning that has emerged over the last twenty years or so in a variety of research and practitioner groups around the world. You may recognise the LPA in other pedagogical approaches such as New Pedagogies for Deep Learning, Visible Thinking, Building Learning Power (BLP),

---

children enter at age 4, roughly) through Years 1 (5–6-year-olds), 2, 3, 4, 5, and 6 (10–11-year-olds). Often these are divided into two "Key Stages": Key Stage 1 comprises Years 1 and 2; Key Stage 2 comprises Years 3 to 6. Key Stage 3 comprises the first three years of high school education (Years 7–9, during which children are aged 11–14). Key Stage 4 comprises the final two years of compulsory schooling (Years 10–11, educating 14–16-year-olds). In the United States, school years are called "grades," and they tend to be one year "behind" the English years, so tenth grade corresponds roughly to Year 11. Post-compulsory education for 16–18-year-olds is usually delivered in sixth forms or colleges, and is sometimes referred to as Key Stage 5. Some of our examples are from Australia, where the year system parallels that of the UK. High school ends with high-stakes exams that have different names in different states (for example, the Higher School Certificate (HSC), in New South Wales), but all are converted into an Australian Tertiary Admissions Rank (ATAR) score which is used to determine university and college admissions.

2   By "parents" we, of course, also mean guardians and caregivers of any sort. In the interests of concision, we hope you'll forgive our use of the term – we don't intend to downplay the role of other carers.

Habits of Mind, Expeditionary Learning, Learning without Limits, Challenging Learning, or a variety of others. Its champions include David Perkins, Carol Dweck, Angela Duckworth, Arthur L. Costa and Bena Kallick, Ron Berger, Ron Ritchhart, Michael Fullan, and a host of others. It doesn't matter what label a school uses, or whether it has a label at all. What matters is the whole-hearted attempt to adjust classroom teaching and whole-school culture so that students do as well in exams as they can and, at the same time, a clearly articulated set of "independent learning strengths" are being deliberately, consciously, and systematically cultivated – this is what we mean when we refer to "the LPA".[3]

Values Precede Style

So *Powering Up Your School* assumes that the roles and responsibilities of school leaders are contingent on this heartfelt sense of moral purpose. Some approaches to school leadership seem to assume that leadership styles are value-free: that is, ways of leading – authoritarian, democratic, transformational, or whatever – can be appraised as good or bad regardless of the underlying vision and principles. We disagree. We think that both leadership style and practice depend critically on where you are heading. Take, for example, the issue of the school principal being some sort of role model for staff and students alike. If the goal is just "better results", there is no strong image for leaders to aspire to – other than a model of efficiency and mutual respect, maybe.

But if the vision is of what we call the LPA – of a school that is dedicated to getting good results, not at any price, but in a way that builds student' confidence, capability, and relish for taking charge of their own learning lives – then, clearly, the principal needs to know what the character traits of the powerful learner are, and take every

---

[3] You might be wondering about the relationship between the LPA and BLP, an approach with which several of the authors have been associated, and one that we will mention throughout the book. Our hope is that this book speaks on behalf of the generic school of thought, rather than any particular version or "brand" of the LPA. Inevitably, a good many of our contributors draw on their experience with BLP, but when we discuss this, we really see it only as one version of the LPA: what we are really talking about is the common underlying philosophy and pedagogy.

opportunity to show colleagues and students that they possess and cherish those traits themselves. They need to model thinking aloud about tricky issues; having the confidence to express uncertainty and ask for help; keeping their own plans and suggestions under review; and owning up quickly when things are not going as they had hoped. One of the best ways to make a school a safe place for both students and teachers to be real learners – to venture, explore, discuss, and experiment – is for the principal to be willing to inhabit that "learning mode" themselves – frequently and visibly. This is just one small example of how the fundamental nature of leadership tasks and roles are critically dependent on the direction and clarity of the school's specific vision for a better future.

It follows that we aren't much concerned about general models or theories of leadership in this book. We will not be discussing academic notions of "professional capital" or the "transactional leadership style". They seem to us to be too abstract to be of much real use. Instead, this book draws on the lessons learned by a wide range of school principals who have successfully undertaken the LPA journey. Their experiences of "what worked well", "how we had to adapt", and "what we would do differently next time" are distilled into a series of detailed case studies, from which we draw out the leadership lessons learned, and offer a compendium of detailed advice.[4] We very much hope that you will see your own ideals, as well as the realities of your school, mirrored in these stories, and that you will find inspiration and guidance here. We want this book to be extremely practical, brimming with guidance about concrete things you can try out to make this culture shift a lived reality in your school. In the chapters that follow you'll find lots of practical ideas and suggestions that are specifically tailored to the job of building a learning-powered culture. We hope that this style, and the vision behind it, will appeal to you. If not, fare thee well on your own chosen course.

---

[4] Some of our "case study principals" co-authored this book: Jann, Rachel, Gemma, and Robert. Others kindly contributed their reflections and are introduced as we go along.

Introduction

Culture Eats Strategy

Management guru Peter Drucker is famously supposed to have said that "culture eats strategy for breakfast". He meant that in organisations (like businesses or schools) deliberate, explicit action plans often fail to create the shift in attitudes and behaviours that were intended. Why? Because they fall foul of underlying assumptions which are often not articulated but, nevertheless, generate a strong, invisible web of habits that determine "the way we do things around here". More precisely, we think of culture as "the way in which we talk and act *as if* we believe and value". Strategy represents what we *say* we value. Culture is a whole collection of habits of speaking, writing, organising, and reacting which implicitly convey our actual beliefs.

For example, a teacher can talk to their students about the importance of having a growth mindset, and put up colourful displays exhorting them not to say "I can't do it" but, instead, "I can't do it *yet*." The teacher consciously wants them to try harder and to not give up so easily when faced with difficulty. Yet other aspects of the way they react to students' questions or performance may still be carrying the message that "Bright students understand and get things right quickly and don't make mistakes", the corollary of which is "If you have to struggle and make use of trial-and-error to get it right, that means you aren't very intelligent." They may be encouraging the students to keep their books neat and tidy, and to rub out mistakes so they seem not to have happened. They may look relieved and happy when one of the usual suspects quickly volunteers the "right answer", the one that they were looking for, while ignoring other answers that weren't what they wanted. And they may be unaware that things like this may be sending strong messages that neutralise the looked-for effect of the growth mindset posters.

Changing the culture of a school as a whole doesn't happen just by creating new policies and delivering exhortations. With the best will in the world, teachers may try to conform to the *letter* of the new policy, but fail to instil its *spirit* into their classrooms. We have seen lots of schools where the students can parrot back the key "learning dispositions" – or list Howard Gardner's "multiple intelligences", or whatever the prevalent model happens to be – without any evidence that they really have become any more powerful as learners, or multiply intelligent in the way in which they respond to challenges. It takes time, continual encouragement and conversation, and coaching and modelling for a new way of being in the classroom to become second nature.

Leading for culture change means having realistic expectations about how long it takes people to change their habits. It means leading a relentless school-wide conversation about what the LPA really means, and why we are doing it. It means working to win hearts and minds, as well as compliant hands. It means identifying your champions and pioneers, and setting up ways in which they can coach and mentor other colleagues who are more cautious or entrenched. It means finding ways to showcase examples of good practice, and to allow good ideas to percolate quickly across the different age phases, subjects, and silos of the school. It might mean reassuring the staff that this is not just another passing fad, perhaps – as Jann Robinson did – by committing yourself to adopting no other initiatives or innovations for the next five years. It might mean thinking about changing the length of lessons, so that students have time to grapple, discuss, and really think about what they are learning. It might mean designing a new system of peer-to-peer professional development within the school. It surely means constantly affirming the value of the approach in meetings with parents, governors or boards of trustees, and inspectors. It means (as we have already argued) walking the talk of powerful learning yourself. And it certainly means finding ways to build the capacity and desire to lead the LPA way in colleagues, so that, when you move on or retire, there is no risk that the LPA will fizzle out and teachers revert to type.

Schools are constellations of a wide variety of structures, practices, ways of doing things, and ways of talking that have usually accreted over time. How timetables are designed and decided; how new staff are interviewed and inducted; how noisy a classroom can be before someone intervenes; how reports are designed and written; how parent–teacher and student–teacher conversations are designed and framed; the extent to which students are involved in thinking about teaching and learning; how often tests and homework are set, what the purpose is, and how the work is marked – all of these, and dozens more aspects of the way in which the school runs, carry messages about how students are supposed to learn and behave. These messages may or may not be congruent with the LPA's overriding intention to build students' capacity for independent thought and learning. A principal won't be able to get all these different aspects aligned overnight. They will need to think carefully about which aspects to tackle when, and how to go about making progress on multiple fronts. The campaign will need planning, prioritising, and coordinating. All of these elements are going to be discussed and detailed, with test-driven suggestions made, in the chapters that follow.

Stability and Morale

Our experience is that having a strong, clear vision for your school reduces stress. Given all the other pressures on schools, it may sound paradoxical to suggest that taking on the task of implementing your own vision can make life easier – but we think that it does. It is like a sailing boat out on the ocean: if it isn't going anywhere, the winds and waves just rock it about. If we, in schools, are just trying to react to and manage all the forces that are impinging on us – budget cuts, government directives, upcoming inspections, parental expectations, and so on – things feel very unstable and difficult. But if the boat has a direction of travel – if a skilful sailor knows where they are heading and are trying to get there – then many of those forces can be harnessed and used to impel forward motion. And this brings a greater feeling of both purpose and stability. Even contrary winds can help to drive you forward. This sense of pride and synergy is transferred to the crew. So too can a clear, explicit sense of moral purpose – of how we want our school to be better – create energy, excitement, and satisfaction among the staff.

This is not for one minute to deny that there are enormous pressures on schools, many of which may be unwelcome. It is only to say that we always have the choice, as Edward de Bono puts it, to be *water thinkers* rather than *rock thinkers*.[5] If you are a rock thinker, what grabs your attention is all the rocks that surround you: all the things you can't do that you would like to, or all the things you have to do that you don't want to. But if you think like water, you don't waste energy worrying about the rocks; it's the gaps that you are after. If there are gaps, water will find them, and it will be on its way. Your goal is to run "downhill" like water: that's the direction of your vision. And then, no matter how many rocks surround you, if you are alert to all the little things that you *can* do to progress your vision, and not preoccupied by all the things that you can't, then you will find those chinks and opportunities, and you will

---

5   Edward de Bono, *I Am Right, You Are Wrong* (London: Viking, 1990).

turn them to your own ends. Here's a well-known quote, often attributed to Johann Wolfgang von Goethe, that make the same point more poetically:

> Concerning all acts of creation, there is one elementary truth, ignorance of which kills countless ideas and splendid plans: that the moment one definitely commits oneself, then Providence moves too. All sorts of things occur to help one that would never otherwise have occurred. A whole stream of events issues from the decision, raising in one's favour all manner of unforeseen incidents and meetings and material assistance, which no man could have dreamed would have come his way.
>
> Whatever you can do, or dream you can, begin it. Boldness has genius, power, and magic in it. Begin it now.[6]

Goethe is right. Half-hearted leadership sets itself up to have only partial success. But of course, what Goethe is talking about isn't really magic. The world does not reorganise itself the minute you commit yourself to something. But *your* world does, because the commitment changes the way in which you perceive it and so act. Lots of things that would have previously passed you by – a chance encounter at a party; an article in a newspaper; a blog post skim read – now look like opportunities to forge a new alliance, find support, pursue funding, or try out a new idea. Both your actions and your words speak loudly to your staff – and, of course, to students and to their parents – about the vision and values you have for the school, and you are constantly refining ways to express your passionate commitment so that they "get it".

Principals for the Future

It is not just for the benefit of ourselves, our schools, and our students that we need to have our own vision. The future of education more generally depends upon it. School leaders are the key to system-wide changes in education. It is our impression that the vast majority of educators know that schools need to change to catch up with the demands, the resources, and the opportunities of the 21st century. The Internet

---

6   This quote is actually a hybrid. Though often presented as the work of Goethe, in fact only the second paragraph is his. The first is from William Hutchison Murray's 1951 book *The Scottish Himalayan Expedition* (London: JM Dent & Sons). The quote as it stands is from Susan Hayward's *Begin It Now: A Book of Motivation* (Sydney: In-Tune Books, 1987).

is here, and has democratised and globalised learning to an extraordinary degree.[7] In their out-of-school lives, probably unbeknownst to their teachers, young people are learning complicated things with and from each other. Children are downloading apps to their smartphones to teach themselves Japanese, law, orthopaedic procedures, and goodness knows what else. Professor of educational technology Sugata Mitra's experiments have forced us to radically rethink our ideas about the extent to which groups of children can self-organise their learning.[8]

Meanwhile, the world of work has dramatically shifted from predominantly "going to a place of work every day and getting a salary" to "posting your skills on a global website such as upwork.com and making deals project by project with a range of employers".[9] Global employers such as Google, PwC, and Pearson are even experimenting with ways of recruiting that do not allow applicants to show off the class of their degree or where it was from, as they find that academic qualifications do not predict the kind of fluid intelligence that they are seeking. It is a whole different ball game out there, and schools must adapt or become a dying anachronism.

In the face of these seismic shifts, the responses of politicians, policymakers, and academics are, as usual, disappointing. What needs to happen is too fine-grain, too subtle, too personal, and too radical to engage the interest of educational bureaucrats who think in terms of pulling the big levers of structural change: curriculum content, forms of assessment, governance, and funding. Tinkering with the structure of education – championing charter schools (in the United States) or academies (in the UK), for example – usually turns out to be an expensive way of having little overall effect. Such structural change does not reach down into the mechanics of teaching and learning, where you find the things that really matter. Also, many policy people have the mindset of an economist: they think in terms of fiscal wealth, not quality of life. Or they focus on raising conventional indicators of school performance – "getting more poor kids into good universities", for example – rather than thinking carefully about the well-being of all those who will *not* get into university, or who may not want

---

[7] See, for example, Douglas Thomas and John Seely Brown, *A New Culture of Learning: Cultivating the Imagination for a World of Constant Change* (Createspace, 2011); and Howard Gardner and Katie Davis, *The App Generation: How Today's Youth Navigate Identity, Intimacy, and Imagination in a Digital World* (New Haven, CT: Yale University Press, 2014).

[8] Sugata Mitra, *The School in the Cloud: The Emergent Future of Learning* (Thousand Oaks, CA: Corwin, 2019).

[9] See David Price, *Open: How We'll Work, Live and Learn in the Future* (Crux Publishing Ltd, 2013).

to go. They like to focus on things that are easy to count. And politicians, with a few honourable exceptions, are prevented by the tribal nature of party politics and the overriding need to win frequent elections from doing anything other than too little, too late.

Academics, too, are unlikely to change the world. Very few, it seems, have the willingness to think big about education while also understanding the constraints, pressures, and possibilities of real schools. Scholarly research is vital, but it has no effect if it falls on deaf or timid ears, or if it is couched in terms that are too abstract or abstruse for busy teachers and principals to make use of. And much educational research punches well below its weight because it is driven by purely academic criteria or by intellectual fashion, and not by the needs of the next generation and the realities of schools. Harvard University's Project Zero has been so influential because its researchers have put as much energy into developing practical suggestions – and communicating them widely and accessibly – as they have into writing scholarly papers.[10]

The future of education lies in the hands of imaginative, courageous, resourceful school leaders – the people on the ground who can orchestrate the necessary kinds of debate, experimentation, and habit change. Though they are constantly buffeted by the whims and diktats of politicians and bureaucrats, it is they who set the cultural tone in schools, and mediate the way in which external policies and pressures are responded to. If schools are to send young people out into the world with minds that are strong and supple enough to cope with the demands of 21st century life – and not just with a clutch of grades and certificates – it will be committed and courageous school principals who must make it happen.

There are thousands of such school principals, in hundreds of countries around the world, who are working hard and smart to develop their school cultures. But there are many others who would like to be doing more, but who need ideas about exactly where they are heading and how to get there. This book distils the wisdom and experience of a handful of those successful pioneers into a guidebook for their fellow leaders. It provides ideas that are certainly grounded in high-quality research, but which are translated into usable, accessible, and adaptable guidelines.

---

10 See www.pz.harvard.edu.

Introduction

Not a Recipe

What the LPA offers, though, is not a pre-processed package to be bought lock, stock, and barrel and implemented according to the instructions on the box. It is a *philosophy*: a set of values about education as a preparation for the tests of life. If you think this is *desirable*, and are serious about offering such an education, then the LPA gives you the *scientific rationale* for believing that it is *possible*. There are a set of habits of mind that underpin both objectives (academic success and character development), and they can indeed be moulded and strengthened through experience at school. And having ticked both the "desirable" and "possible" boxes, the LPA offers a set of *frameworks, design principles, illustrations,* and *practical "tweaks" and "seeds"* that any teacher in any school can begin to implant in their practice.

So to understand the LPA, think "garden" rather than "model aeroplane kit". The seeds will only grow if they are embedded in the soil of your existing culture and connect with the needs and beliefs of your community. The LPA requires school leaders not just to impose a new set of ideas on their school, but to experiment, customise, discuss, reflect, and change tack — to be the leaders of a growing, thinking, learning culture. As with a garden, it takes time, thought, and effort to bring it to fruition. As you will see from some of the stories in this book, what worked seamlessly in one school sometimes turns out to be problematic in another. So if you are looking for a magic bullet, a flat-pack, or even just a new badge to put on the school website or notepaper, then the LPA is not for you. It is harder, slower, and infinitely more rewarding than bolting on shiny new initiatives like "flipped classrooms" or a "knowledge-rich curriculum".

To engage with the LPA, you have to accept that culture change in an organisation involves habit change in people. Teachers, like everyone, are creatures of habit. We get so used to doing things "our way" that it feels awkward, unnatural, or even plain stupid to try doing them differently. Changing habits requires efforts of will and awareness. The psychological research shows that we are unlikely to succeed without at least the following ingredients: real commitment to the benefits of "being different"; forgiving ourselves when we forget and back-slide; becoming sensitised to what triggers the habit; and having the kinship of friends, mentors, and role models who can support us during the transition.[11] Think organisations that help you lose weight or stop smoking, for example. Principals need to invest in creating such a culture of support, experimentation, and mentoring among their staff – and that takes time and skill. It won't happen just because a superintendent of schools or a secretary of state for education says so. If they are to change, teachers need to be inspired by a vision, fed with practical ideas, supported by colleagues, and guided by a mentor. Officials can't do that – but school principals can.

Leading a school to become an ever-stronger incubator of learning power is a complicated business. It requires a deep understanding of what matters and of what is possible, as well as patient, skilful attention paid to how to get there. Take heart: the LPA does deliver many quick wins in terms of students' engagement and achievement. But shifting deeply engrained habits, in both teachers and students – that can take months of patient watching, talking, and coaching. A principal has to think like Bob Bowman, Michael Phelps's swimming coach: keeping the long game constantly in mind while looking for those precious marginal gains every day.[12]

About This Book

This book is the fourth in a series of books about the LPA. Ideally, it should be read in conjunction with the others. The first, *The Learning Power Approach*, explains the LPA in some detail, goes into the reasons why it is important and timely, and provides the research basis on which it rests.[13] It is very helpful in giving school leaders the confidence and information they need to get buy-in from others (though Chapter 2 in this book offers you a highly condensed version to get you going). The second and third books are written for primary and high school classroom teachers respectively.

---

11 For the psychology of habit change, see Charles Duhigg, *The Power of Habit: Why We Do What We Do and How to Change* (London: Random House Books, 2013).

12 Bob Bowman, with Charles Butler, *The Golden Rules: 10 Steps to World-Class Excellence in Your Life and Work* (New York: St Martin's Press, 2016).

13 Guy Claxton, *The Learning Power Approach: Teaching Learners to Teach Themselves* (Carmarthen: Crown House Publishing, and Thousand Oaks, CA: Corwin Press, 2018).

They are *Powering Up Children* and *Powering Up Students*.[14] They provide masses of examples and ideas about how to implement the LPA in any classroom. If school leaders are to adopt the important role of head pedagogical coach, they need to get their heads around whichever of these two books is relevant to their school. And it will be useful if there are copies for teachers to consult as well.

Finally, allow Guy to briefly introduce the team behind this book. (Fuller biographies can be found at the end.) Jann Robinson is the principal of St Luke's Grammar School in Sydney, New South Wales, Australia. St Luke's is an independent Anglican all-through school that teaches 1,000 boys and girls aged 4 to 18. Rachel Macfarlane has been head teacher of Walthamstow School for Girls and principal of Isaac Newton Academy, both in North-East London, England. Both are state comprehensive schools in a highly multicultural area of the city. Walthamstow has 900 girls between the ages of 11 and 16 on roll. Isaac Newton is a brand-new co-educational all-through school for students aged 4 to 19. Rachel is now director of education services at Herts for Learning Ltd.

Graham Powell has worked at all levels across the UK education system. As well as being a schools inspector and secondary phase advisor for a local authority, he was head of an 11–18 comprehensive school in Wiltshire, England. He went on to become a principal consultant on BLP at TLO Limited, and has worked with hundreds of leadership teams in schools throughout the UK, Ireland, and latterly Spain.

Robert Cleary is head teacher of Sandringham Primary School in Newham, a deprived borough in East London. Sandringham has nearly 1,000 students aged 2 to 11 on roll. Gemma Goldenberg was, until 2019, Robert's deputy in charge of professional development at Sandringham. She is now studying full-time for a PhD.

And Guy is a theoretical cognitive and life scientist with a special passion for education and a deeply held conviction about the learnability of learning. He has been professor of the learning sciences at the University of Bristol Graduate School of Education, and co-founder (with his friend Bill Lucas) and research director of the Centre for Real-World Learning at the University of Winchester.

---

14 Guy Claxton and Becky Carlzon, *Powering Up Children: The Learning Power Approach to Primary Teaching* (Carmarthen: Crown House Publishing, 2018); and Guy Claxton and Graham Powell, *Powering Up Students: The Learning Power Approach to High School Teaching* (Carmarthen: Crown House Publishing, 2019).

In addition to the experiences of the authors, the book draws on the learning power journeys of a wide range of other schools, from a special school for autistic adolescent boys and nursery, primary, and high schools in England, to international schools in Madrid and private colleges in Australia. From such a variety of establishments, we have distilled many of the common issues faced by innovative leaders, and tried to identify the range of smart, successful strategies which they have used to grow an LPA culture in their schools.[15] As we have said, schools are really complicated places, and culture change leadership relies on being sensitive to the assumptions and pressures that characterise the specific place in which you work. If "one size fits no one" applies to the classroom, it applies all the more to a whole school. Schools are, to put it technically, complex, dynamic systems. When you poke a system, one of three things can happen – and it is not easy to tell ahead of time which kind of response you will get. First, it can wobble and then settle back into "business as usual". Second, it can shudder and then reorganise itself into a new, often more complex arrangement. Or, third, it can disintegrate. Our job is to find the smart pokes that will cause the second type of response, and create an embedded, sustained culture change that aligns better with our vision and values.

So while we will try to draw out common issues and promising methods that might apply to your school, their success will always depend on issues of timing, prioritisation, and nuance that only you can judge. And even then, you – just like the pioneering principals in this book – will get it wrong sometimes, and will have to rethink and rework your approach. Occasionally, good principals (with good principles) with the best of intentions get it so wrong that the system hardens itself against them, and the only solution may be to move on and start afresh. We hope this book will ensure that such a fate does not befall you and your current school. You won't find recipes here. But you will, we hope, find lots of stories and good ideas for smart pokes that ring bells with your own situation, and prompt you to be adventurous, and to avoid some of the more obvious pitfalls that our pioneers have mapped out for you.

And with that, let's begin the learning power journey, and tackle the first challenge: beginning to get the feeling that the LPA is something important, well-founded, and doable.

---

15 These leaders' titles and positions are correct as of the time of interview. Of course, some may well have retired or moved on by the time you are reading this.

Chapter 1

Getting the Bug

The LPA is, like all educational approaches, a moral business. It derives from a set of value judgements about what we think is "better" – what outcomes of a child's schooldays are to be judged more desirable than others. If you think it is all about getting as many as possible into "top universities" (and we are not really bothered about the rest), that's a value judgement. So is the desire for "all our children to be happy". In particular, the LPA rests on a vision of what we want *young people to be like* when they leave our schools (whichever phase of schooling we are concerned with). We don't want them to be greedy, glib, smug, or dishonest (whether they end up as prime minister of their country or not). We don't want them to be cowed, incurious jobsworths. We would prefer them to be inquisitive, adventurous, honourable, kind, and resilient, for example. Or we would like them to be disposed to think clearly and debate respectfully. So whether the LPA appeals to you depends on where your heart is. And whether you want to lead a successful LPA school depends on your clear and unswerving commitment to those heartfelt values. Without it, you won't get going. And without it, you are more likely to be despondent or lose faith when things don't go smoothly first time. From passion comes grit and determination. Remember Machiavelli's honest appraisal of the leader's task:

> There is nothing more hazardous to undertake, nor more uncertain of success, than to be involved in the bringing about of a new order of things. For the reformer will have as enemies all those who have done well under the old order, and only lukewarm defenders and supporters in those who would profit by the new. This lukewarmness arises partly from timidity, and partly from the incredulity of people who do not readily believe in anything new until they have seen it with their own eyes.[1]

In this first chapter, we are going to share with you the stories of how some school leaders came to that commitment – why they decided to embark on the slow and demanding process of developing a robust learning-powered culture in their schools. This journey, as you will see, often starts with an itchy dissatisfaction with the status

---

1 Paraphrased by Guy from Niccolò Machiavelli, *The Prince*, tr. George Bull (London: Penguin, 1995 [1532]), p. 19.

quo: perhaps a feeling that there has to be more to a 21st century education than the current obsession with grades, tests, and university or college entrance. Sometimes that itch is scarcely felt until it is activated by a chance conversation, a magazine article or a TED Talk, a professional development seminar, or a poignant event at school. And then you become receptive to other sources of information about how it might be possible to scratch the itch. The LPA journey starts with the personal recognition that "there has to be a better way", and with a sense of (cautious) optimism that such a way can be found. Without that wholehearted commitment from the school principal, it is unlikely that anything like the LPA will take root and flourish.

Obviously, not all of the stories we tell will ring a bell with everyone. Schools vary enormously in their starting points, and we are all at different stages in our own educational journeys. But we hope that some of them will fire you up and encourage you to take the next step. In truth, 21st century education depends on it!

Jann's Story

Jann Robinson is principal of St Luke's Grammar School in Dee Why, a suburb of Sydney. St Luke's is a non-selective, independent school, serving families from the area around the northern beaches of Sydney. As you might expect, many of these families are well off, and, being near the famous Manly Beach, there is something of a laid-back atmosphere in the neighbourhood. Here is Jann's account of how she got the bug about the LPA:

> Making the decision to go with BLP – our preferred version of the LPA – has been the outcome of a long personal journey. It has been the culmination of all the experiences I have had in my years as a teacher and in leadership roles.
>
> My pathway to leadership has been through pastoral care. I have always had a commitment to the well-being of students, and a fundamental belief that if we look after this then the academic results will follow. This commitment reflects a number of experiences. I was particularly affected by the suicides of two of my high school students, one in 1999 and the other the following year, while I was a year coordinator in a previous school.[2] Both students were bright and yet this did

---

2 Year coordinator in Australia in equivalent to head of year in the UK.

not prevent them from feeling despair. It set me on a path of wanting to work out how to make students more resilient to the pressures they would inevitably face in life. What could we do that might promote resilience and what does it take to make a person flourish, not just at school but in their lives beyond it? These two questions have stayed with me long term, shaping my work. I began, in that school, to design pastoral care programmes for my students, with an explicit emphasis on resilience.

In 2001, I became the dean of students for Years 7–10 in a different school, where I had overall responsibility for the welfare programmes. At this time I came across Art Costa's Habits of Mind framework, which instantly resonated with my own beliefs. I felt that this really was a way to build resilience in the students. I introduced the habits into the pastoral care programmes – but I couldn't get any real traction with them. Upon reflection, there just wasn't enough regular exposure to the habits for the students to really internalise and develop them. Perhaps if I had been able to get them into classrooms more it might have worked. I was also finding it hard in that role to feel that I could have any real impact on the school. And in some ways this dissatisfaction gave me the push I needed to look at becoming a head.

In 2005, I arrived as principal of St Luke's Grammar School with great plans, but there were so many other issues to be addressed, so I couldn't just leap straight into building a "Habits of Mind" school. In retrospect, I think I was right to take my time. To lead a culture change programme you must have a foundation of trust with the staff. At St Luke's, for various reasons, that foundation didn't exist, and I had to devote the first few years of my headship to building it.

By 2013, when I had been the head of St Luke's for eight years, I was still looking at how we might do better for our students. I'm not even sure if I knew clearly what "better" would look like at the time, but there were a number of things in play which were making me search for answers. For example, we were seeing a number of high-achieving kids from our junior school who were not coming through to the senior school because there was a feeling in the community that we weren't good enough academically. In trying to address that concern we focused staff professional development around a range of themes, one of which was Carol Dweck's work on growth mindset. We wanted to get teachers to explore the idea that all students are able to learn, and we spent time on differentiation to try to overcome the underperformance of our more academic kids. While we did see some improvements, it was hard going.

There was a lot of pushback from teachers at being asked to change their practice, partly because there was a culture of blaming the students for any underperformance. They were saying that it was the students' fault that they were so passive, and there was a general attitude that kids growing up near Sydney's northern beaches were too "laid back" and simply could not be roused to work hard. So when Year 12 students did poorly in their Trial Higher School Certificate exams, staff tended to complain that they were "really hard to motivate" and "just couldn't pick themselves up from any disappointment with their marks". In addition, I was aware of evidence that, even when they did do well in the university entrance exams (Australian Tertiary Admission Rank (ATAR)), students from our type of school often dropped out.

While all this was swirling around in my head, I heard a colleague present on BLP, so I bought both *Building Learning Power* and *The Learning Powered School*.[3] It sounded good, but I left the books sitting on the shelf for about six months. In mid-2013, when I had some study leave, I finally got around to reading them. I can't really describe my reaction. It was as though this was what I had been searching for all my teaching career. I think it was seeing resilience featured so prominently in the model that excited me. But it was more than that: it just resonated with all the things I had read previously, and its foundation in neuroscience added to my buy-in. I remember thinking about how it aligned with Howard Gardner's book *Five Minds for the Future*.[4] The 4Rs of BLP – resilience, resourcefulness, reflection, and reciprocity (or learning relationships) – gave me four out of Gardner's five minds, and the fifth – his "ethical mind" – could naturally be added through a fifth R, "restoration", reflecting our school's Christian foundation.

I remember sitting in the education faculty library in Cambridge, England, reading both books and planning out the strategy for how we would do it. I believed I could get buy-in from the staff by promising them four things: a unified approach to professional development; an answer to the problem of students' passivity as learners; a solid foundation in neuroscientific research; and a promise that we would, as a whole school, be totally committed to this *and only this* for five years. I was excited by the idea that the BLP framework would be for every student in every classroom. Critically, not only would it make them powerful learners in school, but it would also develop the dispositions that they needed to be confident and well-rounded people. For me, the LPA has always been bigger than school learning. If we could develop the dispositions that would enable our students to meet academic learning challenges, these same dispositions would allow them to meet life's challenges too. It is why I am so passionate about it and want to give it as a gift to each and every student. It is about who they are becoming, and giving them the attitudes they need in order to *flourish*: to be resilient; to know what to

---

3   Guy Claxton, *Building Learning Power: Helping Young People Become Better Learners* (Bristol: TLO Limited, 2002); and Guy Claxton, Maryl Chambers, Graham Powell, and Bill Lucas, *The Learning Powered School: Pioneering 21st Century Education* (Bristol: TLO Limited, 2011).
4   Howard Gardner, *Five Minds for the Future* (Cambridge, MA: Harvard University Press, 2006).

> do when they don't know what to do; to work with others; and to be reflective about themselves.

Before we go on to our second story, take a moment to reflect on how Jann's journey towards the LPA is similar to or different from your own.

Wondering

Which bits of Jann's story resonated with you, and which did not?

Did the fact that St Luke's is an independent school colour your reading?

Have you had any experiences that shocked you into thinking hard about your educational values and priorities, like the suicides of Jann's two students did for her?

Robert and Gemma's Story

Our second story concerns a very different kind of school. It has two narrators: Robert Cleary and Gemma Goldenberg. Robert is head teacher of Sandringham Primary School, which, as we mentioned, is in the borough of Newham in East London. Gemma was, until 2019, Robert's deputy in charge of curriculum and professional learning. Sandringham is a large state-funded school. Including its day-care and pre-school provision, the school serves around 1,000 students aged 1–11. The school is located in a densely populated inner-city area with high levels of social deprivation. The majority of the students are from minority ethnic backgrounds, predominantly of Indian, Pakistani, and Bangladeshi heritage. Around 98% of the student population speak English as an additional language (EAL). The school has specialised resource provision for children with autism, and around 20% of the students are registered as having special educational needs and/or disabilities (SEN or SEND).[5]

First, let's hear from Robert:

> In April 2010 I was promoted from deputy head of Sandringham to head. On my appointment, the governing body made it clear to the SLT that they wanted the school to "think big" and look outwards for ideas, not just locally but nationally and internationally. The school had been referred to by local authority officials as "Sleepy Sandringham", and the governors wanted me and my newly appointed deputy, Owen O'Regan, to wake it up. Neither Owen nor I are the sleepy type, and we were keen to get the school moving.
>
> There were a number of events over the first six months that galvanised us into action, and cumulatively resulted in our commitment to our version of the LPA. There was no single blinding moment of realisation. Rather, there was an accumulation of discussions, reading, shared experiences, and being nudged or pushed in a certain direction.
>
> One of these stimuli was an Ofsted inspection. We were told of the visit on the Friday lunchtime of our very first week in charge, and the inspectors arrived on the Monday: quite a baptism by fire! One week in and we managed to get the school upgraded to "good". (There is a whole other story about that inspection, but the important part here is that the school did not need to worry about an inspection agenda for the next few years.)
>
> Following the inspection of "Sleepy Sandringham", we were asked by someone from the local authority if we would like to meet two academics from the University of Winchester who had written a book on becoming smarter. The book was *New Kinds of Smart* by Bill Lucas and Guy Claxton.[6] I still have my well-thumbed copy in my office. The book falls open to Chapter 2, the most well-read, which was a revelation to me. It opens with this quote, written in 1909, by Alfred Binet, often thought of as the father of the IQ test:
>
>> *Some recent philosophers have given their moral approval to the deplorable verdict that an individual's intelligence is a fixed quantity, one which cannot be augmented. We must protest and act against this brutal pessimism ... It has*

---

5   The school made a short video to showcase their establishment: Sandringham Primary School, "Introducing Sandringham Primary School" [video] (19 January 2016). Available at: https://www.youtube.com/watch?v=Ah0JRQikKhQ.

6   Bill Lucas and Guy Claxton, *New Kinds of Smart: How the Science of Learnable Intelligence Is Changing Education* (Maidenhead: Open University Press, 2010).

> *no foundation whatsoever ... What [slow learners] should learn first is not the subjects ordinarily taught, however important they may be; they should be given lessons of will, of attention, of discipline. Before exercises in grammar, they need to be exercised in mental orthopedics; in a word, they must learn how to learn.*[7]

Well! I had never before read or heard anyone advocate that intelligence is not a fixed commodity; that it is expandable; that humans are more than an IQ "number on their forehead". And here was Binet insisting that his IQ test was not to be used to support the idea that we are born with a fixed intelligence. How could educators, parents, and policymakers appear to have been so keen to make the mistake that Alfred Binet had warned against? The idea of a fixed intelligence was something I had unquestioningly believed in throughout my own education. At the high school I attended, the boys were reported on at the end of each year on their ability and effort. The badge of honour was to achieve a high grade for ability with a low grade for effort. We were unable to articulate what we were trying to achieve, but on reflection, we all wanted to be "effortlessly superior". So *New Kinds of Smart* was quite an eye-opener for me.

Another significant event occurred back in 2011. One family who were very aspirational for their daughter had spoken to me about applying to high schools outside of Newham, and even the possibility of boarding. We supported the family in visiting a number of prestigious private schools where I thought their daughter could be successful. At the school they wanted, there was an involved admissions process for the children to go through, and I went with them on the assessment day. Initially, they sat a straightforward academic test, which the girl was able to pass comfortably. Then they moved onto the next stage of selection in which they had to undertake tasks collaboratively with the other children – and here she struggled.

Many of the other children had received an education that had explicitly taught them to be articulate, cooperative, and resilient – skills that, under pressure, the "bright" girl from our school seemed to lack. A colleague put it quite bluntly when she observed that the children that ours was up against seemed much more "polished". Their schools had provided opportunities beyond the national curriculum. These children were confident in English and maths, just like our Sandringham children, but they benefited from being able to articulate their thoughts confidently. They were reflective and curious about the experiences that they were undertaking. And they showed intelligent determination in pursuing the challenges they were set. They had been taught how to learn – and our children had not. Seeing this, I was

---

[7] Alfred Binet, *Les Idées Modernes sur les Enfants* (Paris: Flammarion, 1909). Quoted in Lucas and Claxton, *New Kinds of Smart*, p. 33.

convinced that all our children were capable of becoming just as "polished". There was only the matter of how we were going to do it, and where we were going to start on this journey.

Now let's see what Gemma has to add:

During my teacher training I was never encouraged to think about children's minds and brains. We were told about lesson plans, curriculum, and assessment, but never about what happens in the brain when we learn and how we can make learning more effective. For me, this has always been a fascinating topic, so I was delighted when, as a newly qualified teacher (NQT), I was introduced to the idea of "accelerated learning", an approach that involved teaching in a way which was designed to make learning easier for students. It advocated the use of a range of techniques – for example, training children to use mind maps to organise their thoughts; using Brain Gym (little physical exercises that were supposed to stimulate the brain); sorting kids into visual, auditory, and kinaesthetic (VAK) learners; and giving them different kinds of activities to suit their "learning style".

Often accompanied by a degree of hype, many of these approaches have turned out to have less effect on learning than we were told they would. But, nevertheless, the training I received so early on in my career was really valuable. It helped me make the critical shift from focusing exclusively on what *I* was doing as a teacher to focusing on what *they*, the children, were doing as learners – and taking the latter into account as I strove to become a better teacher. I continued to be interested in children's learning long after the VAK approach had been cast aside, but I didn't know where to start and for some time was unaware of approaches which chimed with my yearning for a more meaningful approach to teaching.

It was some years later that I joined Sandringham to lead on curriculum and teaching development. It was a time of change and an exciting moment to join the school. I noticed straightaway that the students were better behaved than in any other school in which I'd taught. At first glance it felt like an easy place to teach. But getting the students to take charge of their own learning was a different challenge. Many were quiet and reluctant to engage; there was a distinct lack of chatter, debate, and questioning. There were lots of good teachers at the school, but pedagogy varied greatly from one class to the next.

Not long after joining the school, Robert asked me to read *New Kinds of Smart*. For the first time, I read something which reflected exactly how I felt about education and the book was able to articulate what I had been trying to achieve since I began my career. The idea of cultivating better learners was empowering. Every lesson could become a potential vehicle for helping young people to develop better learning skills – no matter what the content of the lesson was. I was excited. For the first time, I felt like an agent of change and not just a technician delivering a prescribed curriculum.

I remember the event that Robert has just relayed – the bright girl who lacked the "polish" to get into the private school. We felt that our curriculum had failed to provide her with the opportunities to develop the confidence and skills she needed in order to stand out and compete against her more privileged counterparts. What got most of us out of bed each morning was the drive to provide our students with the life chances they needed to change the course of their future, so this experience felt like a kick in the teeth. It felt urgent: we needed an approach that didn't just make children more knowledgeable, but made them feel that they had a place at the table, that could help them to become articulate, tolerant, and resilient so that they had equal access to all of life's opportunities. Of course, the challenge was that we did need children to become much more knowledgeable too – and with their starting points far lower than the national average, there was a lot of ground to make up!

Over the next few years, the school embarked on introducing many new approaches under the umbrellas of "making students better learners" and delivering "a broad range of experiences". Singapore maths, reciprocal reading, Philosophy for Children (P4C), growth mindset, Alison Peacock's work on learning without limits,[8] and the mastery approach were all thrown into the mix. There was a lot of "good stuff" going on – but I increasingly felt like we were lacking something which tied it all together. It was hard to pinpoint exactly why we had chosen these ideas and approaches and what they all had in common. I kept asking, "What is all of this leading towards?" In the end I wrote my own vision of what I thought education should be. I shared it with the deputy who passed it onto Robert. It felt like blue sky thinking at the time, but I kept referring back to it over the years. It was soon after that I joined the SLT.

After attending a course on values-led leadership, Robert put the SLT to work rewriting our school vision, purpose, and values. This was a long process which involved much discussion, debate, drafting, and redrafting as we wrestled with putting our ethos, beliefs, and passions into words. The LPA came to our attention at around this time and it helped us enormously in articulating our vision. By combining all of the approaches we had introduced and articulating how they link together under one framework, the LPA helped us distil everything we had put into place over the last few years into a coherent, rational framework. We were able to tie these approaches together with our underlying beliefs and values. It offered us a new way to hold ourselves and one another to account and to make sure that

---

8   For more on which, see: https://learningwithoutlimits.educ.cam.ac.uk/.

> what we did, and the way in which we did it, reflected our core values and ethos. It also made it easier to share our vision with others and to induct new staff.

Again, you might like to pause and reflect on any points which gibe with your own experience.

Wondering

Were there any aspects of Robert and Gemma's story that stirred any memories or sympathies from your own professional life?

How much attention does your school give to cultivating the "polish" which that girl from Sandringham seemed to lack?

Do you notice and care, in your school, about how your students are behaving and thinking as learners, in the way that Robert and Gemma do?

Gavin and John's Story

Here is our third story. It comes from another school in London, Wren Academy, an all-through school in the Borough of Barnet, which is north of the city. Again, there are two narrators. One is Gavin Smith, now executive principal but originally a deputy to the inaugural principal, Michael Whitworth, who has since moved on. The other is John Keohane, originally an advanced skills teacher (AST) and now assistant principal for teaching and learning. John was introduced to the LPA (in the form of BLP) when he first interviewed for a job at the school. Wren was a brand-new high school that opened its doors in September 2008 with an initial cohort of just Year 7 students.[9] John was attracted by the advert for the job, and the way in which the selection process was organised. He explains:

> The emphasis on developing learning character shone through in the information provided by Wren for applicants. This was of great appeal to me. Since my initial teacher training at Newcastle University under Professor David Leat, a learning to learn enthusiast, I had been convinced that the development of students' curiosity and thinking skills should be central to the role of a teacher. (David used to challenge us not to simply "fill empty vessels" but to expand the vessels' capacity.) In my previous schools I had led staff training on thinking skills and, latterly, I had become the learning to learn coordinator. The learning to learn curriculum we were using then was based on the work of Alistair Smith, an education consultant and trainer. It revolved around discrete lessons aimed at developing what Smith calls the 5Rs: resilience, resourcefulness, reflection, reasoning, and responsibility.[10] I had become a great advocate of the approach, yet I also had reservations about the value of trying to teach such skills through discrete lessons as I was not convinced that students would transfer this thinking into other parts of the curriculum, or out into "real life".
>
> On receiving the application pack from Wren, I was very excited to read about BLP – I had not heard of it before. Here was an approach which fitted well with what I already believed: that developing children as learners should *infuse* the school curriculum rather than being the kind of "bolt-on" approach that I had experienced in my previous school.

As a further indication of Wren's commitment to the LPA, the inaugural principal, Michael Whitworth, had arranged for all the candidates to go to a local primary school to be observed teaching a lesson that, to quote the application pack, "would have some element of helping the children to become more independent learners". John's previous experience left him feeling well placed to respond to this challenge. Gavin Smith was involved in the appointment, and he told us that John's teaching stood out: he was clearly "a natural" at the LPA – to his initial disadvantage, as it turned out. John had applied for a role on the leadership team, but the selectors decided that they really needed someone like him to be "one of the troops" in the staffroom, so they offered him a job as an AST instead. Luckily, he took it, and has played a major part in making Wren not only an outstanding

---

9   You can take a video tour of the school at: https://secondary.wrenacademy.org.
10 Alistair Smith, with Mark Lovatt and John Turner, *Learning to Learn in Practice: The L2L Approach* (Carmarthen: Crown House Publishing, 2009).

school in conventional terms, but in developing it into one of the leading BLP high schools in the UK, regularly hosting showcase days for inquisitive visitors from other countries, including Iceland, Spain, and Australia.

Gavin Smith also remembers his first encounter with the LPA. Like John, he had been familiar with learning to learn lessons as an add-on to the curriculum, but the LPA's emphasis on permeating teaching with problem-solving approaches was new. In retrospect, he was even more critical than John was of the stand-alone learning to learn lessons:

> Before taking up my post of vice principal at the new Wren Academy I had been tasked with developing learners in a number of schools. I had put a lot of effort into creating learning review days, study skills (learning to learn) lessons, and other initiatives, but had always been disappointed with the outcomes. Despite some wonderful learning-focused conversations and short-term benefits, I was left dissatisfied with how little had really changed for the students. I found that what happened in these set-piece events did not transfer to other lessons or play a significant part in enhancing their all-round learning habits.
>
> So when I found out about BLP, I immediately saw the value of an approach which touched every area of the curriculum and required all teachers to contribute to the development of each student's learning dispositions. I welcomed the opportunity, at Wren, to create a coordinated approach to curriculum and lesson design which would empower all teachers to do just this.
>
> I liked the fact that we were being offered a common language with which to think about learning, and about our students as people who are growing in their capacity as learners. I liked the fact that it offered a consistent approach that had to be taken by all members of the school, and that the language for learning gave us a way of making links across the different subjects of the curriculum. We didn't go for a cross-curricular, thematic approach, but BLP enables teachers to talk about how students are learning in their different subjects, and to see where there are commonalities and differences. The language didn't feel like a straitjacket, it just helped us all to think and talk about learning. We wanted a clear focus on learning that could easily be explained to new members of staff, and BLP fitted the bill. We took it on board, and we just went for it, really. We did read around the subject and look at other people's work, but it was always to see how it would enrich the framework and help us deliver the vision that BLP had encapsulated for us.

> ## Wondering
>
> In your teaching career, have you been on a similar path to that outlined by John and Gavin?
>
> Have you changed your own style of teaching as your career has progressed? If so, what changes have you made and why?
>
> Does your evolution as a teacher reflect any underlying shifts in your beliefs about the purpose of education?

Having seen how these leaders have taken different pathways to arrive at their commitment to the LPA, let's pull out some of the common factors that predisposed them to find value in the approach.

Concerns Over Existing Ways of Doing Things

We have seen a range of *concerns* that made these school leaders receptive to something like the LPA. Jann's background in pastoral care made her sensitive to issues of *student well-being and mental health*. She was on the lookout for ideas about how to help her students become more emotionally resilient and better able to cope with stress. Gemma and Robert had concerns about how to give their students the kind of attitudinal "polish" that children from more privileged backgrounds seem to have.

Others have expressed concerns about the *narrow academic focus* of the curriculum. For example, we spoke to three senior teachers – Jonny Spowart, Lee Beskeen, and Rebecca Archer – at Heath Mount School, a fee-paying but academically non-selective preparatory school in the south of England. English prep schools often take their students up to the age of 13, preparing them to take a high-stakes academic test called the Common Entrance, or – as is becoming more common practice– pre-tests taken at age 11, which are either standardised versions or set by the senior schools to which the students are applying. Based on these, students may or may not be accepted by the independent high school of their choice. Jonny told us:

> We've been concerned for some time that a curriculum focused purely on preparing our students for these tests was not actually preparing them for the world in which they are growing up, and not providing the holistic education they deserve. We were on the lookout for something that would provide a far greater "value-added" education for the whole child. Our hope was to balance the current emphasis on the high-stakes tests with the development of a passion for lifelong learning, and the identification of unique strengths for each student. Most importantly, we required an approach which matched the school's values, and enabled us to nurture every one of our students to be thirsty, confident, inquisitive, independent learners, better equipped to navigate their way through a turbulent and rapidly changing 21st century.

In contrast, some school leaders come to the LPA by way of a concern over their students' lack of academic attainment. Jann was worried by St Luke's reputation in the local community as not very high-achieving. She was – as many other principals are – concerned by students' *apparent passivity* and lack of ownership of their own learning. Lorrae Sampson, principal of Nowra Anglican College in New South Wales, Australia, said:

> My students really need to take more accountability for their own learning. They need to understand that they are key in their learning journey, rather than sitting placidly in classes waiting for teachers to provide them with information. I believe that teaching students about how they learn will help them develop the necessary skills and abilities to understand each lesson better, give them the skills to transfer their learning to other situations, and create a better classroom environment in which students will be able to focus on their learning more effectively.

We heard similar concerns about the appropriateness of conventional educational methods for students at the lower end of the achievement range. Tessa Hodgson, head of Oaklands Primary School, near Heathrow airport in West London, had been working with children with SEND, across the London Borough of Ealing. Like Lorrae, she was dismayed by the passivity of many such children. She told us:

> After spending three years as a local authority advisor for SEND, I was very concerned by the results of the 2009 *Deployment and Impact of Support Staff* (DISS) report carried out by the University College London (UCL) Institute of Education into the effectiveness of teaching assistants, especially on the development of children with

SEND.[11] I had seen it with my own eyes: children in classrooms all over Ealing displaying signs of "learned helplessness" as they waited for their dedicated one-to-one teaching assistants to "help them learn". But, in my opinion, the DISS report did not go far enough. Teachers and SEND coordinators were delegating responsibility for teaching these children to teaching assistants because they themselves were not sure how to teach them successfully. In addition, senior leaders were being forced by government policy to focus on hitting data targets, so these very low-attaining children were not a key concern for them. And, on top of that, teacher training was not providing enough support.

I read widely to try to find a way to break through. David Mitchell's learning theory, in his book *What Really Works in Special and Inclusive Education*, touched a nerve as it explained why children with low self-esteem and self-belief do not engage in learning.[12] Reading about metacognition in Guy Claxton's *Building Learning Power* and John Hattie's *Visible Learning* seemed to show me a way of teaching that could empower all students.[13]

I was excited to take on the interim headship of Oaklands in September 2014 because the school had already implemented some BLP ideas. However, when I arrived, I found that children with SEND were not my only concern. I realised that I needed to ensure that BLP was embedded in the whole-school ethos, with systems and practice that supported it, before it could successfully impact on children's learning ... and so my journey began!

Jane Bellamy, who was, at the time of interview, head of Leigham Primary School in Plymouth, South-West England, also stressed the value of the LPA for children from disadvantaged communities:

That's why the LPA is so important, because aspirational families are probably giving their children some of the LPA's attitudes and beliefs — for example, "bettering yourself through hard work" — at home, whereas the kids from non-aspirational families desperately need to get those attitudes and habits of mind from school. We need to stimulate their curiosity — to get them interested in the world — because they might not be getting that at home. For instance, we trained our children to use Visible Thinking routines such as "See-Think-Wonder", in which we get them to look carefully

---

11 See Peter Blatchford, Paul Bassett, Penelope Brown, Clare Martin, Anthony Russell, and Rob Webster, *Deployment and Impact of Support Staff in Schools: Report on Findings from the Second National Questionnaire Survey of Schools, Support Staff and Teachers (Strand 1, Wave 2 – 2006)*. Research Report DCSF-RR005 (London: Institute of Education and Department for Children, Schools and Families, 2009).

12 David Mitchell, *What Really Works in Special and Inclusive Education: Using Evidence-Based Teaching Strategies* (Abingdon and New York: Routledge, 2008).

13 Claxton, *Building Learning Power*; and John Hattie, *Visible Learning: A Synthesis of Over 800 Meta-Analyses Relating to Achievement* (Abingdon and New York: Routledge, 2009).

at a puzzling picture, think about what might be going on, and then come up with a good question to ask. For some of our children, even this little technique made a big difference. It gave them a structured way of exercising their curiosity and imagination, and it was a real shift for them. We led them deeper into the "thinking zone" – maybe without them even realising it. Some school communities might not need this kind of induction – but they would probably benefit from a focus on some other of the LPA's learning habits.

Another worry that we have encountered was over students' high levels of extrinsic rather than intrinsic motivation. They were only interested in the grades that they were getting for their work, and seemed to have lost any interest in learning for its own sake. For example, Mark Fenton, the then head teacher of Dr Challoner's Grammar School in Amersham, Buckinghamshire, England, told us:

> As a high-performing school, the margins for increasing academic achievement at Dr Challoner's were pretty limited, but the opportunity to think about learning outcomes that stretched beyond school – the kinds of things that BLP talks about – were significant. In particular, we were finding that although our students were by and large bright, and appeared driven, they were often very extrinsically motivated. They were learning for the grades, and not for the pleasure of digging deep into a new subject or stretching their understanding. And we came to see, looking through the lens of BLP, that we might be able to shift that mindset.

We heard repeated concerns about whether schools were doing enough to prepare their students for life beyond education; in particular, for the challenges and opportunities of the globalised, digitalised world that they are going to inhabit. Jonny, Lee, and Rebecca at Heath Mount told us:

> We were also very conscious of how the big wide world is changing – especially the world of work – and of how our children were going to need to become very flexible and agile to flourish in that world. They are really going to need to be 21st century learners. And a purely knowledge-based curriculum doesn't, by itself, give the children the requisite qualities.

When we asked Simon Buckingham Shum, then chair of governors at Bushfield School – a junior school for children aged 7–11 on the outskirts of Milton Keynes, a large town in the East Midlands, England – what he saw as the core purpose of education at Bushfield, he said without hesitation:

> It's our job not just to help children master literacy and numeracy but to prepare them for a very turbulent and complex world. We are failing if we don't prepare them with the skills they need to cope with uncertainty; to cope with differing perspectives; to cope

with working with different kinds of people; and to equip them to ask good questions. Our children are at a very crucial age. We need to get those skills right into the DNA of the way our children think and learn – before it's too late.

You can hear the passionate concern in Simon's choice of language. It is not surprising that Bushfield has been a pioneer of BLP. Interestingly, Simon is now professor of learning informatics at the University of Technology Sydney, Australia.

Dissatisfactions with Existing Ways of Doing Things

We found that the LPA tended to look like a promising approach to those who had been disappointed with other purported responses to their concerns. In particular, earlier approaches to learning to learn, or the teaching of "thinking skills", seemed – for many of the school leaders who responded to our survey – not to have hit the spot. We saw how two senior leaders at Wren Academy, Gavin Smith and John Keohane, had had disappointing experiences with these earlier approaches. So did Gemma Goldenberg at Sandringham, though she was quick to acknowledge the value of some of these pioneering efforts in quickening her own interest in the nature of learning, and in how teachers might help children to become better learners. One of the problems seemed to be that treating learning to learn as a "subject", to be taught separately from "normal lessons", didn't work very well.

Many of our interviewees told us that, when they finally encountered the LPA in one guise or another, they had been looking for something more infused, more coherent, and more long-term than what they had met so far. They were not interested in chasing the latest fad. You'll remember Gemma talking about her quest for something that would coherently underpin the variety of initiatives taking place in her school, each of which seemed useful, but which lacked an overarching rationale. Robert Cleary reflected:

> I think we sometimes suffer from a short attention span in education. We expect new initiatives and strategies to have an immediate impact – and if they don't, they get discarded and we go looking for the next "magic bullet". But I've learned that creating a team that has stickability and persistence is essential to building an LPA school. You

need advocates who will constantly remind everyone why we embarked on the LPA, what we are going to do with it, and how we are going to use it to achieve our aims.

Mark Fenton, head teacher at Dr Challoner's, told us:

> I was beginning to look around for what was "out there" concerning learning in general. I found lots of different approaches, but nothing that really made coherent sense, nothing which excited me … And then I met Graham Powell at a conference. We got chatting and it sounded as if BLP might be the kind of thing I had been looking for. I arranged for Graham to come in and talk to my SLT, and his approach landed very well with them. That was an important test: if I couldn't "sell it" to them, there was no way I could hope to get the whole staff on board.

Lorrae Sampson at Nowra Anglican College said:

> I am sure that the students will reap the benefits. But this may take a while to see … The commitment to the LPA is for the long haul; it is not just a rapid fix.

Several leaders told us that they were looking for something that would help to bind different bits of the school together into a more coherent whole. You'll remember Gavin Smith saying that he liked being offered a coherent language for learning, and the consistent approach that had to be taken by everyone in the school. Similarly, the team at Heath Mount sought something that would bind the different age groups together more tightly. They said:

> We had a concern about the fragmentation that had crept into the school. It had been organised into four "bands" – the pre-prep (with children aged up to 7), and then the lower school, the middle school, and the senior school – and each had rather gone its own way. So we were looking for a philosophy or a vision that would help us join up the dots, and secure an overview of the children's development and progression across the whole school. When the head came back from a conference enthusing about the LPA, it seemed to tick all of those boxes, and our ears pricked up. It seemed like a philosophy that the whole school could get behind.

Critical Events and Encounters

As we've already seen, there were often critical incidents that strengthened our leaders' resolve to go looking for that "something more". Jann Robinson was powerfully moved by the suicides of her bright students. Gemma Goldenberg and Robert Cleary were both galvanised by the experience of seeing an academically able but "unpolished" girl not get a place at the school she wanted.

Sometimes the critical event was an encounter with an idea that "clicked". Remember Robert reading *New Kinds of Smart* and being hit by the idea that intelligence wasn't a fixed commodity, but was something that teachers could – and should – aim to strengthen. Rachel Macfarlane was struck by listening to a lecture. She said:

> I first heard about the LPA – in the guise of BLP, as it was then – in 2003 when I attended a conference at which Guy Claxton was speaking. I remember how fresh, logical, clear, and articulate the presentation was; it made perfect sense! And how powerful the multitude of glimpses into the classroom practice of BLP teachers given were; I wanted to know more because I could see that it worked.

She went on to explain how the LPA opened her eyes to the wider and deeper potential of an approach to teaching which she was already pursuing in her own subject:

> As a history teacher who had regularly attended Schools History Project (SHP) conferences and taught the SHP GCSE syllabus for many years, I was very familiar with – and had long been convinced by – arguments around the power of a skills-rich, rather than purely knowledge-led, approach to the curriculum. I knew the importance of supporting students in developing learning skills such as empathy, curiosity, questioning, and linking in order to become strong historians. I had seen first-hand that students become more effective and powerful historians – better able to cope with the discipline at A level and beyond – when taught how to interrogate evidence, analyse provenance, and see links and themes over time and between time periods and continents, rather than study eras in disjointed and unconnected chunks, as I had done at university. I was in my first headship at the time, and sitting listening to Guy, I could see that the way in which I taught – and had guided others to teach – was the way in which, as a school leader, I should be supporting staff to develop learners across the entire curriculum.

Often, an important step on the way to buying into the LPA has been a visit to another school that is already using the approach, and seeing it working on the ground.

Summary

As we said at the beginning of this chapter, the LPA journey typically starts with some kind of an educational itch that prompts the search for a satisfactory scratch. There is a sense that the existing way of organising the school, and designing the learning in its classrooms, is missing something important. But in each of our interviewees, that feeling of dissatisfaction is balanced by a sense of hope that there might be a better way, if only they could find it. And then comes a small insight, or a glimpse of a possibility, that begins to crystallise that hope into a cautious optimism. There might be a false dawn, in which an approach fails to satisfy deeply enough, and so the search is resumed. And then an encounter with a version of the LPA kick-starts a process of further research, reading, critical reflection, and trying the ideas out on colleagues, to see if they hold water and fulfil their early promise. Crucially, then there may come that moment of conviction and commitment – and the LPA journey begins in earnest. But getting to that moment is critical, for the journey is lengthy, energy-consuming, and usually not without its downs as well as its ups. Without conviction, it is easy to engage only half-heartedly, and to give up when difficulties appear.

So, to conclude this chapter, now that you have heard about a variety of other leaders' experiences, you might like to reflect again on your own. Here are some questions to guide your pondering.

Wondering

What in all these stories and accounts struck you or touched you? Was there anything that spoke directly to your own idealism?

Were there things that aroused your scepticism – or even cynicism, maybe?

Do you have a sense of "cautious optimism" that things could be more as you would like them in education? Or have you become disheartened about the possibility of significant improvement within the mainstream?

What paralleled most closely your own experience of innovation?

Have you come across one version or another of the LPA already? If so, how did you respond to it? Were your reactions different from those we have offered you in this chapter?

Do you still have any lingering doubts about the validity or feasibility of the LPA? If so, what would you need to do to address them? Visit an LPA school and see it in action? Talk it over with someone whose fair-mindedness you trust? Read more about the research behind it? (If the last of these, we hope the next chapter will help.)

Chapter 2

Learning Power: The Facts at Your Fingertips

Chapter 1 was designed to help you see if the LPA chimed with your own values, ambitions, and aspirations for your school. If all has gone well so far, you are on your way to generating the conviction and commitment that will be needed to turn your school into a hotbed of self-reliant learning. But you will need more than fire in your belly. You will need evidence and knowledge too in order to bring others on board, respond to doubts and scepticism effectively, and feel confident in talking the talk of the LPA. So, having hopefully engaged the heart, it is time to reassure the head (pun intended) and tool it up for the job ahead. This chapter provides the information you will need in order to set about instilling the LPA in your school.

If you want or need more detail, the first book in the LPA series, *The Learning Power Approach*, will give you much more on the rationale and research background. And we provide – at the end of this chapter and at the end of the book – information about other reading material and resources that will help you flesh out your understanding. But for now, here is your starter kit for dealing with the following questions:

- What are the values behind the LPA?
- What exactly is the LPA?
- Why is the LPA needed?
- What is the research evidence behind the LPA?
- Where does the LPA come from and who is behind it?
- How does the LPA look at the classroom?
- What practical resources does the LPA offer teachers?
- What should we be reading and watching?

You might like to orient yourself by reading the following case study about Sunnydown School. It will give you a real-life example on which to hang the information and ideas in the rest of the chapter.

> When Paul Jensen took over as head of Sunnydown School in September 2014, he soon realised he had inherited quite a traditional educational culture. Sunnydown is a maintained (state-funded) special school in Surrey, south of London, England, for boys aged 11–16 with communication and interaction needs (CoIN), commonly associated with autistic spectrum disorder (ASD). There were eighty-four boys and twenty-three teaching staff on roll. Although many of the boys are academically able, when they first arrive at the school they often suffer from high levels of anxiety coupled with an inability to tolerate frustration and uncertainty, can be heavily dependent on adult support, and may find it hard to get along cooperatively with each other. Paul found that, in the existing culture, there was a rigid GCSE-orientated curriculum with limited scope for flexibility, a lot of help from teaching assistants, and a rather traditional, sanction-orientated attitude to "bad behaviour". Exclusions were high. Teachers appeared to be under a lot of pressure to "get the results", and appraisal could potentially be used to deny pay increments if they failed to deliver. There was much compliance and little flexibility and originality in both the staffroom and the classrooms. In Paul's words, the school felt creatively stifled. However, he recognised the potential, the desire, and the enthusiasm in all staff.
>
> One of Paul's first moves was to ask for a voluntary Ofsted inspection, which confirmed that all was not well. He then set about shifting the mindsets of teachers, students, and their parents. Paul remains convinced that some autistic learning characteristics are not set in stone, and that, with help, the boys can become more able to grow the qualities of *resilience, independence,* and *cooperation* which they may have been lacking. These core values of the school are now captured in the acronym RICE[3] – the three Es stand for *enabling, encouraging,* and *empowering* the boys to demonstrate stronger habits of mind so they can "do it for themselves". In recognising that some of the boys may be starting from a lower baseline than others, and that their learning journeys might be unique and need more support, Paul also identified that they had it in them to grow

in confidence, comradeship, creativity, adventurousness, self-awareness, and self-control. His belief was that if these attributes could be developed in them, then, consequently, their innate academic potential could be realised. The freedom and encouragement to design an innovative curriculum, delivered creatively by dedicated staff, was a large part of the solution. Although he didn't know it at the time, Paul's vision echoed closely the LPA ambition to develop all students as confident and capable active learners.

Andrea Jensen, head of English and whole-school literacy, said:

> For many of the boys that come here, they already feel like they have failed; some feel like they've failed in their schools; others feel they've failed in their families, as sons, as brothers. They are mostly quite high-functioning, so they have quite a lot of awareness of their differences with peers and perceive these as "deficiencies" and "failings". And then we say to them, "Learning is all about failing and, more importantly, trying again." You can see why they might baulk at it! But steadily we get them to reframe the struggle to learn so it stops being so frightening.

Paul set about changing things – and constantly talked to staff about his vision and beliefs, inviting their ideas and explaining why the evidence suggested that the shift was both desirable and possible. *Transparency* is one of Paul's watchwords. In our conversation, Andrea commented wryly:

> In any organisation there are people who don't like what's going on, and I'm sure there are here. But at least nobody's confused about what Paul believes in or what his values and assumptions are, or where we are heading.

Paul sowed seeds of curiosity by mentioning key influences such as Carol Dweck's work on growth mindset and by offering staff things to read on mindfulness and active learning. He mentioned an alarming statistic: only 32% of adults with ASD are in any form of paid employment[1] – unemployment is, therefore, a fate that could await two in three of their boys. The potential in his staff, recognised early on, was now able to be nurtured to fruition. As a staff they discussed the impact of stifling their creativity and the possibilities should it be encouraged. Immediately, one teacher offered to lead on finding a better approach to careers education. A teaching assistant suggested that they could offer drama and music

---

1 See https://www.autism.org.uk/about/what-is/myths-facts-stats.aspx.

opportunities and that she could lead it. (Not all the boys went for it, but many did, and learned to love it.) One of the kitchen staff said that she was looking for a new challenge and wanted to try being a teaching assistant. She was brilliant and is now, to use Paul's word, indispensable – as all of his staff are. Teaching assistants are training to be teachers; teachers are doing second degrees; trainee teachers are regularly requesting Sunnydown as their SEN placement; and there is a constant buzz of learning throughout the whole school – which rubs off on the boys. Andrea said:

> It is very encouraging for the boys for their teacher to come in on a Monday morning and tell them how they were struggling with their coursework over the weekend. (*Modelling* is Paul's second watchword.)

Of course, Paul met with some initial scepticism and resistance. Teachers were going to have to change their ways – and habit change is always effortful. Paul met this with a constant emphasis not on performance but on *continuous improvement*. Now, staff appraisals revolve not around a potentially punitive reaction to a teacher's exam results, but around a conversation about how they are going to contribute to building confident, self-regulating, independent learners in the coming year and what innovations they are going to try. It is hard to maintain a cynical stance when your fellow teachers are clearly responding enthusiastically to taking ownership of the school's vision and development, making their own contributions, and seeing the boys growing and blooming.

Some pushback still occurs – some staff (and students) are wary of the recent introduction of mindfulness meditation sessions, for example – but Paul recognises that it is steadily diminishing. And the growing independence of the boys means that teachers can try out other innovations. With invaluable and unflappable support from the leadership team, a Monday to Thursday national-curriculum-focused timetable was established, with active and independent learning facilitated throughout each day. On a Friday, however, some of the boys will be off in town doing work experience with local employers. Others might be doing drama; learning to service a bicycle in the innovative cycle mechanic workshop; designing and making an outdoor chess set; studying horticulture; or contributing to the local community while touring the neighbourhood and selling food from the Sunnydown burger van.

And what about the results of all this innovation? Academically, according to Progress 8 scores, Sunnydown was the best performing maintained special school in England in 2018. Paul seldom advertises this, preferring to remind audiences that his students and staff always had the potential, it just had to be unlocked and nurtured. In their most recent Ofsted inspection, standards had risen from "requires improvement" to "good". Annual surveys have shown that 100% of parents would recommend the school to other parents – five years running. The school gets four applications for every place they can offer; they remain oversubscribed and in demand. And their own home-grown RICE[3] profiling tool (based on the well-known Boxall profile[2]) documents the reality of the boys' growth in resilience, self-awareness, self-control, and sociability from Year 6 (before they arrive at Sunnydown) to Year 9. By Year 10, there is a much-reduced need for the boys to have the constant individual support of a teaching assistant. They have been weaned off it as their own "learning muscles" have steadily strengthened. In Years 10 and 11, one teacher in a class is often sufficient. One boy regularly takes himself off to a local high school to study history – his passion – because Sunnydown doesn't have the capacity to employ a history specialist. This would have been an unimaginable feat of social bravery for that young man two years earlier. The art teacher is now teaching four different GCSE syllabuses in the same class (drawing, sculpture, photography, and textiles) because the boys have learned how to teach themselves – and they notice if they are becoming anxious and fretful, and know how to handle it without help, or when to seek appropriate pastoral support.

As in any school, not all students will get the GCSEs they hoped for. But when that happens (as it did when Guy visited on results day) they do not go to pieces. They ring up the local college and calmly explain why they had a bad day, and why they still deserve the place they had been offered. And that self-confidence, says Paul Jensen, is what matters most in the long run; more than those exam results themselves. This is the LPA in action: students who could easily have been written off in a different education culture as needing only care and containment are now in control of their education and lifelong learning.

---

2   See https://boxallprofile.org/.

> ## Wondering
>
> How do you react to this case study? Does it conform to your own views about the education of youngsters with special needs and/or disabilities, or does it surprise, challenge, or inspire you?
>
> Would you agree or disagree with the idea that, if we can build habits of self-regulation and independence in young people who have "special needs", we can certainly do it in mainstream education?

What Are the Values Behind the LPA?

As we have seen, the LPA is values-led. It starts from a good hard look at the demands and opportunities that today's young people are likely to meet in their lives, and the resources – social, psychological, and material – that they are likely to need to flourish in the face of those demands and to make the most of those opportunities. We value providing an education that will equip them with the necessary skills. Of course people will need to be able to read, write, and calculate. Of course they will need knowledge to help them comprehend and navigate the world. Of course they need the grades to get onto the university or college course they want. But we are interested in what the other residual benefits of their time in school might be.

So the second value asserts that at the heart of every school must be a concern with the development of character. The most valuable residues of schooling are a set of broad attitudes and dispositions that will steer young people towards finding love, respect, and fulfilment in whatever paths their lives take. Some of these dispositions, the *pro-social* ones, concern the ways in which they behave towards other people. Are they more likely to be honest than shifty; kind than callous? Other dispositions, the *epistemic* ones, concern general reactions to uncertainty, challenge, and strangeness. Are they inclined to be inquisitive, or are they narrow-minded or arrogant? We are convinced that school has a part to play in shaping these characteristics, and should do it consciously and deliberately to the best of its ability.

And the third core value is this: not only should education be a preparation for life, but it should be a preparation *for all* – the practically minded as well as the academically minded; those who will be self-employed as well as those who might want to enter a traditional profession. Too many schools still measure their success by the roll call of admissions to prestigious universities and, in dozens of small ways, signal that those who become nurses rather than surgeons, or plumbers rather than professors, are somehow second class.

Every culture, every school leader, is of course free to choose different values than these to underpin their educational philosophy, or to spurn such philosophical talk altogether, and their schools will reflect those choices.

What Exactly Is the LPA?

Put formally, the goal of the LPA is this:

> To develop all students as confident and capable learners – ready, willing, and able to choose, design, research, pursue, troubleshoot, and evaluate learning for themselves, alone and with others, in school and out, for grades and for life.

All of the words in this statement matter. *Develop* reminds us that cultivating these character traits takes time and conscious attention. *All* says that this is vital for every student, regardless of their background or their "academic ability". High achievers need it if they are going to cope with the demands of their academic/vocational pursuits beyond school. And low achievers need it even more, because without these dispositions, they are condemned to stay in the slow lane of learning.

We need to help students become *ready* and *willing* to learn on their own, and not just *able* to. We want them to be keen to learn, as well as capable of learning. It is not enough to train students in learning or thinking "skills", because a skill is just something you *can* do, not something you are *inclined* to do. And we want students to be inclined to be resourceful, creative, and cooperative, not just able to be when prodded.

The next string of words – *choose, design, research, pursue, troubleshoot, and evaluate* – begins to unpack what it means to be a powerful learner. In a traditional classroom it is the teacher who does most of the choosing, designing, troubleshooting, and evaluating of learning, thus depriving the students of the necessity – and the opportunity – to learn how to do these things for themselves. LPA teachers organise their classrooms so that, over time, they do less and less managing and organising of learning, and their students become more and more confident, capable, and keen to do it for themselves.

Alone and with others stresses the importance of being able to take charge of learning in collaboration with others, as well as on your own. *In school and out* reminds us that the whole point of the LPA is to prepare students not just for the next stage of their formal education, but to give them a broad, positive orientation to learning – to grapple with things that are hard or confusing – whatever and wherever they may be, for the rest of their lives. And *for grades and for life* tells us not to see "life skills" and "good grades" as in competition with each other. The LPA offers a way to cultivate both, side by side.

Why Is the LPA Needed?

As a school leader embarking on the LPA journey, your job is to get buy-in from the staff, and that means being able to explain convincingly why it is a good idea. Here are ten good reasons why any school should seriously consider the LPA.[3]

1. **The LPA improves learning at school.** For example, in a 2001 review of research entitled "Learning about learning enhances performance", Chris Watkins – then of the UCL Institute of Education – wrote, "For nearly 20 years it has been known that students with more elaborated conceptions of

---

3 Fuller discussion of, and references for, these claims are provided in Chapter 5 of *The Learning Power Approach*. In the interest of keeping this discussion concise, we repeat only a handful of those references here.

learning perform better in public examinations at age 16."[4] That is, students who have been encouraged to think and talk about learning and about themselves as learners, and to develop a richer vocabulary with which to do so, show gains in their test scores. They are more engaged, and they learn more effectively.

2. **The LPA mitigates the effects of poverty and deprivation.** A recent large-scale study of 145,000 15-year-olds in Chile showed that children from poor or challenging backgrounds who have a *positive and optimistic attitude to learning* (rather than a "fixed mindset") show levels of school achievement that are indistinguishable from those of youngsters from much wealthier families.[5] Of course, this doesn't mean that we should ignore pressing social and political issues of inequity. But while we work for a better society, there are things that teachers can do right now to help.

3. **Disadvantaged children benefit the most from the LPA.** All students show higher levels of engagement and make faster progress in LPA classrooms. But children from low socio-economic backgrounds gain the most from being in classrooms where teachers demystify the processes and strategies of learning, strengthen students' understanding of what it takes to produce good work, and build their capacity for – and sense of enjoyment in – grappling with tricky problems.[6] It is also the case that poorer students who have been over-helped to get the grades they need to get into college are much more likely to drop

---

4   Chris Watkins, Learning about learning enhances performance. *National School Improvement Network Research Matters*, No. 13 (Spring 2001), p. 5. Available at: https://discovery.ucl.ac.uk/id/eprint/10002803/1/Watkins2001Learning.pdf. Chris is referring to research by Noel Entwistle and Béla Kozéki, Relationships between school motivation, approaches to studying, and attainment among British and Hungarian adolescents. *British Journal of Educational Psychology* (1985), 55(2): 124–137.
5   Susana Claro, David Paunesku, and Carol Dweck, Growth mindset tempers the effect of poverty on academic achievement. *Proceedings of the National Academy of Sciences* (2016), 113(31): 8664–8668.
6   See Cheryl Flink, Ann Boggiano, and Marty Barrett, Controlling teaching strategies: undermining children's self-determination and performance. *Journal of Personality and Social Psychology* (1990), 59(5): 916–924; James Mannion and Neil Mercer, Learning to learn: improving attainment, closing the gap at Key Stage 3. *The Curriculum Journal* (2016), 27(2): 246–271. Available at: http://dx.doi.org/10.1080/09585176.2015.1137778; Ron Berger, *An Ethic of Excellence: Building a Culture of Craftsmanship with Students* (Portsmouth, NH: Heinemann, 2003); and Bethan Burge, Jenny Lenkeit, and Juliet Sizmur, *PISA in Practice: Cognitive Activation in Maths* (Slough: National Foundation for Educational Research, 2015).

out in their first year than those who have developed greater resilience and resourcefulness by being taught the LPA way.[7]

4. **Even high achievers suffer if they have not developed their learning power.** For example, the heads of the counselling services at both Oxford and Cambridge universities are seeing a rise in the number of students who are inclined to "go to pieces", or suffer from so-called "imposter syndrome", when confronted with demanding learning challenges and deadlines. Alan Percy at Oxford was quoted in the *TES* as saying, "Students [today] often don't grasp the full meaning of learning. Learning is finding out something you did not know and struggling with it. It is almost as if, if they do not know or understand something immediately they feel as though they are failing."[8]

5. **Learning power is an antidote to mental health issues.** Put simply, stress is what happens when the demands that you perceive are on you chronically exceed the resources that you think you have in order to deal with those demands. Anxiety, depression, rigidity, and fundamentalism (of all kinds) can all be responses to feeling inadequate in the face of complexity and uncertainty. Education ought to offer a way of enhancing your resourcefulness, and thus reducing stress. For many youngsters, however, their schooling simply seems to add to their burdens. It is a net stressor, not a reducer of stress.

6. **Learning power makes you more employable.** Time and again, surveys show that employers value attributes such as initiative, resourcefulness, and fluid intelligence – often more highly than qualifications. Some big firms like Google and PwC routinely hire people who can think on their feet in preference to those with impressive degrees.

7. **Learning power predicts life satisfaction.** Large-scale studies have shown that traits such as curiosity, perseverance, self-discipline, imagination, concentration, and empathy correlate significantly with how stable, successful, and satisfied people are with their lives in adulthood. They also show that

---

7 See Paul Tough, *How Children Succeed: Grit, Curiosity and the Hidden Power of Character* (Boston, MA: Houghton Mifflin Harcourt, 2012).
8 Quoted in Warwick Mansell, "Spoonfed" students lack confidence at Oxbridge, *TES* (10 December 2010). Available at: https://www.tes.com/news/spoonfed-students-lack-confidence-oxbridge.

these attributes are affected by early experience – at home, with friends, and in school.

8. **The LPA helps people cope with the escalation of everyday cognitive demands.** It is a cliché, but we do live in a world where the routine mental demands of modern life can threaten to overwhelm us.[9] New technologies to be mastered; new relationships to negotiate online; new forms of threat to personal and financial security; new possibilities for risky fun; new belief systems to be tried on for size; fake news to be weighed and sifted; dozens of complicated passwords to remember … it is a learning world out there, and we need to be lifelong learners.

9. **The LPA makes teachers' lives easier and more rewarding.** Learning power doesn't just benefit the learners themselves; it can make teaching more interesting and less stressful. Students who are more curious – open to being engaged and intrigued by things – and more determined to work things out for themselves – more likely to relish a challenge than be floored by it – are more rewarding and enjoyable to teach.

10. Finally, **powerful learners are just plain happier**, more of the time. People who have discovered difficult, worthwhile things they want to accomplish, and who feel empowered to pursue those goals with all their hearts, have access to a world of unselfconscious absorption, wrestling with challenges and making progress in overcoming them, in which (they report in retrospect) they feel happy.

---

9 See, for example, Robert Kegan, *In Over Our Heads: The Mental Demands of Modern Life* (Cambridge, MA: Harvard University Press, 1995).

What Is the Research Evidence Behind the LPA?

In the last twenty years or so, there has been a sea change in the view of the human mind. When Guy was an undergraduate psychology student, many moons ago, the general assumption in scientific psychology was that the most important things about the mind were fixed and universal. The hunt was on for the basic structures and functions that could be identified regardless of culture and tuition. "Short-term memory" (STM) was a fixed capacity bottleneck that gave constricted access to a virtually limitless "long-term memory" (LTM) that had, supposedly, a universal architecture – as if all libraries everywhere were bound to rely on the Dewey Decimal System of organisation. Researchers Allen Newell and Herbert A. Simon (the latter went on to win a Nobel Prize for Economics) went in search of a computer model of the Generalised Problem-Solver that was supposed to describe all of us, everywhere, all of the time.[10]

Now, people are talking about the mind not as a monolith but as a shape-shifter. STM morphed first into "working memory", like a laptop's central processing unit, and then into a more nebulous cloud of "executive functions" and "self-regulation strategies" that can be both task- and subject-specific. And these functions also change, grow, or diminish over time as a result of experience, both incidental and intentional. Perhaps most importantly, the notion of intelligence itself has evolved from something perceived as a fixed reservoir of general-purpose and genetically capped cognitive resources, to, as Lauren Resnick calls it, "the sum total of one's habits of mind".[11] And habits are things you acquire; things that can change; and things that may have quite specific triggers.

There may indeed be some hardware constraints, but genes are not the masters of our behaviour; they are protein-making recipes that are turned on and off in complicated ways by the experiences we are having, and by the acquired habits of mind that

---

10 Allen Newell and Herbert A. Simon, *Human Problem Solving* (Englewood Cliffs, NJ: Prentice-Hall, 1972).
11 Lauren B. Resnick, Making America smarter. *Education Week* (1999), 18(40): 38–40 at 39. Available at: http://www.edweek.org/ew/articles/1999/06/16/40resnick.h18.html.

dynamically mediate and modulate the relationships between genes and experience.[12] The intelligent mind comprises – in addition to some basic structures and constraints – a set of malleable habits that are picked up from the families, friendship groups, and schools to which people belong.

So, in the olden days, we felt confident in speaking about the causes of children's achievement, behaviour, and well-being in terms of quite a simple psychological model: a fixed commodity, their "ability", modulated by their "motivation" and their "social situation". Children behaved badly or flunked the test because (a) they aren't very bright; (b) they didn't try; and/or (c) they got in with a bad crowd/had trouble at home/had a poor teacher. If there were no obvious concerns about poor motivation stemming from a disruptive social milieu, teachers felt quite justified in inferring ability from performance – and then completing a circular argument by confidently attributing performance to "ability".

Now, however, the research demands that we add into the mix another set of factors to do with feelings, expectations, self-regulation strategies, attitudes, values, and dispositions. Our personalities and mental aptitudes are not set in stone. They change and develop over our lifespan and can be modulated by the momentary triggering of a stereotype or a self-critical belief. Our apparent intelligence can change in a moment depending who is on the other end of the phone – or behind the teacher's desk. What this means is that teachers have the opportunity to deliberately influence the development of these *habits and dispositions* in positive directions.[13]

Some people resist this increase in the complexity of the stories we tell about children. They prefer to stick with the old, simplistic set of categories and narratives because it is less cognitively demanding to do so. But, as the tax authorities say, ignorance is no defence. And it is not innocuous, because shrinking children to fit an outmoded model of the mind leads to very real, noxious consequences. It is hard to maintain your self-esteem when you are constantly being told, or shown, that you aren't very "bright" – and that there is nothing you can do about it.

---

12 See, for example, Ken Richardson, *Genes, Brains and Human Potential: The Science and Ideology of Intelligence* (New York: Columbia University Press, 2017).
13 See, for example, Resnick, Making America smarter; Cecilia Heyes, *Cognitive Gadgets: The Cultural Evolution of Thinking* (Cambridge, MA: Harvard University Press, 2018).

The research on the modifiability of basic dispositions such as curiosity, resilience, playfulness of mind, reflectiveness, and conviviality – and the influence of such dispositions on learning behaviour and attainment – is reviewed in more detail in Chapter 9 of *The Learning Power Approach*, and in more detail still in *Wise Up: The Challenge of Lifelong Learning*.[14] The evidence base is developing all the time, through the work of such prestigious research centres as Angela Duckworth's Character Lab at the University of Pennsylvania, and Project Zero at Harvard. Please refer any sceptics to those sources.

Wondering

Do you now feel more able to talk convincingly about the new view of the young mind that lies behind the LPA, and the evidence that underpins it?

What else would you need to know in order to feel on firmer ground?

Are there other things you have read, or heard about, that put these ideas in a way that you find more accessible or congenial?

Where Does the LPA Come From and Who Is Behind It?

The LPA charts a middle way between the extremes of "traditional" and "progressive" teaching. It preserves the traditionalists' focus on the importance of knowledge and understanding, and on helping all students achieve the grades of which they are capable. But it combines this with the progressives' concern with the development of epistemic character: that set of positive attitudes and mindsets towards dealing with challenge and uncertainty.

---

14 Guy Claxton, *Wise Up: The Challenge of Lifelong Learning* (London and New York: Bloomsbury, 1999).

Over the last twenty years or so, a number of groups have been homing in on this possibility, refining its specification, and researching practical ways of making it a reality in today's busy classrooms. Though they each have a distinct flavour, they agree about much more than they argue about. The LPA aims to distil the essence of this emerging school of thought. Its principal architects and contributors include:

- The Expeditionary Learning – now called EL Education – schools.
- Ron Ritchhart's work on classrooms as "cultures of thinking", and the development of "intellectual character".
- The Habits of Mind school of thought, with its complementary idea of "dispositional teaching", developed over many years by Arthur L. Costa and Bena Kallick.
- The highly successful International Baccalaureate (IB) programmes used in thousands of schools around the world.
- The Tools of the Mind approach to early childhood education, developed by Elena Bodrova and Deborah Leong.[15]
- The New Pedagogies for Deep Learning work of Michael Fullan and his colleagues.
- The Learning without Limits approach of Susan Hart, Alison Peacock, and their colleagues.
- The venerable Project for the Enhancement of Effective Learning (PEEL) developed by a combination of academics and teachers at Monash University in Melbourne, Australia.
- Our own development, with other colleagues, of BLP.

There are many more contributors to this school of thought, both contemporary and historical, that are covered in more detail in *The Learning Power Approach*. From the pioneering work of great educators such as Maria Montessori and John Dewey,

---

15 Elena Bodrova and Deborah J. Leong, *Tools of the Mind: A Vygotskian Approach to Early Childhood Education* (New York: Pearson, 1995). Details of the other approaches referenced here can be found in *The Learning Power Approach*.

to contemporary scholars such as Carol Dweck and David Perkins, there is a long tradition of rigorous thinking and research that leads in the direction of the LPA.

How Does the LPA Look at the Classroom?

In every classroom there are three different kinds of learning going on: knowledge is being accumulated; specific skills and techniques are being acquired; and more general attitudes and habits of mind are being formed. We find it useful to think of these as different levels or layers in a flowing river.

On the surface, quite fast moving and most visible, are the subjects of the curriculum – the knowledge. As you sit on the bank, you can watch the different topics floating by. There go the Tudors. Close behind come simultaneous equations. Ah, here come figures of speech. And so on.

Then, just below the surface of the river, come the forms of expertise that enable students to acquire and make sense of that content – linguistic, numerical, and digital literacies; the skills and disciplines of mathematical and historical thinking; the ability to read musical notation; and so on. Both of these layers are very familiar to teachers, and of great concern.

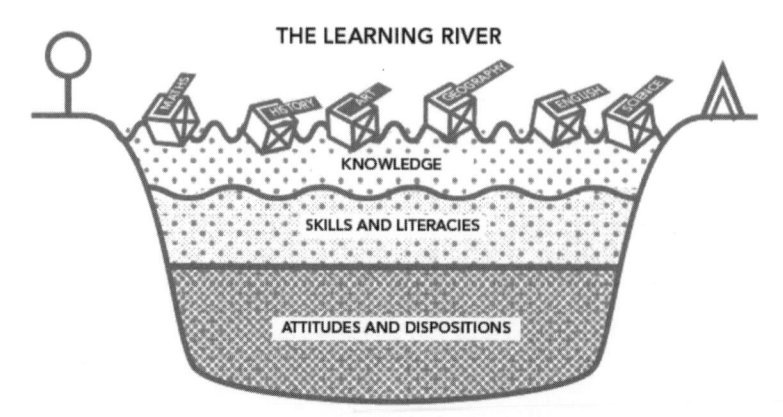

Figure 2.1: The Layers of Learning in the Classroom
Source: By kind permission of Juan and Becky Carlzon

But lower down in the depths of the river, slower moving and less easy to see, the attitudes that shape students' engagement with learning more generally are being formed. Questions we might ask ourselves about these attitudes include:

- Are students becoming more able to sort things out for themselves as they go through school, or less?

- Are they becoming more imaginative in their thinking, or more literal-minded?

- Are they learning to question what they read, or becoming more uncritical?

- Are they learning to enjoy digging deeper into questions and problems, or becoming more focused only on the marks they get on tests?

- Are they becoming more subtle in their thinking – and able to handle more complex material – or are they only interested in the "right answer"?

- Are they learning to appraise their own and each other's work in an honest and respectful way, or becoming more fragile in the face of feedback?

Learning at each of these layers is going on all the time. They don't compete for time and attention. You don't have to stop practising spelling in order to work on your resilience. Resilience is being strengthened – or weakened – by the way in which the teacher is "doing spelling" with the children. Some ways of doing spelling encourage the children to be more tolerant of mistakes, and more able to spot and fix them for themselves. And other ways of doing spelling make the children more passive and dependent on the teacher. As a teacher – or as a parent, come to that – you can't *not* be affecting the habits of mind that are slowly developing at layer 3 in the river – for good or ill.

So developing epistemic character is not optional. It's not an extra layer that you can choose to paste on top of business as usual. The only choice a teacher has is whether to create a cultural undertow in the classroom that pulls students towards becoming more independent, inquisitive, reflective, and imaginative; or whether to allow students to be drawn in the direction of becoming more passive, compliant, unadventurous, and extrinsically motivated. The first move in the LPA is to interest teachers in the kind of impact they are already having to see if, on reflection, they can identify any room for improvement.

What Practical Resources Does the LPA Offer Teachers?

The LPA offers teachers and schools a number of useful tools for thinking about the aims and methods of education. They include two major frameworks for thinking about teaching and learning. The first offers clarity about the desired outcomes, and the second lays out the classroom design principles that will bring those outcomes about. Of course, different members of the LPA family will articulate these two frameworks slightly differently, and some are more explicit about them than others. But they are always present, and they offer strong guidance as to how a learning-powered culture can be cultivated.

The elements of learning power

You can't design a school to achieve certain ends if you are not clear about what those ends are. In the absence of a detailed description of the kinds of habits of mind we want students to develop while they are at school, it is all too easy to fall back on chasing examination results and validation from inspection reports. If all we say about the plus (in *results plus*) is that we want children to become "successful learners", for example, without spelling out what we mean by success, and at what kinds of learning, it is all too easy to slip back into thinking that "successful learners" just means biddable students who get good grades. Likewise, merely wishing them to become "active citizens" begs all the interesting and important questions about what that means. If we can't say what observable behaviours are manifestations of that grand ambition, we have no way of knowing if we are achieving the aim successfully.

If we don't know what we are talking about when we say we want them to "fulfil their potential", that aim becomes vacuous. Ask yourself whether *you* have fulfilled *your* potential. Can you remember when it happened, and what you were doing at the time? How did it feel to say to yourself, "That's it. Fulfilled it! I'll just coast along now …"? Or imagine that you are having to report sadly to your governors or board of trustees that "Only 43% of our Year 10s were able to fulfil at least three-quarters of their potential this year." See what we mean?

The elements of learning power rubric is a tool. It is not to be adopted slavishly, or unthinkingly. It is an aid to thinking, so your school can start to clarify which positive learning dispositions it values, how they are going to be introduced, and what measures you are going to take to review and improve your attempts to achieve them, year by year.

Chapter 6 in *The Learning Power Approach* talks you through these "learning muscles" in more detail. This framework enables you to keep in mind the big picture of learning power, so you are less likely to neglect some of the important, but maybe less obvious, ingredients.

Curiosity:	Having an inquisitive attitude to life. *Wondering*: being alive to puzzles and incongruities. *Questioning*: seeking deeper understanding. *Exploring*: actively and adventurously investigating. *Experimenting and Tinkering*: trying things out to see what happens.
Attention:	Locking your mind onto learning. *Noticing*: being attentive to details and patterns. *Concentrating*: maintaining focus despite distractions. *Contemplating*: letting perception unfold. *Immersing*: being engrossed in learning.
Determination:	Sticking with challenges that matter to you. *Persevering*: staying intelligently engaged with difficult things. *Recovering*: bouncing back quickly from frustration or failure. *Practising*: mastering the hard parts through repetition.
Imagination:	Creatively exploring possibilities. *Connecting*: using metaphor and association to leverage new ideas from what you know. *Playing with Ideas*: allowing the mind to bubble with possibilities.

	Visualising: using mental rehearsal to refine skills and explore consequences. *Intuiting*: tapping into bodily based hunches and inklings.
Thinking:	Working things out with clarity and accuracy. *Analysing*: reasoning with logic and precision. *Deducing*: drawing inferences from explanations. *Critiquing*: questioning the validity of knowledge claims. *Systems Thinking*: thinking about complex states of affairs.
Socialising:	Benefiting from and contributing to the social world of learning. *Collaborating*: being an effective and supportive team member. *Accepting*: being open to ideas and feedback. *Imitating*: being permeable to other people's good habits. *Empathising*: adopting multiple perspectives. *Leading*: playing a role in guiding and developing groups and teams.
Reflection:	Standing back and taking stock of learning. *Evaluating*: appraising the quality of your own work. *Self-evaluating*: knowing yourself as a learner. *Thinkering*: blending doing and thinking together. *Witnessing*: quietly watching the flow of your own experience.
Organisation:	Managing and controlling your own learning. *Learning Designing*: creating your own learning activities. *Planning*: anticipating needs and pitfalls of the learning journey. *Resourcing*: building your bank of learning resources. *Adapting*: being able to change tack when needed.

Figure 2.2: The Elements of Learning Power[16]

---

16 If you have already read *The Learning Power Approach*, you might have spotted some small changes to this list from the one that appears there. We have since revised the wording of some of the design principles too, and added a few words to our definition of the approach. Apologies: we are inveterate thinkerers! And we hope you will be too.

> # **Wondering**
>
> Have a look through this list of putative features of the confident and independent learner.
>
> How might you rate them (on a scale of 1 to 5, 5 being very important) in terms of how important you think each of them is for young people growing up in today's world?
>
> How would you rate them in terms of how well you think your school currently does to help students develop those strengths?
>
> Pick out one or two that you think are highly important which you are not yet strong on. What could you change in order to do better?
>
> Do you think this activity would be a useful one to try with your staff? With parents? With the students themselves?

Design principles

The second framework is what we call *the design principles for learning power teaching*. These are general guidelines that identify the aspects of teachers' styles and methods that have greatest impact on the development of positive learning dispositions. They will help to steer the development of pedagogy, so that the classrooms in your school become ever more effective incubators of students' learning power attitudes and habits. Of course, the list is not exhaustive: we could have elaborated in more detail. But it should serve as effective guidance as you think about the kinds of teachers you want your staff to be.

1. Create a feeling of safety.
2. Distinguish between learning mode and performance mode.
3. Organise compelling things to learn.
4. Make ample time for collaboration and conversation.
5. Create challenge.
6. Make difficulty adjustable.
7. Talk about and demonstrate the innards of learning.
8. Make use of protocols, templates, and routines.
9. Use the environment.
10. Develop craftsmanship.
11. Allow increasing amounts of independence.
12. Give students more responsibility.
13. Focus on improvement, not achievement.
14. Lead by example.

Figure 2.3: The Design Principles for Learning Power Teaching

Seeds, illustrations, routines, protocols, and habits

In addition to those two overarching frameworks, the LPA offers teachers a variety of tools for growing an LPA culture in their classrooms. There are *seeds*: small tweaks or techniques which convey the spirit of the LPA, and which teachers can insert into any lesson. We offer many *illustrations*: examples of how these tweaks work out in practice. Then there are *routines*: small, well-defined procedures that teachers can use to get students to stretch their minds in a variety of different ways, in any subject. Well-known routines are Edward de Bono's Plus-Minus-Interesting (PMI), used to explore the pros and cons of an idea; and Ron Ritchhart's Think-Pair-Share that sequences students' thinking on their own, then talking with a partner, and finally sharing thoughts with the whole class.

Then there are *protocols*, which are general templates for designing lessons. In *The Learning Power Approach*, Guy details EL Education's protocol called "Workshop 2.0" and the BLP protocol called "Split-Screen Teaching" that designs lessons explicitly with two ends in mind: mastery of content, *and* the stretching of a specific learning muscle. We won't go into these in depth in this volume as they are a little less relevant to school leadership, but we'd certainly recommend introducing your staff to the concepts so that they can explore further.

Finally, there are our own personal *habits* which may need to be brought a little more into line with the aims of the LPA. We are all creatures of habit – we couldn't get through the day without them. But sometimes we may need to expend a bit of effort to become aware of those habits and adjust them. For example, some teachers have a strong impulse to rescue and reassure students who are on the brink of getting upset at their inability to do or understand something. They like to seize the "teachable moment" to do a neat bit of explaining. But if we jump in too quickly, we may be depriving students of a vital opportunity to build up their learning stamina, and to feel the pride that comes with having wrestled with something hard and worked it out for themselves. That may be a habit that we could retrain a little.

Getting Her Head Around the LPA: Jann's Story

Jann Robinson always had an interest in the science of learning: how learning happened; what good learners did; and why some learners gave up. Since becoming a principal, her professional learning has been focused on school improvement and its interplay with leadership. She cares deeply about the welfare and well-being of her students, but there was pressure from her governors to improve academic outcomes, and so her reading was targeting this area.

She read a lot, including: Art Costa's *Habits of Mind*;[17] John Hattie's *Visible Learning* and his latter research on the differing effect sizes of the factors that impact on learning;[18] Carol Dweck's growth mindset;[19] Angela Duckworth's *Grit*;[20] Martin Seligman's *Flourish*;[21] and Michael Fullan's *Leading in a Culture of Change* and *The Principal*.[22] These authors were all looking at the cognitive and the emotional aspects of learning.

The work of the Project Zero team at Harvard – and, in particular, the work of Ron Ritchhart, Mark Church, and Karin Morrison in *Making Thinking Visible*[23] – started Jann thinking about what classroom routines could impact on the students' understanding of their own learning. Howard Gardner's *Multiple Intelligences*[24] and

---

17 Full references to the volumes in this series can be found in the Further Reading section at the end of the book.
18 Hattie, *Visible Learning*; and John Hattie, *Visible Learning for Teachers: Maximizing Impact on Learning* (Abingdon and New York: Routledge, 2012).
19 Carol S. Dweck, *Mindset: The New Psychology of Success* (New York: Ballantine Books, 2007).
20 Angela Duckworth, *Grit: Why Passion and Resilience Are the Secrets of Success* (London: Vermilion, 2017).
21 Martin Seligman, *Flourish: A New Understanding of Happiness and Well-Being – and How to Achieve Them* (London: Nicholas Brealey Publishing, 2011).
22 Michael Fullan, *Leading in a Culture of Change* (San Francisco, CA: Jossey-Bass, 2001) and *The Principal: Three Keys to Maximizing Impact* (San Francisco, CA: Jossey-Bass, 2014).
23 Ron Ritchhart, Mark Church, and Karin Morrison, *Making Thinking Visible: How to Promote Engagement, Understanding and Independence for All Learners* (San Francisco, CA: Jossey-Bass, 2011).
24 Howard Gardner, *Multiple Intelligences* (New York: Basic Books, 1993).

Five Minds for the Future were also shaping her thinking. Gardner's work was critical as it was challenging the status quo of schooling. It was looking at what needed to change if students were going to be prepared for a world which was no longer the same as the world that their parents – and, in many cases, their teachers – had experienced. Six months prior to first reading about BLP, Jann had used Gardner's books as the basis for an address to the parents and students at the annual senior school presentation night because she felt that it was important to get them thinking about what was needed to be an educated person in the 21st century.

Jann says:

> I had done a lot of reading and thinking, and I was really aware that we needed to change what we were doing, but I didn't really have a clear idea of how I could bring everything I had read together. Everything was thought-provoking. All of it had a solid research base. I was just struggling with how it all fitted together. I knew that I wanted to be preparing the students for the future. I knew we had to change what we were doing. I just needed to find something that would unify all the ideas. When I read about BLP, I saw the same rigorous research base. In this case it was the neuroscience of learning. It immediately resonated because it separated the areas of learning into cognitive, emotional, and social. It gave me a clear sense of how teachers could develop the students as learners by developing the dispositions which were characteristic of good learners. The BLP framework brought together all of the different ideas I had been reading about.

Wondering

In what ways would your story be similar to, and different from, Jann's?

What have been the key influences on your thinking so far? How have they changed the way in which you talk about the school and its vision to staff, parents, and children?

What Should We Be Reading and Watching?

While we hope that we've given you enough information to whet your appetite and get you started, if you are like Jann and want to read around for greater depth, you might be interested in some recommendations.[25] First, here are our top ten books for consolidating your understanding of the science behind the LPA.

Ten best books to read about the foundations of the LPA

All of these books are suitable for both primary and high school contexts, unless otherwise stated.

1. David Perkins, *Outsmarting IQ: The Emerging Science of Learnable Intelligence*. Anything by Perkins is worth reading. He writes very simply, and thinks very deeply, about education. This seminal book introduces the idea of "learnable intelligence", on which the whole field of the LPA rests.

2. David Perkins, *Making Learning Whole: How Seven Principles of Teaching Can Transform Education*. In this book, Perkins lays out a way of organising classrooms so that children are more engaged and, as a result, they get better results *and* their minds are stretched and strengthened.

3. Carol Dweck, *Mindset: The New Psychology of Success*. A classic. Dweck's very accessible exploration of the practical implications of her discoveries that, first, people's buried beliefs about the nature of intelligence dramatically affect their resilience and curiosity as learners, and that, second, these beliefs can be changed by teachers.

4. Ron Berger, *An Ethic of Excellence: Building a Culture of Craftsmanship with Students*. Berger is the patron saint of the LPA. This book documents his discovery that virtually all children, with the right amount of time and support, are capable of producing "high-quality work".

---

25 Full bibliographic details can be found in the Further Reading section.

5. Ron Ritchhart, *Intellectual Character: What It Is, Why It Matters, and How to Get It*. In this ground-breaking book, the second of "the two Ronnies" from Project Zero reports the results of his PhD, which developed and researched the dispositional view of intelligence.

6. Howard Gardner, *Five Minds for the Future*. "Further, the world of the future [...] will demand capacities that until now have been mere options," says Gardner.[26] Erudite and lucid, Gardner explains what those "five minds" are, why they are so important, and how to grow them in school.

7. David Price, *Open: How We'll Work, Live and Learn in the Future*. An easy-to-read eye-opener about how far and how fast the worlds of work, leisure, and learning have already changed with the explosion of digital and social media. With even low-attaining students doing things online and after hours that are way more cognitively complex that what gets served up in the traditional classroom, schools are going to have to change.

8. Neil Postman, *The End of Education*. Pun intended: if we don't think hard about the proper ends – the goals – of education, it may well be the end of schools as we know them, as they become more and more out of step with the world. Postman thinks deeply and writes beautifully.

9. Paul Tough, *How Children Succeed: Grit, Curiosity and the Hidden Power of Character*. An accessible and authoritative review of the research that shows conclusively why "results" are not enough, and why all children are capable, given the right environment, of acquiring the traits of "epistemic character".

10. David Robson, *The Intelligence Trap: Why Smart People Do Stupid Things and How to Make Wiser Decisions*. Part 1 of this fascinating book explains how schools contribute to developing the kind of stupidity that characterises clever people. Parts 2 and 3 review a wealth of research about how it could and should be different.

---

26 Gardner, *Five Minds for the Future*, p. 2.

Ten best practical books

These books are packed full of practical, tried-and-tested classroom strategies and activities for turning the theory of the LPA into a living reality.

1. Arthur L. Costa and Bena Kallick, *Activating and Engaging Habits of Mind, Assessing and Reporting on Habits of Mind, Discovering and Exploring Habits of Mind*, and *Integrating and Sustaining Habits of Mind*. A set of four slim volumes packed with ideas and illustrations for working with their Habits of Mind framework.

2. Ron Berger, Libby Woodfin, and Anne Vilen, *Learning That Lasts: Challenging, Engaging, and Empowering Students with Deeper Instruction*. A very detailed manual of the teaching approached developed by the EL Education schools. Comes with a really useful DVD of classroom examples of how to get great results and build learning character at the same time.

3. Ron Ritchhart, *Creating Cultures of Thinking: The 8 Forces We Must Master to Truly Transform Our Schools*. A very practical guide to different aspects of the culture or ethos we can create in classrooms, including the ways in which we communicate our expectations, and the ways in which we model different attitudes towards learning.

4. Kath Murdoch, *The Power of Inquiry: Teaching and Learning with Curiosity, Creativity and Purpose in the Contemporary Classroom*. Aimed mainly at primary teachers, this is a treasure trove of exciting ideas for developing enquiry-based learning in your classroom.

5. Hywel Roberts and Debra Kidd, *Uncharted Territories: Adventures in Learning*. Trained by Dorothy Heathcote – originator of the influential "mantle of the expert" approach to primary project-based learning – Debra and Hywel offer hundreds of ingenious ideas to fire your imagination, making learning in every subject, and across all age groups, more dramatic and engaging.

6. Joanna Haynes, *Children as Philosophers: Learning Through Enquiry and Dialogue*. A great introduction to P4C, with lots of good ideas to get you going, and thoughtful discussions of the rationale and benefits.

7. James Nottingham, *Challenging Learning: Theory, Effective Practice and Lesson Ideas to Create Optimal Learning in the Classroom*. Using his well-known image of the learning pit, James illustrates a variety of strategies for teachers to use to challenge their students to think more skilfully and logically.

8. Gordon Stobart, *The Expert Learner: Challenging the Myth of Ability*. An accessible handbook of arguments in favour of the "learning is learnable" concept, as well as practical, research-based suggestions as to how to go about it.

9. Paul Ginnis, *The Teacher's Toolkit: Raise Classroom Achievement with Strategies for Every Learner*. A mine of practical activities to engage and stretch students of all ages across a wide variety of subjects.

10. Wendy Berliner and Deborah Eyre, *Great Minds and How to Grow Them*. Aimed principally at parents, this is nevertheless a very useful distillation of research and practice for anyone interested in helping children grow the attributes and attitudes they will need in order to thrive in the 21st century.

More books by Guy Claxton and his colleagues, past and present

Obviously, your first port of call will be the other books in the Learning Power series, but if you would like to delve deeper, here are ten more books by Guy and his colleagues and collaborators.

1. *What's the Point of School? Rediscovering the Heart of Education*. An examination of why school so often adds to young people's stress rather than giving them the mindset to cope with it.

2. *Wise Up: The Challenge of Lifelong Learning*. A comprehensive digest of the cognitive science behind "learning to learn". Shows the importance – and the learnability – of curiosity, imagination, resilience, reflection, and empathy.

3. *Building Learning Power: Helping Young People Become Better Learners.* The bestseller that launched a wave of practical resources for building children's confidence and capacity to be independent learners.

4. *Teaching to Learn: A Direction for Education.* Develops a simple but powerful set of ideas about how the learning mind can be helped to function more elegantly and efficiently. The first "outing" for the explicit concept of "learning power".

5. *Learning to Learn: The Fourth Generation.* Charts the progress that has been made in developing learning to learn from its beginnings in study skills and revision guides, through the hints-and-tips era to teaching thinking skills, and the present interest in *infusing* learning to learn into every lesson.

6. *The Learning Powered School: Pioneering 21st Century Education* (with Maryl Chambers, Graham Powell, and Bill Lucas). A research-based road map of the layers of change necessary to build a school-wide culture of learning.

7. *The Creative Thinking Plan: How to Generate Ideas and Solve Problems in Your Work and Life* (with Bill Lucas). A workbook for developing a mind that just bubbles with fresh ideas when you need them, teaching you how to toggle productively between focused and diffuse ways of seeing, thinking, and remembering.

8. *New Kinds of Smart: How the Science of Learnable Intelligence Is Changing Education* (with Bill Lucas). Explains the new science showing that intelligence is a conglomerate of learnable habits of mind that rely on social and technological connections as much as internal brainpower.

9. *Educating Ruby: What Our Children Really Need to Learn* (with Bill Lucas). A book for parents, explaining what their children's education could be, and how they can pester their children's schools to get it.

10. *Expansive Education: Teaching Learners for the Real World* (with Bill Lucas and Ellen Spencer). A worldwide survey of innovative classroom practice, including examples from the UK, the United States, Canada, Finland, Romania, Singapore, Australia, and Argentina.

Ten best things to watch

Finally, here are our top ten things to watch or check out online in order to get a feel for the LPA.

1. www.voice21.org. Resources for building your students' capacity for sophisticated, respectful, productive, collaborative talk in the classroom – learning *to* talk, and learning *through* talk.

2. www.chriswatkins.net. Chris Watkins, formerly of the UCL Institute of Education, has assembled a website full of giveaway resources for building students' capacity for and interest in learning. Really useful – and generous. (Chris has had to retire through ill-health. If you find his website useful, we are sure that he would be delighted for you to contact him and tell him.)

3. Eduardo Briceño, "How to get better at the things you care about", *TED.com* (2016) [video]. Available at: https://www.ted.com/talks/eduardo_briceno_how_to_get_better_at_the_things_you_care_about. Eduardo is head honcho of MindSet Works, the spin-off organisation that supports Carol Dweck's work. In this excellent TED Talk, he offers an improved way of thinking about what have come to be known as fixed and growth mindsets.

4. www.expansiveeducation.net. Founded by Guy Claxton and Bill Lucas, the Expansive Education Network is a sharing platform for teachers who are interested in learning with and from each other about how to develop a learning power culture in their classrooms. It also offers useful tailored professional development about how to try out ideas in an action research framework.

5. www.learningpowerkids.com. This is the website of Becky Carlzon, Guy's co-author on *Powering Up Children*. Here Becky blogs about her classroom practice, and freely shares her resources with a growing band of followers.

6. www.youcubed.org. This is the website of Stanford professor Jo Boaler, full of ideas and resources for making maths (or "math" if you are American) more

adventurous and less intimidating. Also watch out for Jo's new book *Limitless Mind*.[27]

7. www.pz.harvard.edu. For fifty years, Harvard's Project Zero has been a constant source of well-researched, deeply thoughtful, and highly accessible ideas about what education can and should be. The website points you to a wide range of resources and professional development opportunities – many of them free.

8. www.dylanwiliam.org. Dylan Wiliam's work on formative assessment is not technically part of the learning power family because his focus is predominantly on improving school achievement rather than (also) building lifelong learning characteristics that are useful in their own right. But his website contains useful free resources and also a wealth of wisdom about how to configure effective self-help teacher learning communities (TLCs) in schools, which can easily be adapted to LPA ends.

9. https://educationendowmentfoundation.org.uk. The Education Endowment Foundation (EEF) website has a load of good evidence-based advice for teachers, some of which – such as their recent work on metacognition and self-regulation[28] – sits squarely within LPA territory.

10. EL Education, "Austin's butterfly: models, critique, and descriptive feedback" [video] (4 October 2016). Available at: https://www.youtube.com/watch?v=E_6PskE3zfQ. Austin's butterfly is a classic video that shows how to build what Ron Berger, chief education officer of EL Education, calls "an ethic of excellence" in even very young children. If you've seen it before, watch again, and think about how the spirit of Berger's work could be infused even more deeply into the day-to-day workings of your own school.

---

27 Jo Boaler, *Limitless Mind: Learn, Lead and Live without Barriers* (London: Thorsons, 2019).
28 See https://educationendowmentfoundation.org.uk/evidence-summaries/teaching-learning-toolkit/meta-cognition-and-self-regulation/.

> **Wondering**
>
> If you were to think about rewriting the vision and values on the home page of your school's website, are there any bits of this chapter that would help you clarify and refresh those fundamentals? What are they? How might you want to phrase them differently?
>
> Who are the people in your school who challenge and stimulate your thinking most? Do you make enough use of them?

Summary

The aim of this chapter has been to give you, as a school leader, the intellectual ammunition you need in order to "talk the talk" of the LPA. If you can't speak articulately and knowledgeably about the vision and values you want to pursue, it is unlikely that you will get the widespread buy-in that you will need if you are to turn the vision into a reality. So we suggest that you not only read and comprehend this chapter, but that you start using the content in your daily interactions with colleagues, parents, and students. Work on refining your own personal LPA-style "elevator pitch" so you don't have to um and er, or retreat into platitudes, when someone asks you what is special about your school. You know what the values behind the LPA are, as well as the scientific rationale. You can explain why it is important, and what the benefits will be for your students. You can describe clearly, in your own words, what the LPA actually is. You can picture what it looks like in a classroom, and what kinds of habit change it asks of teachers. And you have a good starter kit of further reading and watching so you can keep deepening your understanding and commitment.

Armed with all this, you are now ready to work on getting buy-in from all the different stakeholder groups in your school.

Chapter 3

Getting Buy-In: Onboarding All the Stakeholders

A school principal can be as passionate about the LPA as we – the authors – are, but if this passion is not communicated to and embraced by the rest of the school community, it will not take root. Hopefully, if you have read this far, you have "got the LPA bug". This chapter explores how to take others along with you so that the LPA can become deeply embedded in your school's culture and ethos, policies and practices, and language and behaviours. This chapter explores several key aspects of getting others on board and fully committed:

- What leader behaviours are most effective for engaging others with the LPA?
- How might you get staff on board?
- Is it important to have a strategic plan or can the LPA grow organically?
- Who should lead the LPA at your school?
- How should you deal with the sceptics, cynics, and blockers?
- How might you introduce the LPA to students?
- How can you ensure that everyone is on board?

What Leader Behaviours Are Most Effective for Engaging Others with the LPA?

We think that the first responsibility of the LPA head teacher is to speak with strength and conviction to staff, students, and parents at every possible opportunity about the purpose of education in the 21st century. They need to hear from the horse's mouth, again and again, that "our job" in school is to foster learning dispositions as well as impart knowledge, and to develop character as well as deliver exam results. LPA principals must learn never to talk as though the sole purpose of education is to produce top grade-getters – as if academic outcomes are the be-all and end-all. LPA leaders must have the courage and confidence to share a compelling narrative of learning power that invites and encourages everyone else to come on board. Constant reiteration of a compelling vision is your best recruiting sergeant!

> LPA principals must learn never to talk as though the sole purpose of education is to produce top grade-getters.

It is important to formulate an educational vision for the school which communicates clear LPA goals and inspires direction. It is vital that this does not rely on vague platitudes about "building self-esteem" or "helping young people to develop their potential" but gives a sharp, explicit message about the aims of developing learning power and key character traits. An LPA vision statement or motto can be extremely useful to this end.

Not everyone finds it natural or easy to be a gregarious, charismatic orator, but the school principal has to work on developing the confidence to be a committed and articulate cheerleader for learning power, even if another member of their team may be fronting a particular presentation. The LPA leader needs to have anticipated misunderstandings and objections (the inevitable "yes, buts") in order to deal with them as they arise. Our arguments in Chapter 2 about why the LPA is needed will hopefully provide you with inspiration here. If you practise talking the talk, you will speak with increasing confidence and conviction! We strongly suggest that you work on honing and refining your elevator pitch, and seek out opportunities to practise it. The "drip-drip" approach of "gentle pressure, relentlessly applied" really works in communicating the LPA message.[1]

In LPA schools, leaders use the language of learning power consistently and naturally and the message is sold at all key events – open days, parent meetings, concerts, sports days, assemblies, fairs, and prize-givings. At Isaac Newton Academy, for example, no opportunity is missed for communicating the LPA vision, starting with the statement of the Isaac Newton philosophy on their website and in their staff recruitment pack:

> At Isaac Newton Academy everyone is a learner with needs and entitlements. We all have a responsibility to support everyone else in the school community with their learning and a role to play in encouraging ambition, hope and optimism in our fellow learners.
>
> [...] we believe that all students have the potential to achieve outstanding educational outcomes.
>
> We know that the brain is like a muscle, in that its intelligence grows with exercise. Scientists are learning that people have more capacity for life-long learning and brain development than they ever thought. Although each person has a unique genetic endowment and starts with different temperaments and aptitudes, we know that experience, training and effort are critically important. It is not always those who start out the smartest who end up the smartest. This has implications for how we teach and communicate with students.[2]

Founding member of the Isaac Newton primary team Farhana Ali said:

> When I saw the website I was drawn by the Dweck quote – "Great teachers believe in the growth of the intellect and talent, and they are fascinated with the process of learning."[3] This was the reason I applied to Isaac Newton, even though I had not come across the LPA before.

---

1 This phrase was used by an Australian educator who was talking to Guy about her efforts to get her teenage son to keep his bedroom tidy! But it stuck in Guy's mind as a useful maxim for the LPA leader too.
2 Isaac Newton Academy, Candidate Information Pack, p. 2, p. 3. Available at: https://isaacnewtonacademy.org/sites/default/files/INA%20Candidate%20Information%20Pack.pdf.
3 Dweck, *Mindset*, p. 194.

> ## Wondering
>
> Do you have an LPA elevator pitch? If not, who could you practise it on? Who would give you honest and constructive feedback?
>
> Do you need to adapt your LPA elevator pitch for different audiences? How?
>
> What opportunities do you currently use to communicate your LPA message?
>
> What opportunities might you be missing?
>
> Is there anything that stops you going full throttle? Can you put your finger on what it might be? What might help you to get over that barrier?

How Might You Get Staff on Board?

Unsurprisingly, we have not been able to identify a single sure-fire method of introducing the LPA to staff. Different leaders – knowing the make-up, nature, and idiosyncrasies of their staff body – will use different approaches.

At Leventhorpe School in Hertfordshire, England, for example, head teacher Malcolm White sent a few members of staff to see the LPA in action in different schools. They fed back to the SLT and, informally, shared their experiences with their colleagues. Malcolm recalls that this led to:

> a sense of expectation and a healthy buzz around the school that we would be doing something different.

Rachel Macfarlane reflected on how she introduced the LPA, in the form of BLP, to her staff on arrival at Walthamstow School for Girls:

I thought hard about how I might go about introducing BLP at Walthamstow. I had no idea how receptive the staff body might be to this approach, or how open they were to change or challenge. This was an outstanding school with a great reputation, and I was coming in as a young head from a less successful and lower-performing setting. I needed to form relationships, establish my credibility, build trust, and choose my priorities. Yet I also wanted to take advantage of my honeymoon period with staff, be upfront about my interest in BLP, and communicate a clear message: "You don't have to be sick to get better." I did believe that Walthamstow could provide an even better education.

I therefore chose to sow the seeds in my very first address to staff on the first day of term. During my speech, I made reference to BLP, told staff that it was an approach to learning that I believed could have impact at Walthamstow, and invited colleagues who were curious to dip into one of Guy's early BLP books (I had brought along half a dozen copies to loan out) and to come to a lunchtime meeting in my office three weeks later. I had no idea how many people to expect. In the event, twelve members of staff (around 10%) turned up and squashed into my room – there was a mixture of heads of department, SLT members, heads of year, and subject teachers, along with the ICT manager, the librarian, and the SEND coordinator, many clutching well-thumbed copies of the book, some books with sticky notes protruding and others with scribbles in the margins. It was apparent that these texts had been passed around from teacher to teacher and were already cherished manuals.

We discussed our first impressions of the book. There was a palpable excitement about its message. We discussed how to most effectively get the entire staff to understand the principles and philosophy of BLP and get them on board with the initiative. I had booked Guy to address all staff later in the autumn term. We started to shape the direction that we would give him for his presentation, deciding that we would like him to begin with the educational philosophy – "What is education for?" We agreed that we wanted lots of practical examples of classroom resources, strategies, and activities.

Everyone at that meeting felt that BLP was relevant and important to Walthamstow, but we needed to communicate this to all staff. We set the next meeting for three weeks later (in a larger venue!), ordered more copies of the book, and agreed that all staff would be welcome. Our preparation task was to give some thought as to the best way to introduce BLP at Walthamstow, considering:

- Taking one of the 4Rs (resilience, resourcefulness, reflection, and reciprocity) at a time and focusing on it for a term.

- Conducting an audit of examples of current good practice at Walthamstow from each of the 4Rs.

> - Working on the 4Rs simultaneously but in different faculty areas/with different year groups.
> - Discussing the concepts of BLP with student groups.
>
> And so began the working group which led the introduction of BLP and determined the strategic direction of travel. Over the 2004/5 academic year the group held thirty lunchtime meetings – almost one per school week. This volume gives an indication of the energy and momentum generated. The membership of the group grew to around twenty, which represented a sizeable proportion of the staff body. Crucially, it contained some influential staffroom characters, including the teaching and learning leader and the NQT tutor.

The Walthamstow working group took a whole year to plan the full introduction of BLP, involving a number of staff meetings and training days, getting feedback and consulting along the way. In a similar way, in the six months prior to launching BLP at St Luke's Grammar School in 2014, Jann Robinson and her team began a soft launch. At the full staff INSET days at the beginnings of Term 3 and Term 4, Jann spoke about BLP and the rationale for change, and Dr Simon Breakspear from Agile Schools talked about the need to prepare students for a rapidly changing world.[4] Jann stressed at each staff meeting that she appreciated that change is always difficult, but that teachers would only be asked to make incremental changes to their practice. She made a long-term commitment that this, and only this, would be the focus of all professional development sessions for the next five years. She made it clear that she understood that deep change needs time to embed, and that she was convinced that BLP was what every student needed in order to be ready for the future. She promised that there wouldn't be a different shiny new idea every time she returned from study leave or a conference!

Jane Bellamy also committed to protecting staff from initiative overload when she introduced the LPA, again in the form of BLP, at Leigham Primary School. She makes the important point:

> Everything you do has to be permeated by BLP, so all the other initiatives and demands that are coming at you, you look at and say, "How does this fit in with our ethos?"

---

4   In most Australian schools, the school year is divided into four terms.

> BLP – its philosophy and its practice – becomes the lens through which you look at everything that happens, or could potentially happen, in the school.

Jane's initial approach at Leigham was to get the staff thinking about learning, before introducing any specific ideas about how teaching might be improved. Jane says:

> We didn't pile straight in and say, "We are going to do BLP." We didn't just plop it in. For example, we had a neuroscientist from a local university come in to talk about learning and the brain, and that really got staff interested in thinking and talking about what was going on at the learners' end of things in the classroom, and wondering what the implications for their teaching might be. So when we did introduce some of the language and methods of BLP, the staff were ready to eat it up.

In a similar vein, Jonny Spowart at Heath Mount School reflected:

> We needed to make it seem manageable for staff, so that they could easily begin to embed one or two LPA-type things in their everyday teaching. The staff here, like the students, are incredibly busy. We pack a huge amount in already. So we had to ensure that the LPA wasn't going to be the straw that broke the camel's back. Becky Carlzon gave us lots of simple ideas and resources that we could use to help staff get going, and that was very helpful.[5] We needed to start small, and then gradually build it up.

At Isaac Newton Academy, Rachel Macfarlane had the opportunity to prepare the staff in the months before the school's opening. As this was a brand-new school, she was able to make explicit the ethos which she wanted for the school from the word go. Integral to this was the BRIDGES framework (which is discussed in detail on page 244), which summed up the dispositions and character traits which she deemed essential for a child to experience and develop: Bravery, Resourcefulness, Integrity, Discovery, Grit, Emotional intelligence, and Self-discipline. She reflected:

> The founding staff team (teaching and operational) assembled for a number of pre-opening training weekends. One of the first activities undertaken was a lecture from and follow-up discussion with Matthew Syed around the theme of growth mindset (supported by some Carol Dweck pre-reading). This established the high-expectations and high-performance culture that would be central to the ethos of the academy. There then followed a session on the vision and mission statement, at which I facilitated a staff activity to unpick the academy's tripartite emphasis on knowledge, learning power, and character. This three-way focus would be central to the policies and procedures at Isaac Newton. In one training session, colleagues were talked through the background context to BRIDGES and they interacted and gained familiarity with the learning

---

5 The co-author of *Powering Up Children: The Learning Power Approach to Primary Teaching*.

dispositions and character traits in the framework. The seven key groups of dispositions making up BRIDGES were examined through the behaviours of great learners.

This was followed up by a day's in-service training (INSET) led by Professor Guy Claxton. The training was designed to increase the founding team's level of confidence with the learning dispositions and characteristics. The day covered what the LPA is, the BRIDGES framework, how we would assess students' mastery of the characteristics, and how to design and lead great BRIDGES lessons. There was a lot to learn, but having a small, committed staff made it easier to develop a shared, consistent understanding of the framework.

Wren Academy, like Isaac Newton, was a new school which introduced the LPA from the outset. Principal Gavin Smith, looking back at the staff induction process, recalls:

> While some time was spent with general introductions and explaining the fundamental procedures of the new school, the "centrepiece" was the introduction to learning power. All the staff who are still with us tell us that this was the most memorable part of the day. BLP consultant Graham Powell led a demonstration of what he called a "stuck challenge". Two volunteer colleagues sat on two chairs on opposite sides of the room; in-between them, in the centre of the room, was a cake hidden under a bowl. Graham had placed various resources by each chair, and the volunteers' task was to uncover the cake, cut it, and share it between them, without leaving their seats. After the activity, the whole staff were invited, in small groups, to try to identify which "learning habits" the guinea pigs had been using, and there was a general discussion of how they had gone about learning and problem-solving. There could not have been a more engaging, interactive, and fun way to introduce the learning habits. There was a real buzz in the room, and I fondly remember working in a small group that afternoon, planning how we could embed BLP philosophy in our lessons. Despite the wide range of teaching experience in the room, there was a great sense of common purpose and shared values – even if they were newly acquired for some colleagues! I don't think anyone could have left that day without realising that this school is really, truly about learning. It was the first time we had all met each other, but it was clear that this school was going to be very hot on the details of teaching and learning.

Graham Powell was also involved in supporting Dr Challoner's Grammar School with the introduction of the LPA. Head teacher Mark Fenton tells the story:

> Graham advised us not to kick the LPA journey off with the traditional whole-staff INSET day. With the best will in the world, these often have limited long-term benefit. Instead, he came into the school to run a learning review with us. This is a kind of audit that focused on the kinds of learning habits that students in different year groups and subjects were using in their lessons; the way these habits were being explicitly mentioned and stretched; and the opportunities that teachers created for students

to make use of these learning habits. [More on this in Chapter 9.] To carry out the audit, Graham convened a working group that comprised six or seven teachers across different subjects and of mixed seniority, plus two or three students, and together they developed an observation schedule to take stock of the kinds of learning that was going on in a variety of lessons, over the course of a few days. Then Graham analysed the results and compiled a report for us to digest and discuss.

Is It Important to Have a Strategic Plan or Can the LPA Grow Organically?

The way in which principals prepare the ground for the LPA depends critically on the context of the school. As in so many areas of school life, there is no "one size fits all" or a particular tried-and-tested "right way" of planning for the introduction of a learning-powered culture, or to embed the practices. Some people naturally want to map out the journey in advance and develop a "strategic plan". Others – as we have already seen – prefer to start gently, or even "indirectly", and read and respond to the mood of the staff as they go along. In general, the majority of the school leaders we spoke to seemed to lean towards the second approach, and even if they wanted the clarity of some kind of road map, they realised that they would need to be flexible, and be willing to adjust their trajectory in the light of experience. Here we include some case studies from across this spectrum. As you read, consider which chime best with your own situation (and, perhaps, personality).

> Different approaches suit different schools, depending on the stage of development, the staff, and the make-up of the community. This is illustrated clearly in the story of the two high schools that Hugh Bellamy led in the first decade of the 21st century.
>
> The first was George Pindar School, an 11–16 state school on the outskirts of Scarborough, a seaside town in North-East England. Near a large, deprived estate of social housing, George Pindar had more than its fair share of difficult and disadvantaged children. When Hugh arrived, children were openly smoking

in the building and female members of staff did not walk down the corridors on their own. Attendance was dreadful: many children would come in to "register" in the morning, and then just drift off during the day. The examination results were dire. A good many of the teachers seemed to have very low expectations of the students' capabilities as well as their behaviour. There was a sense of, "Well, what can you do with Eastfield kids?" And the attitude towards the school from the local community was unsupportive, to put it mildly. In fact, relationships generally had broken down.

Hugh wanted to introduce the LPA, but he had to spend the best part of his first year in the school re-establishing basic order and rebuilding trust and engagement with the community. There was no point in trying to talk about learning when kids were running wild and parents were disengaged. So Hugh and his SLT set up some practical initiatives, such as accompanying police patrols on Friday nights, establishing a community football club, and meeting parents in the local café on Friday afternoons. Over that first year or so, these initiatives had a massive impact, not only on children's behaviour, but also on their attitudes to school and their levels of achievement. And the parents started to support the school and engage with it much more. As Hugh gently chipped away at their negative views of education, they began to see that school could actually be different from how it was in their day, and also that, under Hugh's headship, the school really did care about their children, wanted the best for them, and believed that they were capable. Now the school was ready for the LPA.

In 2008, Hugh took up the headship of South Dartmoor Community College in rural Devon, England. Though South Dartmoor, like George Pindar, catered overwhelmingly for white British families, the cultures were in some ways strikingly different. South Dartmoor had received a grade of "outstanding" in a recent inspection: students' behaviour and levels of achievement were good, and the staff were rather complacent. There was a general attitude of "It ain't broke, so what have we got to fix?" But despite that, the teaching itself was – with some conspicuous exceptions – quite dull and didactic. There was a lot of copying down from the board. Hugh was keen to develop a more challenging style of teaching – which, in turn, would build the more useful attitudes of confidence, curiosity, and resilience towards learning – rather than continue with the passive spoon-feeding which students were often getting. But his challenge at South Dartmoor was to get the teachers themselves to become more inquisitive about teaching and learning, and to realise that having compliant students and achieving reasonably good results wasn't necessarily "as good as it gets".

If you were in Hugh's position, how would your approach to planning for the introduction of the LPA at the two schools be different?

Whether to take the planned or the organic route clearly depends on the school and its culture – as you can see from Hugh Bellamy's experience. Rachel Macfarlane also used contrasting approaches in the two schools she led. At Walthamstow School for Girls, there was already an experienced and supportive staff who were able to take the LPA and run with it. However, Isaac Newton Academy was a brand-new school, with many teachers unused to LPA styles of teaching, and here Rachel judged that it would be better to take a more structured and directive approach. Let her explain:

> At Isaac Newton, the LPA initiative was strategically planned in detail and then launched, following training, with the whole school community in one go. Everyone was required to be on board from day one, and there were clear non-negotiables. Subject leaders planned and designed their schemes of learning in the months before opening and discussed them with their line managers. The SLT could thus ensure that the full range of learning dispositions were covered across the curriculum and that the LPA was well-embedded. The standard for a high-quality Isaac Newton scheme of learning was set and could be replicated again and again over the coming years as more were written. Once staff were ready to write individual lesson plans – each with split-screen teaching objectives – the expectation was communicated that these should be uploaded onto a shared staff drive, so that they could be quality-assured and reviewed before delivery.
>
> The expectation of having a full written plan for every lesson was maintained for a number of years as the school grew. It was not always popular with staff, and undoubtedly impacted on workload. However, it enabled the SLT to ensure that all lesson planning was of a high quality, to showcase the best practice for others to learn from, and to check that BRIDGES dispositions and character traits were featuring in every classroom. It made monitoring the implementation of the vision

much easier; if a subject leader dipped into lesson plans and saw that BRIDGES objectives weren't being interwoven, they could have a quiet and discreet word with the colleague concerned, offer help or support, and then check again or pop into a lesson a few days later to see that the support had had the desired impact. As a new school with no established schemes of learning, the requirement for each lesson to be documented was invaluable for building up a resource bank for subsequent years, and for new colleagues to see how BRIDGES was delivered in practice.

At Walthamstow, by contrast, Rachel introduced BLP somewhat more gradually and collegially. A year of research, taking soundings, and trialling and testing the ground preceded a phased introduction – one year group at a time – and staff were permitted to buy in to varying degrees. Rachel recalls:

Early on I asked for volunteers to help think through the introduction of BLP, and I had many enthusiastic applicants. The BLP working group put together a draft strategic plan for the formal introduction. The proposal was that we focus on introducing BLP each year to the Year 7s, giving them a thorough grounding in the skills and learning habits of the 4Rs though a fortnightly tutor session. Every two weeks we would focus on a different sub-skill from one of the 4Rs, which we put into student-friendly language and circulated well in advance to tutors and subject teachers, along with supportive materials detailing what the learning disposition was and how it could be introduced in a tutor lesson. We also shared ideas for subject lesson starters and plenaries, so all teachers could refer to and reinforce the skill in their subject lessons over the fortnight. This model would require a set of Year 7 tutors who were passionate about BLP and who could be relied upon to support students in reflecting on their development as learners. At the same time, all teachers would be requested to consider how they could build the learning muscle of the fortnight into at least one of their lessons with each class over that ten-day period – for example, through a five-minute starter activity, a longer discussion, or a whole-lesson task. Heads of department would be asked to amend schemes of learning as we went along, building in BLP activities that had been trialled in lessons.

In many ways this was a deliberately pragmatic approach. We knew that we had enough BLP cheerleaders to establish a strong tutor team for the incoming Year 7s. If we had tried to launch BLP with all year groups simultaneously, we would not, at that stage, have had a sufficient number of confident tutors to ensure high and consistent quality. And we felt it appropriate to go for a bit-by-bit approach with those staff who were less enthusiastic: as long as they addressed the learning disposition of the fortnight in some way and with each of their classes, that was fine. If they planned whole lessons around developing a learning habit, great, but

> if they just used a five-minute starter, that was OK too. In hindsight, I believe that this was the right decision. In effect, we were saying that everyone must play, but how adventurous they were was up to them. This way, no one could feel out of control or too threatened by the initiative.

In other schools the approach developed even more informally. Robert Cleary, head teacher at Sandringham Primary School, says:

> The implementation of the LPA began organically. We used the interest of a small group of staff to create a number of book groups. We read *New Kinds of Smart* before moving onto *Building Learning Power*. Whole-school training was delivered by Gemma Goldenberg and other members of staff. This raised the profile of the LPA.

Gemma adds:

> Staff meetings began to shift from information-sharing and admin to being more of a learning community. We began by setting aside the first part of each meeting to look at an article or some research and discuss it together before moving onto the more traditional "chalk and talk" training.
>
> Before long we pretty much abandoned whole-staff training sessions in which one member of the SLT stood at the front talking. We replaced those passive whole-staff "lessons" with smaller, opt-in study groups, in which members engaged in pre-reading before the sessions and all took responsibility to explore, trial, and feed back on various approaches.

Two years ago, the LPA was formally added to the school improvement plan. Two members of staff were appointed to lead on the LPA alongside Gemma. Their job is primarily to advocate for the LPA and offer the opportunity for staff to watch them teaching using LPA techniques.

Similarly, at Maple Cross Junior Mixed Infant and Nursery School in Hertfordshire, head teacher Hannah Trickett describes:

> … quite an organic introduction. I had an original plan, but this inevitably changed in many directions along the way based on the responses of students and adults. The message never changes but the approach can!

Hannah joined the school as a deputy head and oversaw the introduction of the LPA. She became head teacher in September 2018 and reflects:

> Supported by a strong SLT, we are now creating our "non-negotiables" linked to our learning to learn agenda.

What do these examples tell us? Certainly, there are many different forms, frameworks, and signature styles of the LPA. We believe that it is important that each school develops an approach that will work best for them, given their unique context. However, leaders need to watch out for lethal mutations that veer too far from the key principles of learning power and character development. And careful thought needs to be given to what is a requirement and an expectation of everyone, and where there is room for individuality and variability. This is an example of the delicate balancing act between "tight" and "loose", which – as we will see in Chapter 4 – school leaders have to learn to perform. If the LPA is too watered down, it will not be impactful; if it is too regimented, there is a risk that it loses the spark of unpredictability and freshness, and that some members of the school community may be lost along the way.

Wondering

Which would work better for your school – a strategically planned initiative or an organically grown one?

What will be the unique features of your LPA?

What will be your non-negotiables?

Where will you allow more freedom for customisation?

Who Should Lead the LPA At Your School?

Establishing, embedding, and maintaining a distinct and impactful LPA requires strong and committed leadership at all levels in the school's "hierarchy". In building that network of leaders throughout the school, it is important to give careful thought to questions like these:

- Who would provide this kind of leadership most effectively?
- Who would command the authority and respect of the staff?
- Who would be good at firing up colleagues' enthusiasm?
- Who would role model the LPA in their classrooms most strikingly?
- Who has the capacity to make the LPA their key priority?
- Who has the determination and courage to take on the cynics and sceptics?

Not surprisingly, in many schools with a head teacher who is committed to LPA, it is they who introduce the LPA to the staff and establish it in the early days. It's human nature that – at least to begin with – staff will often listen and respond to the head particularly keenly. Mark Fenton, head teacher of Dr Challoner's, recalled:

> I appointed a senior colleague, Mark Sturgeon, to be in charge of the day-to-day operation of learning at Dr Challoner's. I delegated a lot to him, but with one very important caveat: I made it very clear to the staff that the LPA was my thing, not just his thing. When we talked about the approach with the whole staff, I thought it was important that I fronted that. They were in no doubt that "the boss" was strongly behind the initiative.

Very often we have seen that heads who are LPA enthusiasts come to realise that they cannot devote the time and attention needed to embed and sustain it. They look to appoint a coordinator or ambassador. But if they do not continue to show their own commitment frequently and vigorously – especially in the early days – there is the risk of losing impetus. Recalling events at Walthamstow School for Girls, Rachel Macfarlane says:

> The appointment of the BLP coordinator was a crucial one. Effectively, I was handing over the oversight of the initiative after twelve months of being centrally involved.

The new post holder would be accountable for the launch of BLP at Walthamstow, for training up and setting the tone with the inaugural BLP tutors, and for leading each year's successive new team of Year 7 tutors until the school had trained enough for all five year groups. The colleague appointed had many strengths: she was an experienced member of staff who was held in high regard, she was a very strong teacher and leader, and she had been involved with the BLP initiative at Walthamstow from the outset.

Under such circumstances, Rachel was able to take a step back without the culture change process losing momentum – but she was able to do so because she judged the person to whom she delegated, and the timing, astutely.

> ... it is important that all of the senior leaders in the school are visibly committed to the LPA, to using growth mindset language, and to role modelling the development of learning dispositions and character traits.

Our conversations with veteran LPA leaders have shown us that it is important that all of the senior leaders in the school are visibly committed to the LPA, to using growth mindset language, and to role modelling the development of learning dispositions and character traits. However, several of our contributors have emphasised the importance of having the LPA championed in the staffroom by people who are not on the SLT. Hugh Bellamy told us that in both his schools, he deliberately chose as his ambassadors colleagues who were capable teachers but who were also well-liked and respected by their peers: as he put it, "people who had the ear of the staffroom". These were the individuals that Hugh drew on to lead group discussions or to act as coaches and mentors to cautious or reluctant colleagues.

Of course, an ambassador needs a band of troops – enthusiastic converts who will spread the message and rouse the masses. At Heath Mount, the SLT started by identifying people who they thought would be good LPA champions, one from each section of the school, and they worked with this group to build up their understanding of the LPA before opening it out and introducing it to the staff as a whole. The LPA leaders at the school – Lee Beskeen, Jonny Spowart, and Rebecca Archer – told us:

> We were on the lookout for teachers who we thought were already showing elements of LPA teaching in their classrooms, and who would be keen to get on board and learn more – people who were looking to push on and would be up for trying something new. Some of them had worked with BLP frameworks in previous schools, and we were keen

to make use of their experience. And we also deliberately chose people who we knew would have the ear of the staff – they would be respected and listened to. We felt that it was important that the LPA wasn't seen as just coming from senior management: that it wasn't viewed as an initiative imposed from on high. We hoped that staff would think, "Well, if they can do it, and seem to value it, we reckon we could give it a go." We thought that there would be less resistance if we did it that way, and we think that we were right.

We have learned that savvy school leaders are wary of giving the impression that the LPA is being imposed on teachers "from the top down", sensing that there is more likely to be pushback from some staff in that case than if it is obviously valued by respected colleagues who are more "at their level".

Many LPA schools form a working group to generate momentum and penetrate into each department. This can be a really effective way of embedding and sustaining the LPA. You've already heard from Rachel Macfarlane about the vital role that the BLP working group played in the exploratory year before the launch at Walthamstow. She reflects:

> After the first term of evidence-gathering and securing staff interest and engagement, the spring and summer terms involved lots of hard work from the BLP working group members, who analysed the information gleaned from staff and students and then action-planned, informed by the findings. In retrospect, it is clear that having a sizeable team of optimistic, enthused, like-minded professionals who enjoyed spending an hour per week developing BLP was invaluable. The depth and breadth of the team enabled us to subdivide into smaller groups to explore different year groups' or subject departments' feedback. Each time we had useful or illuminating findings we took them to staff meetings and asked colleagues to consider the evidence in more detail. For example, we presented subject teams with the summary of their responses to the staff questionnaire about which learning muscles they used already and which they felt more or less confidence in developing, and requested that they compared it to the feedback from the staff as a whole, discussing differences, implications, and possible next steps.

Similarly, at Dr Challoner's, Mark Fenton recalls:

> The experience for the members of the working group was a really powerful one, for several reasons. Just to go into their peers' lessons and see how they were "doing teaching" was quite a novelty for many of the group. And for all of them, learning to focus not so much on what the teacher was doing, and more on how the students were behaving as learners, was quite an eye-opener. The discussions between the observers after lesson visits were very engaged and insightful. As far as the teachers

being observed were concerned, we tried to make it quite low-key, allowing them to opt in or out as they wished. But we made it clear that this was in no way an appraisal exercise, and no one was going to be judged.

Because the members of the working group were talking positively about their experience to their colleagues, the mood was generally receptive, and not one of suspicion that "another initiative" was being foisted on them. Rather than trying to push water uphill, people were coming to Mark Sturgeon and saying, "When are you going to do another one of these?" We never went in and said, "You've got to start teaching like this", but gradually people started coming up with their own ideas about how to tweak their teaching in order to allow the boys to take greater control over their own learning. I knew we were making real headway when some of the heads of department started coming to me and saying, "Hold on, why aren't we involved in this?"

The key role that LPA converts can have in winning over sceptics will be explored further shortly.

Finally, some schools have involved students in leading and maintaining the LPA culture in the school, giving them responsibility for conducting lesson observations, planning activities, and mentoring their peers. At Isaac Newton Academy, senior school students visit their primary school counterparts termly for a one-to-one appointment to discuss and review the younger children's BRIDGES dispositions. They support the 6- and 7-year-olds in completing their BRIDGES handbooks, leading both the mentors and the mentees to develop their learning muscles. Figure 3.1 shows a sample page from this handbook.

Bravery

Date:

By myself	• I am always positive and hopeful. • I try out new ideas and ways of doing things. • I am happy to experiment and I am open to new ideas. • I learn through trying things out. • I show confidence and courage even when I am unsure. • I am a positive influence on others. • I like to find out how something works and why something happens in a particular way. • I love to learn.
Mostly by myself	• I am positive and optimistic most of the time. • I like to try new things and new ideas, though I may need some encouragement. • I have shown bravery lots of times. • I am growing in confidence. • I like to discuss ideas in class.
With some adult support	• I try to be positive and am beginning to show my bravery more often. • I usually attempt to be brave. • I am learning to try new things and not to be afraid of getting it wrong, although I still get upset sometimes when things do go wrong.

With lots of adult help	• I am learning to be positive and optimistic. • I am learning what it means to be brave. • Sometimes I have tried to be brave. • I am learning to share my ideas with other pupils in the class without being shy.

Figure 3.1: An Extract from the Isaac Newton Academy Primary BRIDGES Handbook

To give a flavour of the benefits of this exercise, some 6- and 7-year-olds were asked to reflect on their experience of being mentored. Their comments included:

"We have mentoring with Year 9s. They ask us questions about the dispositions we are learning about. If we're learning about responsibility, they'll ask us, 'How do you use it?' We get to ask them questions."

"If we didn't know some of the dispositions, we'd tell them and they'd explain it."

"Mentoring helps so that when we get to high school, we'll understand it more."

Wondering

Who would make a great LPA leader in your school? What qualities make them an ideal choice?

What role will you play in the introduction, implementation, and sustaining of the LPA?

How will you judge the moment when you can safely step back a little without risking the gains already achieved?

How might you convene and use a working group? Would you let it grow organically or how much might you need to "manage" its make-up and remit?

> Is there a role for student LPA ambassadors or leaders at your school, do you think?

How Should You Deal with Any Sceptics, Cynics, and Blockers?

In each of our leaders' schools, the LPA has revolutionised the practice of some staff and filled them with enthusiasm. At Dr Challoner's, one very experienced teacher who had seen a multitude of innovations come and go remarked, "This has had real impact. It has reinvigorated my career." Yet however well you have planned for the introduction of the LPA, however strategic and bespoke your approach, however charismatic the leadership, and however persuasive your arguments, there will always be some who fail to be filled with that excitement. We should not be surprised by this. As leaders, we know that change is tricky, that it can be threatening and unnerving, and that it usually meets with some degree of pushback. The key is to ascertain what type of resistance you are facing and what lies at the root of it. Each reason will require a different response.

The key is to ascertain what type of resistance you are facing and what lies at the root of it.

Hugh Bellamy had some useful insights on this topic:

> You have to see winning hearts and minds as a long-term project. It takes time for people to get their heads around the key ideas of the LPA, let alone make and embed the requisite changes in their practice. And there will be legitimate questions of the "Yes, but ..." and "What if ..." kind, some of which will be veiled attempts to stop change from happening, but many of which will be quite rational and often useful in sharpening and deepening everyone's understanding of where the school is heading.

In *Leadership Plain and Simple,* Steve Radcliffe suggests that people typically fall into the following six categories in their response to any new vision or initiative presented to them:[6]

1. Committed.

2. Enrolled.

3. Willingly compliant.

4. Grudgingly compliant.

5. Apathetic.

6. Resistant.

In establishing a strong culture of learning power, leaders are striving to convert any apathetic or compliant colleagues to a position of enrolment or commitment. The resistant will, of course, require a different approach, but they do need to be tackled! You might like to sort your staff into Steve Radcliffe's six types in relation to how you anticipate they will react to the LPA. This could help you to anticipate the likely blockers and how you might deal with them.

Your enthusiasts and pioneers can be used to support, reassure, and cajole your cautious bystanders or nervous wait-and-see-ers. Principled questioners can be won over by the evidence and research presented in Chapter 2. The diehard cynics and those who revel in blocking new initiatives and resisting any change may need a one-to-one tough conversation with you or your LPA coordinator. It's essential that you have your counterarguments to hand to respond to the yes-but-ers; that you practise your replies to blockers' objections; and that you train your ambassadors and pioneers to do likewise.

People push back for different reasons. Let's look at some of the common reasons for resistance to the LPA and rehearse effective responses and strategies for addressing them.

---

[6] Steve Radcliffe, *Leadership Plain and Simple,* 2nd edn (Harlow: Pearson, 2012), pp. 50–53.

Limiting assumptions

At Isaac Newton Academy, all interview candidates, regardless of the post they are applying for, are asked to read the staff expectations policy which starts with the core purpose:

> To demonstrate belief in the potential of all students to develop the skills and character necessary for success at university and beyond.

Rachel Macfarlane says:

> We would rather not appoint and tolerate a vacancy than offer a job to someone with a fixed mindset.

Rachel was in the enviable position of being able to appoint her staff from scratch, picking only those who would sign up to such a code of expectations, but, of course, not all leaders will be. They might find themselves coming up against some fixed mindsets. Some teachers have different beliefs and expectations about the learning potential of different students. Some have been taught that intelligence and character are fixed, and they find it hard to shift their viewpoint. Sometimes you will hear comments like "Our kids just couldn't" or "Our parents wouldn't get it." These limited assumptions are dangerous and need to be challenged head-on – patiently and politely, but firmly. The research of Carol Dweck and others (see Chapter 2) provides plenty of ammunition, as do the countless stories in every school of learners (young and adult) developing from modest starting points and blossoming through hard work, deliberate practice, and great teaching from educators who believed in them.

Remember Jane Bellamy, head teacher at Leigham Primary School, who brought in a neuroscientist to talk to the staff in the early days of the LPA? Well, interestingly she commented on the impact of that visit:

> The staffroom culture changed – for example, in student review meetings there was less fatalism about children, and a dawning realisation that everyone can learn, and you can't write children off because of their background or the family they come from.

The pressure of course delivery

You might hear staff saying that they don't have time to engage with the LPA on top of covering the content/preparing children for SATs/GCSEs/A levels, etc. These colleagues need to be pointed to the evidence suggesting that teaching using the LPA saves time as it supports students to become better, more self-regulated learners, so that knowledge sticks and they can learn beyond the classroom and outside of taught hours. Far from their results suffering, schools with a well-embedded LPA tend to enjoy impressive academic outcomes.

The following cartoon makes the point:[7]

Figure 3.2: A Common Misconception

---

[7] This concept was presented to Guy a long time ago by a participant in a workshop he was running. Unfortunately, we're not able to trace the originator.

Jane Bellamy agrees. She told us:

> One of my staff's most common concerns is the pressure to get through subject matter, and there is a widespread feeling of time-poverty. Some teachers said, "We haven't got time for this LPA stuff; there's so much content we've got to get through." But I said, "You'll get through the content much more quickly if you have a bunch of confident, powerful learners in the room!"

Some teachers get sidetracked by a belief in the false opposition between traditionalist and progressive models of education. They may think that what the students need in order to get great grades is knowledge, not skills – but, of course, the LPA delivers both. They may have formed an assumption that attention to skills is always at the cost of knowledge, yet the LPA combines the two.

Gavin Smith recalls that there was some pushback from staff at Wren Academy when the curriculum in England moved, under Secretary of State for Education Michael Gove, towards what came to be called a "knowledge-rich" approach (meaning that there was more prescribed content to cover, and more traditional, recall-based exams at the end). Gavin explains:

> When we first spoke to staff about the planned reforms to GCSEs and A levels and the focus on a knowledge-rich curriculum, one teacher asked whether this would be the end of BLP. I responded by saying that, in fact, BLP had never been more important for our students. If they were to thrive in the new exam regime, then it was all the more important that we helped them to become highly effective learners. Rote learning and drilling were not good enough, given the challenges they faced. I informed the staff that we would be renewing and refreshing our learning-focused approach to ensure that students across the school were well-equipped to engage with the increased subject knowledge that they now required in order to be successful. The staff responded brilliantly in ensuring that this happened. Our first GCSE Progress 8 score placed us 21st in the country, and since then our progress levels have consistently been in the top 1%.[8] To assume that there is some inherent conflict between subject knowledge and developing learning power is just nonsense – and quite unnecessary.

---

8   Progress 8 scores are a method used in England to show how much progress students in a particular high school have made in their learning during their first five years in that school (roughly from age 11 to 16). The measure compares the progress made in that school to the average progress students have made across the whole country.

Fear of having to teach in a different way

In some cases, staff are not against the LPA, but rather lack confidence in their ability to teach in an LPA way. They may fear being left behind by others or worry that adapting their lesson style will take too much time. Typically, these teachers are either more fragile or very experienced and somewhat set in their ways. If you have a John Keohane on your staff, it would be invaluable to pair them up with such a character.

Sometimes, reluctance to try the LPA can be framed as a "traditional" view about the role of the teacher as the imparter of knowledge. You may have staff members who rather like being "the knower". They can sometimes be your less secure practitioners, for whom pedagogical coaching would be beneficial. Others are lukewarm about the LPA because they, consciously or subconsciously, rather like "rescuing" children as opposed to teaching them to be self-sufficient learners. Showing them what happens to fragile, over-reliant learners when they no longer have their over-caring and dominant teacher by their side can be salutary!

Some examples of how to effectively tackle the "awkward squad"

In some schools there may be a few recalcitrant colleagues who need to be cajoled into engaging with the LPA. Smart leaders use their antennae to spot them or have reliable "informers" to apprise them of who might be swimming against the tide. Here are a few examples of how LPA leaders have worked with this level of resistance.

Malcolm White, head teacher at Leventhorpe School, recalls:

> We had some staff who were not keen to change. Our approach of training staff in waves meant that the laggards self-selected and were slow to step up for training. This approach actually helped, as with successive groups of staff undergoing training, the climate of the school gradually changed. The reluctant staff slowly became more isolated as all the others were confident in the benefits of the LPA. The norms of the school moved, and the resistance to change eased. Staff in the reluctant group eventually had their training and were no longer vocally resistant as the culture and climate had moved on.

Jann Robinson found a canny way of winning over the blockers at St Luke's:

> Teachers were asked to share with others how they were introducing the dispositions in their classrooms. The "early adopters" were naturally keen to share and gave freely of their practical insights. However, a stronger impact was made when some teachers who had a reputation for being sceptical about BLP were asked to share how they were using the framework in their classes. This really helped to shift the mood in the staffroom, especially among those who had initially been wary or reluctant. I can still remember the feeling of, "Well, if X can give it a go, and succeed, I can give it a go too." It felt like a breakthrough in overcoming the natural resistance which occurs with any change.

Wondering

Who might the blockers be in your school?

How will you know?

What might their reasons for resistance be?

How could you most effectively get them on board or work around them?

How Might You Introduce the LPA to Students?

The ways in which you introduce your students to the LPA are likely to depend on their age and prior exposure to such methods of learning. Some of our schools have used intrigue to get the students speculating about what the LPA involves. At Walthamstow, a few weeks before the formal launch of BLP, giant letter Rs started to appear around the school in random places. The girls could be heard chattering about what they were, speculating as to what they meant, and hypothesising as to how they had come to be there. As you might recall, the 4Rs represent the four major "learning muscle groups" of the BLP framework: resilience, resourcefulness, reflection, and reciprocity.

There are many ways of introducing students to the elements of learning power. Some schools have opted for discrete LPA lessons, often delivered by a class or form teacher. We find that these are fine, as long as they are accompanied by the sustained effort to create those shifts in routine pedagogy which lie at the heart of the LPA. Just talking about the "learning muscles" by itself doesn't achieve the culture change we want. At nursery and primary level, LPA "characters" are often used to personify the learning characteristics. At Icknield Infant and Nursery School, for example, Rocky the Tortoise (who embodies resilience) can often be seen sitting on a table to remind a child or a group to persevere with their learning.

However, Woolenwick Infant and Nursery School in Stevenage, England, have taken a different view. Usha Dhorajiwala, the head teacher, explains:

> We felt that the characters diluted the message and created confusion in the language. There was a danger that the children would become hooked on the story of the characters and see them as separate from the dispositions.

At Woolenwick, the values and ideas of BLP are communicated in many ways, including through forest school, yoga, and mindfulness. Usha says:

> BLP values are woven through our forest school and woodland learning experiences. Similarly, our allotment project, in which the children are involved in developing an edible garden, has allowed them to become immersed in BLP principles, as well as foster an intimate relationship with nature and an understanding of the changing seasons. The learning powers are supported through whole-school participation in daily mindfulness practice and weekly yoga practice. In our weekly celebration assembly, selected children are awarded BLP super learner certificates. Their names are added to the BLP tree in the hall. These awards are shared via our weekly newsletter, reaching families, staff, and governors.

Many schools incorporate the learning dispositions and character traits into assemblies, during which staff members, parents, and the children themselves may tell stories about their own learning lives, and stress the virtues of being resilient and resourceful. Jann Robinson says that at St Luke's:

> Student buy-in came through using the assemblies each week to talk about learning and what a good learner does. I spoke endlessly about how school is about more than getting good marks, about it being to help them become adults who would be ready

to meet the challenges of a rapidly changing world. I used assemblies to talk about the dispositions and what they looked like, and I tried to always have a story to illustrate them. I often spoke about the challenges I experience in my own learning.

Similarly, at Isaac Newton, each Monday morning – prior to the tutor-led BRIDGES lesson in Period 1 – Years 7 and 8 have a BRIDGES assembly. Whoever delivers the assembly (it might be a senior leader, a head of department, or a member of the operational staff – every adult is invited) will link it to the BRIDGES disposition of the fortnight, usually giving a personal story of how they have struggled with and practised that characteristic. For example, the finance officer talked about living in Japan and having to find her way around Tokyo on her own with no knowledge of the language or alphabet, making her unable to read the signs, and the head of art showed a video of how she had practised free kicks every day of the summer holidays, proving the power of practice as her football skills improved markedly by the end of the six weeks. The form tutor can then build on the messages of the assembly. In the primary phase, the dispositions are introduced in the Monday morning assembly and explored throughout the week during lessons and circle time. The teachers focus on those characteristics and look to encourage their use within the children's wider school life. Every child who has demonstrated the dispositions of the week is awarded a certificate during the Friday celebration assembly.

Explaining, illustrating, and exemplifying the learning dispositions is also a good way of getting teachers – in fact, all the adults in the school – talking and thinking about the nature of learning and what makes a good learner. It helps them to deepen their own understanding and appreciation of what the LPA is about. The culture changes for everyone as they come to use the language and embody the values of the LPA.

Wondering

What would be the most impactful way to introduce the LPA to your students? Why?

How will you judge how effective your strategy has been?

How Can You Ensure That Everyone Is on Board?

Even with the best-laid plans, many leaders have reflected on the fact that there were groups of stakeholders who, in retrospect, they wished they had engaged more inclusively from the outset. It is easy to overlook governors when inducting the school community into the LPA, for example. At Woolenwick, the governors regularly review the language for learning and their visits focus on the practice of BLP in classrooms. At St Luke's, Jann Robinson shared the importance of BLP with her governors. Having laid the groundwork, she was able to gain their approval for the appointment of a dean of professional development and learning. The governors have remained supportive of this work as they have seen the impact on the students, and on their results.

Hannah Trickett at Maple Cross reflected:

> I wish we had more engagement from lunchtime staff. Also, it can be very challenging when external professionals (for example, a librarian or music teacher) have limited understanding of the school's approach. Without meaning to, their language or actions can contradict the LPA. For example, they may unthinkingly do too much for the children, and deprive them of opportunities to find out how to do things for themselves.

Similarly, Rachel Macfarlane learned an important lesson from initially overlooking support staff in the introduction of BLP at Walthamstow. For reasons that echo what Hannah has said, Rachel discovered that the engagement of operational staff is vital and so, when she moved to Isaac Newton, she made sure that *all* members of staff were involved in the BRIDGES programme from the word go. All staff at the academy, both teaching and operational, agree a personal BRIDGES professional development target with their line manager as part of the annual review cycle. They explicitly identify a particular disposition that they wish to develop further during the year.

Here is a sample of BRIDGES professional development targets adopted by staff:

- To develop the disposition of leadership with a larger team, including the development of team members as leaders – particularly [names staff members].

- To develop the disposition of resourcefulness in using different materials and finding ways around obstacles when planning the refit of the medical room.
- To further develop the disposition of planning in developing a Key Stage 4 curriculum that provides clear progression into Key Stage 5.
- To develop the disposition of creativity in designing resources for EAL learners.

Another way in which the leaders at Isaac Newton ensure that absolutely every member of staff is involved with the LPA is by using them all as BRIDGES mentors. Each student has one (usually either their tutor or an attached member of staff – either teaching or operational) and meets with them for a twenty-minute, one-to-one session every six months. Students prepare in advance, detailing their strengths and outlining the dispositions they intend to develop further, supported by evidence and concrete actions. Staff receive regular training on how to be effective BRIDGES mentors.

Wondering

How will you engage your governing body with the LPA?

What systems or structures might you introduce to ensure that everyone is engaged?

Who on your staff body will you rely on to tell you honestly about those who are not yet on board?

Summary

It may not be realistic to expect to take absolutely everyone in the school community with you on your LPA journey. However, it is well worth the effort to get as many staff, students, parents, and governors on board as possible. Never lose your energy and passion for communicating the vision, and leave no stone unturned in your efforts to ensure that you have engaged all stakeholder groups. But, at the same time, don't allow complacency to set in and remember that it is better that you know who is not yet fully convinced than to have silent and hard-to-detect cynicism in the staffroom.

To conclude, we'd like to offer some top tips; these are our strong recommendations.

- Never overlook an opportunity to promote and enthuse about the benefits of the LPA: the influence you have as leader is invaluable.

- Gauge carefully when you can step back from the leadership of the LPA. And ensure that you are handing over to someone who is definitely up to the challenges of this vital role.

- Whatever you do, *do* something with the LPA. Don't just stick up posters and think that you have done the job.

However, we have given plenty of ideas and options to help you on your way, rather than advocating one single path of action. This is because, as Dylan Wiliam says, "Everything works somewhere and nothing works everywhere."[9]

---

9   Dylan Wiliam, *Leadership for Teacher Learning: Creating a Culture Where All Teachers Improve So That All Students Succeed* (Palm Beach, FL: Learning Sciences International, 2016), p. 66.

Chapter 4

Creating a Staff Culture of Learning

All schools speak about the importance of creating lifelong learners, but they are often only talking about the students. In this chapter we explore how teachers might be helped to become exemplary learners for life too. We ponder what our schools would look like if there were a really strong culture of learning among the staff. We explore how we can strengthen (or, in some cases, maybe even create from scratch) a culture characterised by collaboration, openness, experimentation, thinking about learning and how to shape it, observation, and stretching oneself: a culture in which professional learning is seen as valuable and not just as another thing to do. We look at both established and new schools and at how they have shaped a learning community. All the leaders we spoke to faced the challenge of how to bring about the desired change and not make teachers feel as though they had no agency over their craft.

The questions we will explore in detail in this chapter are:

- How do school leaders cope with balancing "tight" and "loose" in building the learning culture?
- What are the characteristics of teacher learning communities (TLCs)?
- How is a staffroom culture of openness, experimentation, and support built?
- How might the traditional walls that isolate practice be broken down?
- How can teachers share their practice?
- How might leaders use external pressures to build culture?

How Do School Leaders Cope with Balancing "Tight" and "Loose" in Building the Learning Culture?

An important issue for school leaders to grapple with, which many of our contributors touch upon, is the tension between centralised control and individual creativity. How tightly do we prescribe the LPA? As Siobhan Leahy and Dylan Wiliam put it, there is a shifting balance to be struck between *fidelity* to the original idea, and *flexibility* in the face of changing circumstances and personnel. They call this the "tight but loose" dilemma, and every change agent has to deal with it. According to them, our job is to:

> combine an obsessive adherence to central design principles (the "tight" part) with accommodations to the needs, resources, constraints and particularities that occur in any school or district (the "loose" part).[1]

As you have seen, the LPA is built around two frameworks: a specification of the habits of mind of powerful learners and a set of pedagogical design principles – drawn from research and teacher experience – which cultivate those habits. Both frameworks are the result of much thinking and research, but both are open to modification, elaboration, and customisation by teachers. Some schools, as we have seen, may need to establish the basic habits of organisation and collaboration before they can start experimenting with imagination and craftsmanship. Others might want to highlight critiquing or determination from the word go. Some schools might want to change the vocabulary so that conversations about learning capitalise more effectively on the everyday language of their students and their communities. Some teachers might welcome the design principles that show them how to build a learning-powered classroom one step at a time. Others might feel constrained by what feels to them like "teaching by numbers" and want to work on embedding the principles in a more holistic way. The leader has to be conscious of these tensions, and find their own balance. And as experience with the LPA grows in a school, so the balance between fidelity and flexibility will necessarily change. While many teachers might have welcomed the frameworks to begin with, as confidence and skills grow, so the

---

1   Siobhan Leahy and Dylan Wiliam, From teachers to schools: scaling up professional development for formative assessment. In John Gardner (ed.), *Assessment and Learning*, 2nd edn (London: Sage, 2012) pp. 49–71 at p. 55.

tools can come to feel restrictive rather than helpful. Leaders have to keep monitoring and questioning whether the balance point between tight and loose that worked well last term, or last year, is still optimal.

What Are the Characteristics of Teacher Learning Communities (TLCs)?

The need to embed coaching, planning, and reflection firmly within the context of everyday classroom experience is well-supported by research. Marnie Thompson and Dylan Wiliam, while working at the Education Testing Service in Princeton, in the United States, summarised the research thus:

> If the practices you are hoping to get teachers to change are recurrent, central, and entrenched within everyday teaching and school culture, then teachers will need sustained support to change them. Not only must the support be sustained over time (at least a year and often much longer [...]), that support must embed teachers' learning within the realities of day-to-day teaching in their own schools and classrooms, and allow for repeated cycles of learning, practice, reflection, and adjustment within their native context.[2]

Thompson and Wiliam are also alert to the difficulties schools may face in implementing this kind of professional development:

> Significant structural barriers to TLCs exist in many schools, including daily and weekly schedules that provide little or no time with colleagues during the normal school day, personnel policies and practices that do not recognize or value teacher expertise, local bargaining agreements that discourage teachers from meeting outside scheduled hours, inadequate resources to support teacher time away from the classroom, competing demands on teacher time, and school cultures that do not easily align with the needs of sustained, school-embedded, collegial work with colleagues.[3]

---

2 Marnie Thompson and Dylan Wiliam, Tight but loose: a conceptual framework for scaling up school reforms. In E. Caroline Wylie (ed.), *Tight but Loose: Scaling Up Teacher Professional Development in Diverse Contexts*. Educational Testing Service Research Report. Ref: ETS RR-08-29 (2008), pp. 1–44 at p. 12. Available at: https://www.ets.org/Media/Research/pdf/RR-08-29.pdf.

3 Thompson and Wiliam, Tight but loose, pp. 16–17.

In the face of these challenges, Dylan Wiliam has developed detailed specifications regarding how these TLCs should be designed if they are to achieve sustained habit change in teachers. A good presentation of these ideas can be found in Chapter 6 of *Leadership for Teacher Learning*. In brief, these monthly meetings of small groups of teachers, which last around ninety minutes, follow a common format. They begin and end with a review of the "learning intentions" which have been set for that meeting. There is a "How's it going?" segment, in which all participants share their recent experiences with trying to implement a new style of teaching (in our case, the LPA design principles; in Dylan Wiliam's case, the focus is on formative assessment). Then comes a segment on personal action planning, in which each teacher writes notes on what they will be experimenting with between now and the next meeting. Their next steps must include arrangements to spend time in each other's classrooms and to collaboratively plan lessons. Finally, there is a second review segment to check that everyone is comfortable with their plans and willing to proceed.

Not everyone will be happy with such a scripted approach. For example, here is John Keohane reflecting on his experience leading professional development at Wren Academy:

> We keep rediscovering that, however hard you try to get it "right", one size never fits all, and we have had to become more flexible in our approaches and keep monitoring how well they are working. Historically, we have been very prescriptive and given the teacher triads a fixed weekly programme that required them to engage with BLP resources and activities.[4] But in the last few years we have built up a teaching and learning resources hub on our intranet and each triad can access that and design their own programme as the weeks go on. We have moved away from relying on one particular "brand" or set of resources, and now draw on a wider range of inputs – for example, the Research Schools Network[5] – that all bear on the question of how to develop and maintain a strong learning culture in the classroom.

Here again we see the tight-but-loose dilemma. While too tight can cause teachers to feel dragooned and chivvied, too loose also has its problems. Teachers are busy people, and it is all too easy for mere good intentions, or general exhortations by school leaders to visit each other's classrooms, to fall by the wayside if there is no time

---

4   Triads are simply groups of three teachers, often orchestrated so that the individuals bring a mixture of different subject specialisms, teaching experience, and enthusiasm for or skill with the LPA to the group.
5   See https://researchschool.org.uk/.

set aside to do these things, no clear purpose, and no sense of accountability if they fail to do so. Thompson and Wiliam summarise research which shows that:

> teachers' awareness that they would be asked to report on their most recent efforts was a helpful, even necessary, spur to action.[6]

How Is A Staffroom Culture of Openness, Experimentation, and Support Built?

With those complexities in mind, let's now look at the ways in which leaders have gone about the business of building a strong culture of learning among their staff. We'll look first at some established schools with contrasting cultures and approaches, and then at a couple of new schools that were able to orchestrate the desired culture from day one.

Established schools

> Walthamstow School for Girls was a well-established school when Rachel Macfarlane took over as head. She says:
>
>> The cultural vision of staff as learners, and the school as an inclusive learning community, had always been strong at Walthamstow. However, there is no doubt that the BLP working group was able to strengthen this.
>
> Sue Milligan was a member of the BLP working group. She reflects:
>
>> I was an assistant head teacher who was approaching retirement at the time (after more than thirty-five years in schools) when Rachel introduced us to BLP. As would be expected, some staff were sceptical (a fear of the new). However, once

---

6 Thompson and Wiliam, Tight but loose, p. 18.

BLP was embedded, few doubted the benefits for our young people. We have a responsibility to ensure that the children we educate are prepared for adulthood and to become lifelong learners. BLP does this. As a teacher it was good to try something really new – even after many years of teaching in a different way – and BLP really energised my lessons.

Through the examples being set by members of the BLP working group, staff naturally started to invite colleagues into their classrooms to see them trying out new activities and techniques and to offer feedback. This evolved very organically and spread beyond the working group, opening up a "safe" culture of practising techniques with the support of a friend. Rachel comments:

A staff reading group was established, following a request from colleagues. Each month a new educational text was chosen by the group. Any staff member could read it and bring their thoughts and reflections to a lunchtime meeting, held in the school library. We deliberately chose the library as the venue so that the girls could see and hear staff in action, discussing their reading and pedagogical ideas. Before too long we had students pulling up a chair, listening in, asking about the books that were being read, and getting involved.

Wondering

Do you like the idea of staff discussing their teaching "in public"? Is this something that you could imagine happening in your school? Are there any cultural factors that might prove inhibiting?

Could you go even further and invite some students to participate in the discussions?

In contrast to Walthamstow, St Luke's Grammar School did not have a strong pre-existing culture of staff learning when Learning@STLUKE'S (L@SL) was introduced in 2014. Prior to L@SL, teachers were generous in sharing resources within their departments, but there wasn't a culture of thinking about pedagogy or sharing practice across departments or between the junior and senior schools. There had always been a lot of resistance in the staffroom to change of any kind, which was linked to the perception that change meant asking hard-working teachers to work even harder. These prevailing attitudes meant that a very intentional approach to culture change had to be taken.

While it was important to be intentional about staff becoming LPA teachers, the working group felt that in order to shift the teachers' attitudes, they would need to get them to experience being learners themselves. They were careful to make the process as non-threatening and manageable as possible by going for small, incremental changes. The working group met twice a term, with Simon Breakspear acting as a "critical friend", to plan the steps that they would take. Jann Robinson says:

> Having the accountability of those meetings helped to make sure that none of us lost focus in the midst of the busyness of a school. Particularly for me, that time was sacrosanct and let me focus just on learning. The working group itself developed a learning culture as we read, experimented, and reflected on what we were doing.

The after-school whole-staff meetings which were already in place were repurposed. Traditionally, these meetings had been used for administrative matters, followed by a presentation by an outside speaker. They now became a time for the staff to learn together. Topics and activities were introduced that invited teachers to think about learning, to be open to learning from each other, and to have ongoing conversations about learning.

For example, at the first meeting, small groups of teachers from different departments and year groups were tasked with studying some of the learning dispositions and designing progression ladders that would track their development. They were then asked to trial the use of one learning ladder in one of their classes. At the next meeting, some teachers volunteered to share how they had been using the ladders, and with what effect. Teachers enjoyed these meetings, and they got them talking about learning. The working group could see the progress that teachers were making and were looking for the right moment to go deeper.

At that point the decision was taken to establish professional learning groups (PLGs), which read and discussed articles about the science of learning. Jann says:

> I had a strong feeling that if the teachers could read what I had read, they would have the same response: an aha moment. I felt there would be greater buy-in and openness to change. I wanted to start reading groups, but I knew there would be resistance by some teachers who had quite a lot of power. So we had to come up with a softly-softly plan.

They began by asking teachers in the senior school if any of them would like to be in a trial PLG, and a number volunteered. They were given pre-readings from *Building Learning Power* and a set of discussion questions that could be used to scaffold conversation – for example, what resonated with you? What challenged your thinking? What might you do as a result of this reading?[7] The volunteers generally enjoyed the group discussions and spoke positively about them to the rest of the staff.

At the beginning of the next school year, all teachers at St Luke's were assigned to a PLG. Each group met twice a term. In the senior school, teachers had the PLG timetabled in one of their non-teaching periods, and every group was cross-faculty. In the junior school, PLGs took place after hours. In each group a chair, a timekeeper, a minute-taker, and a convenor were appointed. Each group had no more than six members: they were deliberately kept quite small to discourage "social loafing". A few groups were handpicked by the working group to "manage" some of the personalities at the time. The same process of pre-reading followed by set discussion questions was followed. Members reported back at the next meeting on how their trialled changes went. The minute-taker was required to submit their records to James Pietsch, the dean of professional development and learning. This was an accountability mechanism. There was some resentment at

---

7   For further advice on setting up reading groups – or journal clubs, as they call them – see the advice from the Chartered College of Teaching: https://chartered.college/journal-club.

being required to report so rigidly, but in the early days it helped to shape the discussion.

In the junior school, the groups were initially designed to contain teachers of different age groups and also included the teachers' aides.[8] However, there was some early pushback from teachers who wanted to work with their grade partners and without the teachers' aides. The groups were redesigned as a result. The decision demonstrated the working group's openness to feedback and willingness to rethink – although in retrospect Jann felt that removing the aides was a mistake as it meant that the framework didn't reach all those involved with the children's learning. After some discussion, in subsequent years the teachers' aides have been included in all professional development and in the PLGs.

Present: Apologies:	Date of meeting: Location:

Reflections on the reading. (10 minutes)

What is the difference between lessons in which students are given opportunities to collaborate and lessons which support students' development as collaborators?

Do we give students support in becoming more powerful learners or do we just give them time in class in which they can ask questions, reflect, collaborate, listen, etc.?

How might we do things differently if we were to have as our goal helping students to become better learners? Would this impact the way we approach:

a. collecting feedback?
b. framing lessons?

---

8   Equivalent to teaching assistants or learning support assistants in the UK.

c. designing learning activities?
Sharing ideas. (10 minutes) Share with your group anything you learned from observing colleagues this term. Share any successes you might have experienced with flipping the classroom.
Planning future lessons. (10 minutes) Do you think students learn best in your subject area with an overarching learning focus which is revisited each lesson (e.g. having a focus on collaboration in Term 2 and a focus on reasoning in Term 3) or having a different learning focus each lesson (or learning activity)? (Note: in Guy Claxton's work with schools in England, both these approaches have been adopted at different schools.) Discuss how you might encourage students in your class to become better learners in terms of their use of one of the dispositions.
One aspect of classroom practice that is rare, even though we know that it is related to better learning outcomes, is providing a time for feedback from students to teachers and for students to reflect on their own learning. How could you give students more opportunities for reflection and providing feedback?

Figure 4.1: An Agenda for the Meeting

Five years on, PLGs continue with the same basic structure but with some changes: readings are taken from a wider range of sources; meetings are held more often; and observation of each other's lessons has been included. The groups display their insights and reflections in the staffroom on big sheets of paper so everyone can see them. They are also digitised and loaded onto a shared drive. The display has replaced minute-taking. Jann reflects:

> PLGs replaced the twice-a-term after-school staff meetings, and I believe that the trading of time was critical for their success. It acknowledged the time pressures teachers feel. It was a strong statement about what was valued: teachers having time to read, think, reflect, and share with each other. I also think that it has been important that I am a member of a PLG. The staff appreciate that I am being a learner too, and my participation has enabled me to see first-hand how the groups have shifted teachers' outlooks.

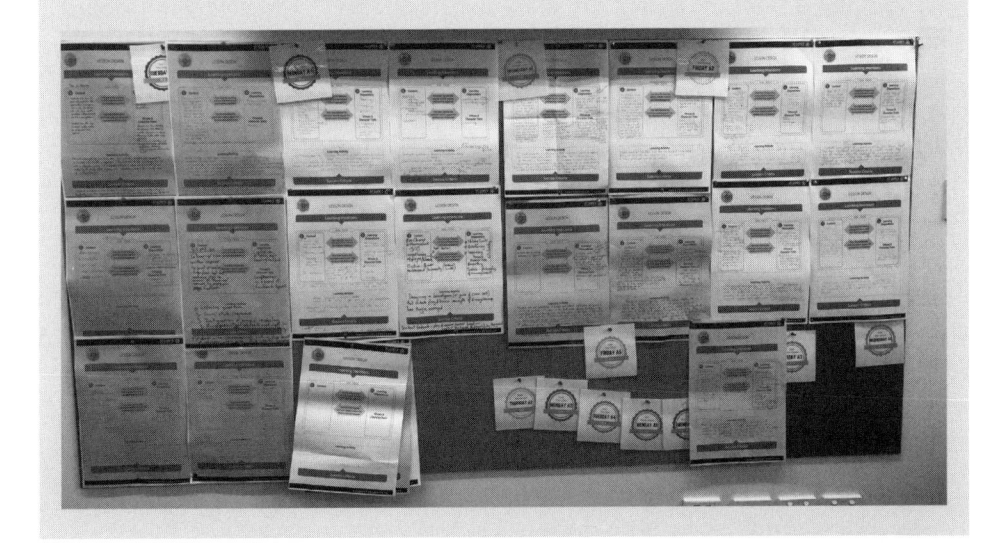

How Might the Traditional Walls That Isolate Practice Be Broken Down?

In 2015, Jann visited South Dartmoor Community College and met with Hugh Bellamy. Here she saw a model of learning observation which was focused on looking at the learners in the classroom, not at the teacher: the learning walk.

This seemed like an unthreatening way to open up classrooms and enable teachers to observe and learn from each other. Staff at St Luke's were generally not comfortable with other adults coming into their classrooms. Jann recalls:

> I have a practice of giving students a card and a chocolate frog on their birthdays, which I deliver during class time. One teacher said to me, "You should get the kids to come to you in your office. That would be more efficient."

Knowing that there might still be some initial resistance to introducing learning walks, Jann used a similar softly-softly approach. In 2015, James Pietsch called for volunteers from the senior school to be part of a trial. Those who responded knew when James would come into their classes, and he made it clear that he was looking at students' learning behaviours, not at their performance *per se*. He committed to sharing his observations with the teachers. Again, the volunteers had a positive experience which they shared informally with their colleagues, so it came as no great shock when, at the beginning of 2016, learning walks were introduced more widely. Members of the working group went into classrooms to look at learning, and they made sure that the observations which they fed back to teachers were framed positively.

To build teachers' confidence, there has been a slow evolution from them knowing when they would be observed to having designated learning walk weeks each term. Now the initiative has broadened to include:

- Peer observation through PLGs visiting classes, discussing what they have seen, and giving feedback to the teacher.
- Teachers requesting a learning walk when they want to share or explore something.
- Targeting a specific focus – for example, asking students about their understanding of the learning intentions and success criteria.

The junior school has developed a slightly different pattern for learning walks. They have small teams of walkers (all teachers and teachers' aides take part), who meet prior to going into classrooms. They visit every classroom in one day, discuss what they have seen, and give feedback. Everyone values being able to observe others. It opens teachers up to trying new things and, as a result, they have productive conversations about learning.

How Can Teachers Share Their Practice?

Creating opportunities for teachers to share their practice more broadly has also helped to shift the learning culture at St Luke's. At the beginning of each term, the teaching staff meet for a professional development day prior to the students' return. These sessions are led by members of the working group and, since 2018, the specially appointed learning mentors (more on which in Chapter 8). These meetings allow time for teachers to work together on planning their teaching and their teaching sprints for the term.[9] Teaching sprints are focused, short-term interventions designed to boost students' understanding of the dispositions. At the end-of-term meeting, there are two or three set-piece presentations given by chosen teachers to the whole staff, and then they all form two concentric circles to conduct a "speed-dating" style exercise to share the effects of their sprints.[10] Teachers also bring examples of students' work to share with each other.

> Creating opportunities for teachers to share their practice more broadly has also helped to shift the learning culture at St Luke's.

Learning conversations are also fostered through teachers telling a "story of impact" (i.e. an example of successful learning) in the regular Monday morning

---

9 See https://teachingsprints.com/.
10 Speed-dating is a classroom protocol in which participants can quickly get feedback from, and give it to, a number of peers. One common (though not the only) way of organising this is to create two concentric circles of people. The inner circle faces the outer circle so that participants can discuss in pairs and then one of the circles moves round so everyone has a new partner.

staff briefings. However, shifting culture takes time and there will inevitably be some pushback along the way. Jann reflects:

> It is important to understand that pushback will come and to know when to persevere and when to pivot. It can be quite discouraging. Depending on where the pushback comes from it can be easier or harder to stand against; the hardest times were when it came from within the working group. Middle leaders fed back that they were experiencing both their own discomfort with change and the discomfort of their group of teachers. This meant that as the principal I had to have a relentless focus on the desired future and to judge when to compromise in the face of resistance. At times it meant we had to pivot on a strategy, but more often than not it was just a matter of persevering and not allowing the everyday to take away from what really mattered. Principals are busy, but we need to set the learning agenda at the heart of the school. It is about being intentional about shifting daily practice. What I think has had a big impact on teachers has been that I am part of every professional development session, I am a member of a PLG, and I model myself as a learner.

Wondering

What in Rachel's and Jann's stories resonates with your school?

Both Rachel and Jann had reading groups in their schools. What do you think is the value of such groups? How might they work in your school?

What practices do you have in your school to allow teachers to see each other's lessons?

What role do you play now in leading learning in your school?

Hugh Bellamy's experience when he took up the headship of South Dartmoor Community College in 2010 was much like Jann's. If you recall, despite an "outstanding" grading in a recent Ofsted inspection, much of the teaching was quite dull. Hugh tried a number of things to wake his staff up to learning. One such initiative was "learning days" for all teachers. In the morning, everyone had to try something that they had never tried before. It could be surfing, knitting, diving, clay pigeon shooting, pottery, playing a new musical instrument, line dancing – anything like that. It had to be something that they were no good at, and they had to give it a good try. Then, in the afternoon, they would all come together and reflect on what it had been like. Self-reflective question prompts were given – for example, how did I go about learning? How did it feel to be a beginner? What did my approach show me about how I treat learning more generally? Hugh was in no doubt that this was one of the most popular and successful things that they did. He says that it really helped his teachers to think about learning, and to become interested in what was going on in learners' minds in their classrooms.

Other deliberate practices which Hugh introduced to try to boost the learning culture involved a series of weekly meetings:

- Every Monday morning Hugh or another member of the SLT would lead a teaching and learning briefing before lessons began. It would be the job of one of the departments – geography, say – to share with the rest of the staff one practical idea for developing LPA teaching which they were currently using or trialling. For the rest of the week, all staff are expected to have a go at exploring that tip or technique in their lessons, and to reflect on its usefulness with the rest of their department.

- Every Wednesday morning the heads of department would meet for three-quarters of an hour to discuss how that technique was being worked with, what was working well, what not so well, and how the students' learning was being impacted. These weekly meetings provided a continual drip-drip-drip of ideas and possibilities, which kept the LPA in the front of people's minds, and kept things moving, preventing them from becoming stagnant. And they also ensured that there was a bit of pressure and accountability; that all teachers were taking part and not hunkering down, waiting for it all to blow over.

- Every Friday at morning break there was a celebration briefing for staff – with doughnuts! Sometimes students would showcase a musical performance, or a sports team would be applauded for an achievement – focusing, of course, on the effort that went into the result. But, equally, staff members were celebrated for particular pieces of LPA-inspired teaching which the SLT had observed to be particularly imaginative or successful.

Instead of having pairs or triads of teachers working together, Hugh tried pairing up whole departments. He says:

> With the whole department working together, it's less "personal". Individual teachers don't feel as in the spotlight or under scrutiny. And there is also a certain pride in wanting your whole team to do well.

The departments met regularly to share the approaches to teaching that they had developed. Some would then be demonstrated in the classroom for the partner department to experiment with in their lessons. Everyone would ultimately be involved in evaluating and fine-tuning.

Hugh is critical of coaching models that revolve predominantly around discussion, concluding:

> While reflective discussions might generate interesting insights and possibilities, they didn't seem to translate very often into sustained changes in behaviour in the classroom.

How Might Leaders Use External Pressures to Build Culture?

Work on creating a staff culture of learning can be threatened by extraneous factors, but that external pressure can also be used to stimulate much-needed change. At Oaklands Primary School in West London, new head teacher Tessa Hodgson had inherited a culture of rather anxious compliance by the staff. Teachers had seemingly become used to doing what they were told, rather than proactively exploring their own questions by reflecting on their practice and looking at the research. The school was under a great deal of pressure to improve results and quality first teaching, and there was the threat of a punitive "requires improvement" judgement from Ofsted. This atmosphere made her staff quite stressed, and they became eager to make things "look better", rather than *be* better. Tessa had to work hard to shift the conversation from "What will Ofsted say?" to "What is best for the children?" She did this largely through focusing on the LPA. Tessa reflects:

> To create long-term change and empowered teachers, I needed to shift the learning culture to one that enabled teachers to reflect on changes to their practice that would positively impact on the children. Five years on, individual teachers and curriculum teams are now experimenting with new ways of working and trialling different practices that are refined and then rolled out across the school.

Here are some of the things that Tessa did to shift her staff away from an attitude of compliance and towards one of greater learning power – for both themselves and the children:

- She established a common language for talking about children's learning and about their development as learners.

- The way learning was celebrated in assemblies was changed to recognise the use of good learning habits as well as achievement and good behaviour. This had the most effect on the language being used around the school, and it also provided a really useful informal source of information about where the teachers and children were in their understanding.

- She discussed Carol Dweck's research on growth mindset with staff, and encouraged them to see risk-taking and making and learning from mistakes as integral to learning.

- She changed the performance management culture from one in which teachers continually felt judged to one in which they became interested in their own improvement.

- She gently but relentlessly insisted on teachers actually using LPA tools and techniques in the classroom, until they became second nature.

- She promoted the idea that they shared the responsibility to *ensure* that each child made good progress and that is was not acceptable to fall into the trap of blaming the child or their background for their "inability to learn". Tessa would explain to staff her conviction that, "If a child wasn't making progress, it was because of something *we* were or were not doing, and it was *our* job to adjust our teaching until we found a way that worked".

- She used staff meetings to discuss and role model different aspects of LPA-style teaching, so all staff were constantly hearing the same kinds of suggestions.

- She facilitated group visits to other schools so that her teachers could undertake lesson study in a different environment and learn by reflecting on what they had seen.

You'll see that these schools – all already established and seeking culture change – have adopted a wide variety of strategies for building that communal culture of learning and experimentation. Particularly if your school is also in this boat, you might like to stop and reflect on the range of strategies we have described and see which appeal to you most.

Wondering

Which would work best in your situation?

Which would work least well? Why do you think that is?

What are some of the dos and don'ts of which you think you might need to be aware?

What could be your next step?

Is there a sweet spot for tight but loose? Does it move? If so, what causes it to move?

Blank canvas opportunities

We have seen what leaders have done in established schools and it is clear that shifting the culture takes persistence. We will now look at how things might be different when building a culture of learning from the beginning.

> When Rachel Macfarlane was appointed to lead the brand-new Isaac Newton Academy, she had a head start. She was able to hand-pick staff who were keen to come on board with her plans for the philosophy and pedagogy of the school, and who were also naturally inquisitive, and keen to research and discuss pedagogy. Building on this fortunate foundation, Rachel was able to hit the ground running, and straightaway instituted a number of practices designed to build a staff culture of learning. Every subject team was timetabled an hour per week in which everyone was free at the same time to co-plan lessons. Time was also given at training days for different teams to work together and cross-fertilise each other's thinking.
>
> When Isaac Newton first opened, many teachers were co-teaching. Rachel comments:
>
>> In the first year, many teachers were co-teachers of a second or third subject – as well as teacher of their specialist subject – because of the way staffing had to work. This created a culture in which everyone was used to and comfortable with having colleagues in their lessons.
>
> Later this developed into a system whereby staff went to peer observe another teacher each term to see good practice. Rachel says:
>
>> We encouraged everyone to use their peer observation time to see BRIDGES lessons from time to time, as well as subject-specific lessons.
>
> Heads of year were kept off timetable during their year group tutors' BRIDGES lessons, so that they could go around the classrooms to see how everyone was tackling them and give extra support where needed. These regular visits enabled the heads of year to evaluate the lessons and to get a sense of who in the team was strong at particular aspects of pedagogy and who might be good at co-planning lessons for a particular BRIDGES disposition. These practices set the tone for

Isaac Newton and established a strong learning culture from the very beginning. This culture has continued.

Wren Academy had a similar focus on creating a staff culture of learning from the outset. As John Keohane says:

> If we are intending to nurture and develop lifelong learners, we need to model that attitude ourselves.

Wren has a number of strands to continuing professional development (CPD). The core purpose of each of the strands is to develop better teaching, and the focus is always on the detailed practicalities of the classroom. The one we want to highlight here involves the professional learning triads, which John Keohane has already mentioned briefly. To elaborate, all teachers in the triad have an equal right and responsibility to contribute, and the triads are carefully designed and monitored. They are always cross-faculty to help teachers to focus on learning and not fall back into conversations about content. There is a mix of more and less enthusiastic LPA practitioners, so, for instance, two teachers who might be more on board are teamed up with someone who may be more set in their ways, or even openly cynical. Triads meet in the open-plan cafeteria area, as there was the sense that this learning and reflection should not take place behind closed doors. They work in cycles of three weeks. In the first week, the triad works to collaboratively plan an LPA-style lesson for one of its members. In the second week, two teachers observe the third delivering the lesson. In the third week, the trio meet to review their reactions to the lesson and to draw out any lessons for the future. Everyone is in a triad and there is an expectation that everyone will improve their practice.

Summary

All of these leaders have created staff learning cultures. They have looked at their situations and developed strategies to cultivate and deepen learning for the teachers. At times they have used a tight model to move the culture forward by insisting that everyone is committed to the same practices. Sometimes they have loosened the model to allow teachers to have greater ownership of and flexibility in their practice. Sometimes they have moved between the models as they have tried to ensure that the essence of the LPA is not lost. They have all grappled with the tight-but-loose dilemma. The challenges have been different in each of the schools, but a number of common approaches have emerged. While they don't look exactly the same in each school, they have led to teachers who openly learn from each other, experiment, plan together, and feel safe to share their attempts to implement the LPA in their classrooms. The most effective practices which have emerged across the schools are:

- Having a small group of leaders (a working group) who originally develop the implementation strategy and openly experiment with ideas.
- Establishing reading groups which encourage teachers to engage with research into learning and the LPA.
- Creating opportunities for peer observation as a means for teachers to see and feel what the LPA is like in the classroom.
- Grouping teachers from across subject boundaries to plan together.
- Developing shared resources which teachers can access easily.
- Providing opportunities for teachers to share their experiences.
- Making the teachers' learning visible by having displays in common areas.
- Taking every opportunity to foster learning conversations.

Wondering

Are all of these approaches needed?

Which of these would be the top ones to try?

What does the learning culture look like currently in your school?

Which of these approaches might work in your setting, do you think?

> What would happen if peer observation was introduced at your school?
>
> What is the effect on students of seeing their teachers become more engaged in learning?

Chapter 5
A Language for Learning

It's curious how schools have an agreed way of talking about – and delivering – *what* they want their children to learn, but there is no such common agreement about *how* we want them to be as learners. National curricula in schools across the world ensure that a body of knowledge is imparted, which the powers that be consider to be important for future citizens and members of the workforce to know. And yet it is arguably even more important to have agreement about those learning skills and habits that all young people should have developed as a result of their education, since this is what they will need in order to operate in a fast-changing and uncertain world. In an LPA school, there has to be a common language for talking about learning: both the process of learning – what it involves and how it feels – and the skills and attributes that make someone a robust and independent learner. It is therefore one of the leader's key responsibilities to ensure that such a language evolves and becomes embedded in the daily conversations of classrooms and staffrooms.

In this chapter we will offer some stories and suggestions that explore the following questions:

- Why is having a common language for learning important?
- How can you open up a debate about students' learning habits?
- How can the vocabulary and concepts of learning power be introduced to students?
- How do you talk about learning with parents?
- How do you weave learning power language into everyday talk?

Why Is Having a Common Language for Learning Important?

There are a number of possible reasons why we might want to enrich the language that staff and students use to talk about the habits of effective learners. Hopefully this list will supplement the resources and arguments we gave you in Chapter 2, and help you to convince any waverers of the value of changing their linguistic habits a little.

- The language for learning defines a clear set of desirable outcomes for students that complement, but go beyond, good exam results. If we are to value these outcomes, we have to be able to talk about them.

- Such a language provides you with a more precise way of articulating the collective vision for education in your school – over and above exam results.

- The vocabulary of learning power enables teachers to plan lessons that target different aspects of students' capacity to learn. Just as elite sports coaches need to have a detailed understanding of fitness to be able to design a range of appropriate exercises for their teams, so teachers need to know what goes into making up "learning fitness" if they are to stretch all of the muscles effectively.

- A language that makes explicit what it is that effective learners actually do – and how they feel – will, if used consistently, allow students to understand the cognitive and emotional effort that learning requires, and therefore not assume that if they are finding something hard, it means they are lacking in "ability".

- A common language for learning gives all young people a better understanding of themselves and enables them to take greater control of and responsibility for their learning – which will equip them better for the future.

- The language allows you to talk to parents about those outcomes that really matter and which they can support through interactions at home and in the world beyond school.

> ## Wondering
>
> Which of these points ring most true for you?
>
> Which do you think will carry the most weight with your staff?
>
> What concepts do you most often use when you are talking about the way in which students learn, and what might make them better or worse at learning?

How Can You Open Up a Debate About Students' Learning Habits?

Has there been any discussion about the crucial outcomes of education in your school? If not, you might like to consider starting one.

You could ask colleagues the following open questions:

- How do we want our young people to be as learners by the time they leave us?
- What kinds of young minds are we aiming to produce?
- Which characteristics do we want them to develop? And which do we hope they will not?
- Are there ways in which we could inadvertently be contributing to the development of undesirable characteristics?

Invite people, perhaps in twos or threes, to choose their top four characteristics. The following list could provide some possibilities, but everyone should feel free to come up with their own.

> Adventurous, reflective, expedient, knowledgeable, creative, anxious, curious, resilient, open-minded, perfectionistic, gullible, self-aware, truthful,

sceptical, courageous, humble, pedantic, conscientious, confident, perceptive, laid-back, collaborative, ethical, empathic, dogmatic, analytical, resourceful, independent-minded.

Then gather their responses in a general discussion – without any guidance from you, other than to probe gently for clarity. For example, if colleagues were to say that young people should be "able to work with others", you might like to dig a bit deeper into the roots of effective collaboration – without telling them what you think. You could ask questions such as:

- What does it take to be an effective collaborator?
- What kinds of collaborative challenges are they likely to meet in school/at college/in work?
- What is the optimal group size? On what does it depend?

If you are able to withhold your own preferences, and act as neutral chair for the discussion, you are more likely to open up the kind of reflective conversation that you need. Having got some suggestions about desirable learning dispositions, you could plan a follow-up session to go a little deeper. The following questions, though perhaps a little challenging, could lead to a very productive exploration of the language:

- To what degree are these habits evident in our learners at the moment?
- Which habits are most evident?
- Are there subjects in which some of the students' learning habits are stronger or weaker?
- Which of those weaker learning habits concern us most?
- Do we perceive differences according to age?
- Do learners generally gain or lose these learning habits as they progress through the school? What happens as high-stakes examinations loom?
- What do we do as teachers to cultivate/develop/enhance effective learning habits?

- Can our students talk about themselves as learners? What kind of language do they use?

Recently, Graham asked four groups of teachers, who teach across the full 5–18 age range at Hastings International School in Madrid, just this question. Their responses are summarised in Figure 5.1.

Before they leave us

- Engaged
- Empowered
- Opinionated
- **Collaborative**
- **Global citizens**
- Thoughtful
- Open-minded
- Challenging
- **Curious**
- Questioning
- Pragmatic
- Ambitious
- Imaginative
- Confident
- Autonomous
- **Independent**
- Adaptable
- **Flexible**
- **Compassionate**
- Empathetic

Figure 5.1: Spider Diagram of Responses

Source: Hastings International School, used with kind permission of Neil Tetley

This led to a lively follow-up discussion about how well students are developing these habits currently, and how any gaps between teachers' aspirations for their students and those students' current attitudes and habits could be filled.

As another provocation to debate, you could get your staff to look at the two contrasting word clouds in Figures 5.2 and 5.3. They were produced by different groups when Graham asked them for their associations with the word "learning".

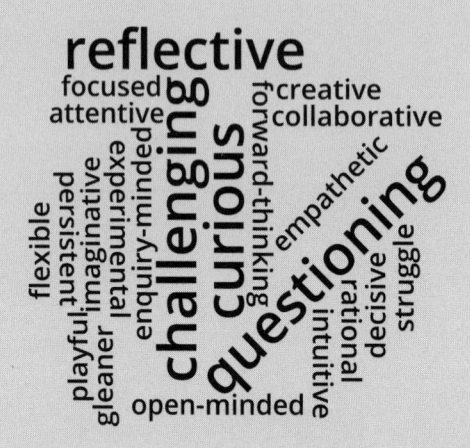

reflective focused creative attentive collaborative challenging curious questioning forward-thinking empathetic experimental rational persistent enquiry-minded intuitive decisive struggle flexible imaginative playful gleaner open-minded

5.2: Learning Word Cloud Option 1

intimidated
risk-averse cautious
diligent closed
anxious persistent
careful quiet indifferent
dependent
frustrated disengaged
bored

5.3: Learning Word Cloud Option 2

Ask yourself:

- Which of the words describe your own students' attitudes to learning?
- What words do you find challenging? Can you say why?
- Which words might you need to think about more closely?

We'll come back to some of these words later in the chapter.

After you have awoken your teachers' interest in the ways in which their students behave as learners, and how they might better direct their energies, it can be useful to introduce some ready-made frameworks for discussion. You could use our elements of learning power, the seventeen habits of mind identified by Art Costa and Bena Kallick, or the original *Building Learning Power* list.[1] You could get groups to look at different frameworks, discuss their pros and cons, and see if there emerges a set of ideas that everyone can get behind.

At Surbiton High School in South London, for example, they took the time to create their own version of the LPA framework, shown in Figure 5.4. EF Academy Torbay in Devon, England, did a similar thing (see Figure 5.5). While these are all variations on the LPA theme, and hold true to the LPA spirit, they are distinctive, and they have significance for the schools that created them.

If you are going to develop your own framework, one thing to bear in mind is the size of your "little list". While you might want to be detailed and comprehensive, there is also virtue in working with a shorter list of dispositions that everyone can understand and remember. For example, Neil Tetley, while headmaster at Woodbridge School in Suffolk, England, started out with a long list, but found that it was too complex to be workable, and decided to slim it down. Looking back on his time at Woodbridge, Neil says:

> What was really important was to keep the language simple. To begin with, we came up with a framework that made perfect sense but was far too complicated for teachers

---

[1] See Arthur L. Costa and Bena Kallick, *Discovering and Exploring Habits of Mind* (Alexandria, VA: Association for Supervision and Curriculum Development, 2000); and Claxton, *Building Learning Power*.

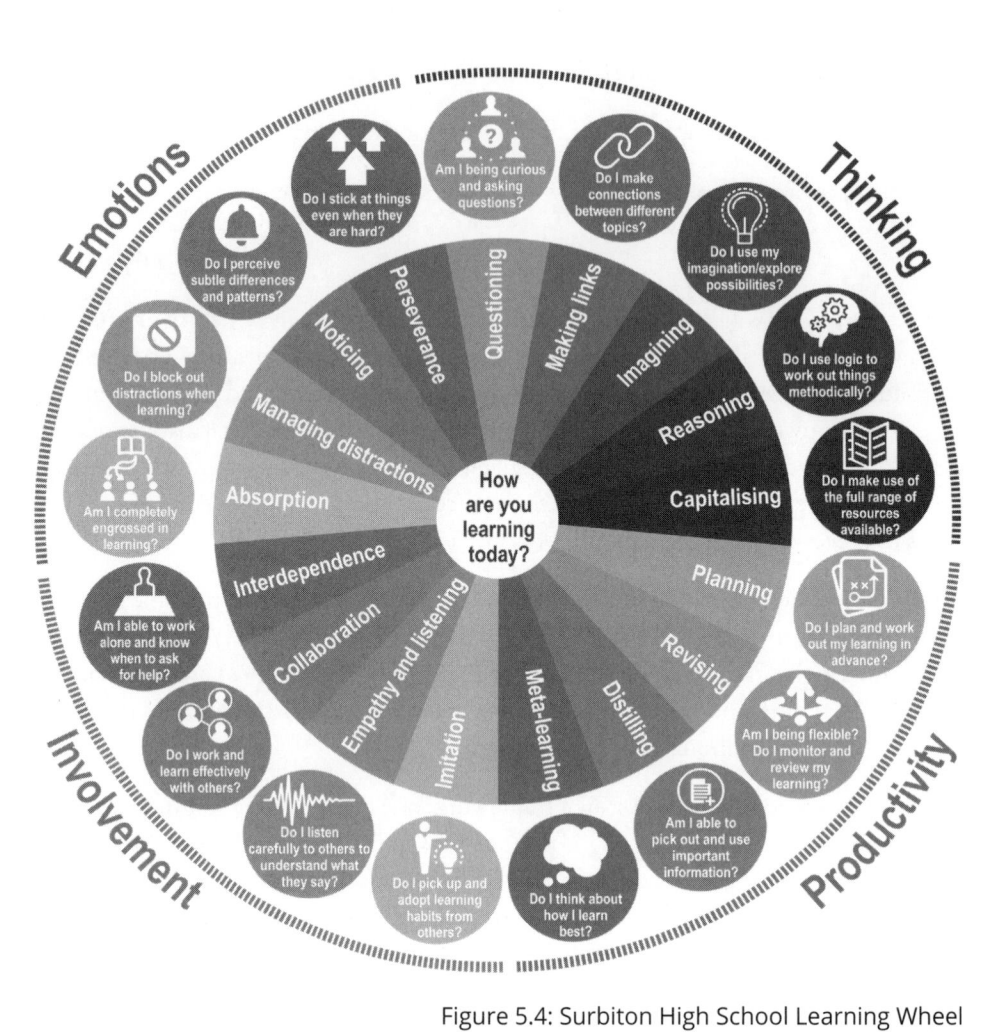

Figure 5.4: Surbiton High School Learning Wheel

Source: Adapted from a resource devised by TLO Limited

A Language for Learning

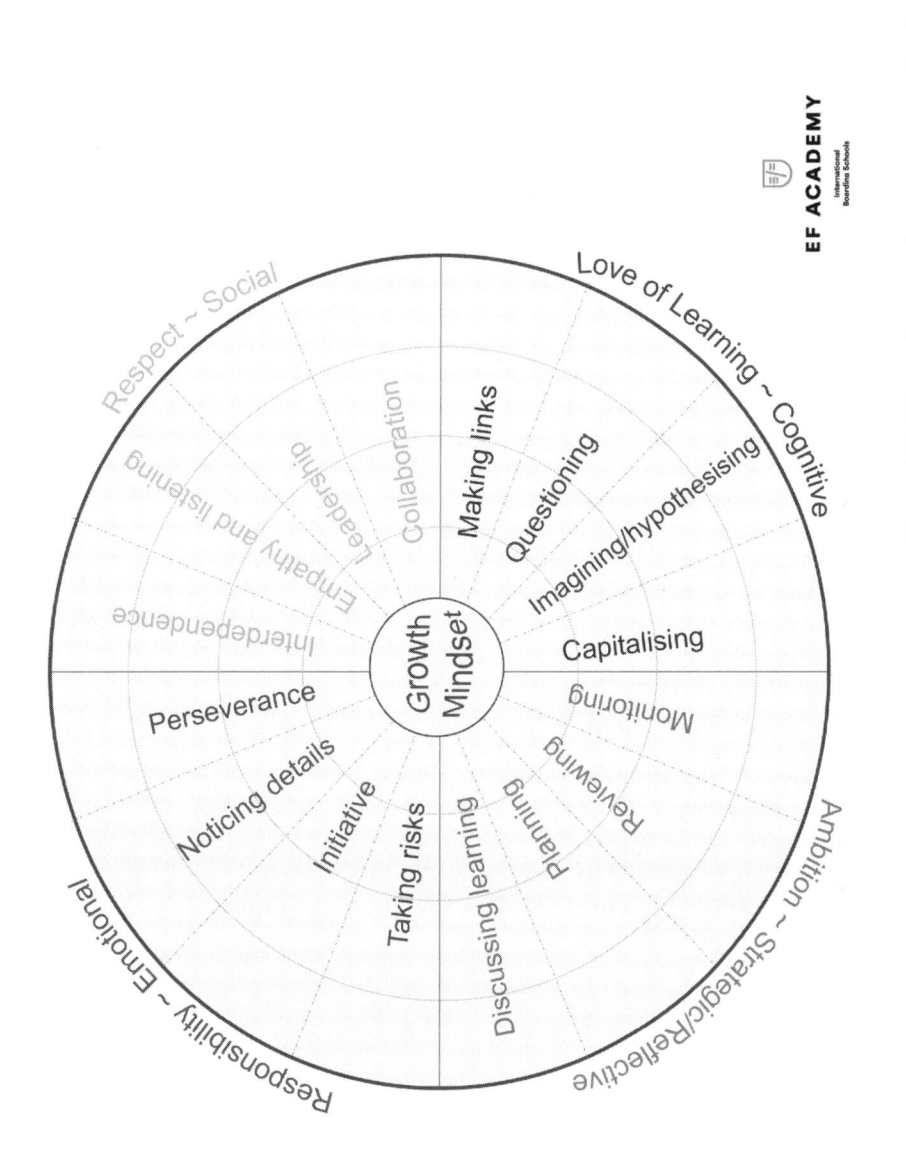

Figure 5.5: EF Academy Torbay Learning Wheel

Source: EF Academy Torbay, used with kind permission of Louise Blondell

The Woodbridge learner seeks to be:

Inquisitive: has a positive attitude to learning and is curious to find out more.

Adventurous: is willing to risk and "have a go" and is keen to embrace new challenges.

Imaginative: comes up with creative ideas and possibilities.

A problem-solver: is able to find solutions even if they are not immediately obvious.

Independent: is able to take responsibility with confidence and shows initiative.

Resilient: stays determined, positive, and persistent in the face of difficulty and is willing to make mistakes in order to learn.

Focused: is able to concentrate on achievable objectives.

Logical: is able to organise evidence and information to arrive at an answer.

Conscientious: is well-organised and plans carefully; shows attention to detail in producing carefully crafted work.

Reflective: is able to identify and act upon areas for improvement.

Articulate: is able to express ideas clearly verbally, and fluently and accurately on paper.

Collaborative: is a good team player and helps groups to work well together.

Open-minded: listens to the views of others and asks thoughtful questions.

Empathic: understands others' emotions as well as their own and is kind.

Figure 5.6: The Woodbridge Learner

Source: Woodbridge School, used with kind permission of Neil Tetley

to get their heads around. Once we had stripped it down to something much clearer, it became much more useful on a lesson-by-lesson basis.

For interest, the original Woodbridge framework is shown in Figure 5.6.

We are inclined to think that whichever way you go is up to you. We have seen a multitude of different frameworks work well in different situations. It may depend on the size of your school, or on the strength of the learning culture among staff. Some staffrooms are more willing to accept "an edict from on high", while others will need a period of debate before they are willing to come on board. And it may be that you already have a set of values, or the beginnings of a learning framework, that you would rather develop and elaborate on, rather than trying to impose something quite new on top of (and possibly in some ways at odds with) what is already familiar. You might remember that even at St Luke's Grammar School, where Jann embraced the BLP framework, the school added a fifth R to recognise the importance of their Christian values.

How Can the Vocabulary and Concepts of Learning Power Be Introduced to Students?

Having gone some way towards developing an agreed language for learning – though it may not (and probably should not) be set in stone – you now have to think about how to introduce it and "sell it" to your students. We will offer you some case studies to illustrate different ways in which school leaders have gone about it. First, let Jann Robinson explain how she tackled it at St Luke's:

> Having a shared language for learning has been the most significant way in which students have been able to own their learning and know how to improve. At St Luke's the BLP language for learning was adopted wholesale, and across the entire school (with all age groups), right from the word go. The language was adopted in its entirety because we felt that it captured all the components of learning (intellectual, emotional, and social) that we wanted to talk about. The language

has not been altered in the five years since we started, in part to reduce change fatigue for the teachers, but also because it has (after some teething troubles) been adopted, confidently and fully, by all members of the school community. The focus from the beginning was on all members of the school (teachers, students, and parents) understanding the language and using it meaningfully to describe learning.

Initially, some teachers found that using the language in their interactions with students did not come naturally. It took them a while to become fluent. They used a variety of visual prompts – for example, magnets with the words on them which they placed on their whiteboards to focus on a particular disposition in the lesson. However, over time the language has become just part of the way in which our teachers talk.

Early on, the students also found the language a bit unnatural and "clunky". As they went from class to class, students would say to their teachers, "Not you too", because the language didn't feel as though it fitted the lesson. However, as teachers became more fluent, the students stopped commenting critically and began using the language themselves. Now they use it naturally and frequently. When they are speaking in class or in public, they use BLP language – and they are not just parroting the words back but using them meaningfully. The words aren't empty; they are used with understanding. The language has given everyone a common way in which to talk about learning – to identify areas for development – and it has changed how students *feel* about learning.

For example, the debating teacher, Maria Caristo, recently wrote to me following a successful regional competition: "Our students won because they argued well, and more importantly because they used language from the L@SL framework. What I noticed was that they were not just using words, they were understanding the meaning behind them. They mentioned that taking risks and being independent thinkers would probably make them more able to adapt to a new environment and to the personal challenges that this experience would offer. The difference I notice now is that the students understand how their learning power can be applied to all facets of life, both in and outside of the classroom."

Recently, a Year 10 student, Samuel, was asked to speak to the parents of incoming students about what learning was like at St Luke's. He said to them, "When I was in the junior school, before we had L@SL, I used to get a hard maths problem and just hope I could get it right. Now when I get a hard problem, I ask myself a series of questions to prompt my thinking. I also think about whether the problem links to anything I have seen before, I am more prepared to ask others for help, and I know how to stick with the challenge."

Another student, 15-year-old Hanna, is an up-and-coming Rugby League referee. (Rugby League is a male-dominated sport in Australia.) She has been selected by the New South Wales Rugby League Referee Development Squad. She referees for the under 21s league. She was asked to speak about her experience in an assembly. Without any prior coaching she said, "I find I use the dispositions of L@SL a lot. I have had to draw on my resilience and I have to be open to listening and to being empathetic. I really feel that the things I am learning at school are helping me as I continue to develop as a referee."

Five years on in our LPA journey, teachers, students, and parents all use BLP vocabulary quite unselfconsciously, and this helps our relationships with families. Parent–teacher interviews always include the student now, and the conversations always make use of learning power language; everyone is focused on how the student's mastery of the dispositions is impacting on their learning, and how their learning power can improve. Teachers have found that it is more meaningful to talk to and about students in terms of dispositions that need to grow, rather than just saying that students need to do better. The language gives students a clearer understanding of what they actually need to do to improve – both in their mastery of content and in their growth as confident independent learners. It is hard to overestimate how much it helps when everyone in the community has a shared understanding of the dispositions that make up learning.

> Teachers have found that it is more meaningful to talk to and about students in terms of dispositions that need to grow, rather than just saying that students need to do better.

One of the ongoing challenges is bringing new staff and students on board with the language. At St Luke's this is done by continuing to have a termly focus on a cluster of dispositions. New teachers are asked to do what we did in the early days: try to use one disposition at a time. They are also allocated a learning mentor who helps them to design lessons, models their own practice, and assists them in getting up to speed. For students, peer-to-peer partnerships are established to assist with the acquisition of the language.

There are many points of interest in Jann's account. One we would like to pick out here is the time it takes for everyone to get used to using a new language for learning. Remember, language is a complicated constellation of habits and, as with all habit change, a new way of speaking feels odd to begin with. So you should be prepared for that, and not be too concerned. Keep reminding everyone to use it, acknowledge them when they do, and reassure them that it will come to feel natural quite quickly.

Jann decided to introduce the BLP framework all at once, across the whole school. Others, like Rachel Macfarlane at Walthamstow, decided to introduce the elements of learning power one by one, giving each a chance to become familiar and take root before adding another.

Many high schools have decided to change attitudes to learning by starting with their intake year and gradually adopting approaches and changing attitudes one new cohort at a time. In fact, a gradual approach to the introduction of a language for learning can be more effective than trying to implement whole-school change, especially when the concept of learning power is very unfamiliar, perhaps even alien, to the existing culture of the school. Nevertheless, as Rachel Macfarlane has shown at Isaac Newton – as has Jann Robinson at St Luke's – when the mood is right, you can proceed much faster. A commitment across the school to the full range of learning dispositions and habits can work if the leadership operates in a coherent and consistent way – as we will show in the next chapter.

At Dr Challoner's Grammar School, Mark Fenton and his team decided that they would introduce the LPA to their high-achieving and articulate teenage boys through the medium of discussion. Tutor time was used to introduce students to what the language for learning meant in practice. Students would regularly work in groups, discussing and refining what it meant to *plan ahead* or *adopt multiple perspectives*, for example, and how they could be developing these and other habits across the curriculum. It was clear to students that their teachers took this approach seriously, that there were clearly articulated benefits for them and their future prospects, and that it was not an unnecessary add-on to the curriculum, but rather an essential constituent of effective learning. Over ten years later, this language for learning has evolved but is still an integral part of the school's culture.

How Do You Keep the LPA Language Alive and Fresh?

One problem with the LPA language – as with many innovations in schools – lies in keeping it current and meaningful. Teachers who do not really understand concepts like "resilience" or "growth mindset" might cling to particular words and phrases in an effort to "do it right", but because there is nothing behind it, it renders the concepts lifeless, dull, and formulaic. So one obvious solution is to keep your language and frameworks under review, and encourage critical and quizzical discussion. Treat every poster and policy document as a work in progress, constantly open to challenge and improvement. Sometimes, when staff have put some time and energy into creating their own framework (or mastering a pre-existing one), they can fall rather in love with it, and assume that it is the last word. (Some of the more entrepreneurial creators of such frameworks have been guilty of the same fault.) Instead of being a living, growing thing, it becomes a treasured object to be revered and, if necessary, defended.

> ... keep your language and frameworks under review, and encourage critical and quizzical discussion.

Dr Challoner's, for example, has always kept learning under review. The school takes a particular focus each year as it continues to pose questions about how the students are learning. The framework that was created initially was in danger of getting tired, with teachers and students using words without digging beneath the surface as they did at the outset. A film on "Learning at Challoner's" that was made eight years ago shows teachers and students debating what individual habits mean in practice, where they are being developed across the curriculum, and why they are important for future success. This high level of serious engagement cannot be allowed to happen only once. Schools that genuinely wish to improve never sit back on their apparent success, and instead are always prepared to review what they are doing, ask questions of themselves and others, and challenge existing practice again and again.

Another good way of keeping your language fresh is to make sure that you have a range of ways of referring to the core concepts, so that children do not get sick and tired of teachers going on about "resilience" or "grit", for example. It may be helpful to do this as a brainstorm with a group of colleagues or, even better, to involve the students in finding phraseology that is meaningful to them. Let's take one of the desirable habits of effective learners and consider the rich variety of phrases that could be used to describe it in a more nuanced and flexible way.

For example, you might talk about the habit of perseverance as:

- Sticking with it.
- Being determined.
- Having tenacity.
- Showing "stickability".
- Taking your time.
- Walking away and coming back later.
- Not giving up.
- Keeping on keeping on.
- Enjoying the struggle.
- Wracking your brain.
- Thinking until your brain hurts.
- Not allowing frustration to overwhelm you.

Take one of the habits that you would like to see your learners develop in your lessons and create your own thesaurus of alternative words and phrases.

Do the graphics matter?

Useful to bear in mind as you develop your distinctive set of "learning virtues" are the pros and cons of different ways of presenting your framework graphically. Some schools use basic lists; others use matrices or wheels. Each has its advantages, but such graphics may also overemphasise the separateness of the dispositions. We take things apart in order to understand them, but they only work if we put them back together again. In practice, concentrating and persevering, for example, share a common root. While curiosity is fed by careful attention and leads to reflection and critical thinking.

> We take things apart in order to understand them, but they only work if we put them back together again.

At John Taylor Free School, principal Sue Plant has chosen a graphic that reinforces the integrated nature of the dispositions. Sue has been committed to the LPA since her days as coordinator of learning at Landau Forte College in Derby, England. Landau, under the leadership of Elizabeth Coffey, had developed its own language for learning that informed classroom practice and was complemented by whole-school practices.[2] At her new high school, Sue's curriculum is underpinned by six elements of learning that are characterised by the acronym, STRIPE, as shown in Figure 5.7.

The headline elements of STRIPE have been broken down – as we have seen elsewhere – into subsets that are displayed around the school. There are five aspects of learning grouped under each of the STRIPE elements. Notice how they have been presented in hexagons in order to underline how each of these habits fits alongside the others and doesn't just stand alone.

Groups of students are given sets of colour-coded plastic hexagonal tiles to work with, each of which has an aspect of learning printed on it. They turn them over and talk through when and how they have used, exercised, stretched, and developed these habits across the curriculum, during recent lessons or across a unit. The shape of the tiles means that students can fit them together to present a profile of what they have

---

2   Landau Forte is also featured as a case study in Claxton and Powell, *Powering Up Students*, pp. 205–206.

Figure 5.7: John Taylor STRIPE

Source: John Taylor Free School, used with kind permission of Sue Plant

Figure 5.8: STRIPE Tile Diagram

Source: John Taylor Free School, used with kind permission of Sue Plant

achieved and what they need to keep improving. Being able to move the tiles around invites conversations between students, and with their teacher, and students write down their achievements and targets as an aid to personal reflection and dialogue. This reflective writing feeds the development of insightful self-awareness, which enables students to lead rich and productive parental consultation sessions.

The Arthur Terry School, a high school in Sutton Coldfield near Birmingham, England, uses graphics in a different way to show both the individual nature of the learning habits, and the fact that they flow together and interweave in real learning situations. You may also like the way in which each of the learning dispositions is illustrated in terms of straightforward statements that students might say if they have made progress in mastering that habit (see Figure 5.10).

Wondering

Do any of these models appeal to you?

What advantages do they each have? What's missing from each?

If you were going to create a model, which features would you want to include? What do you think could be improved upon or adapted for your context?

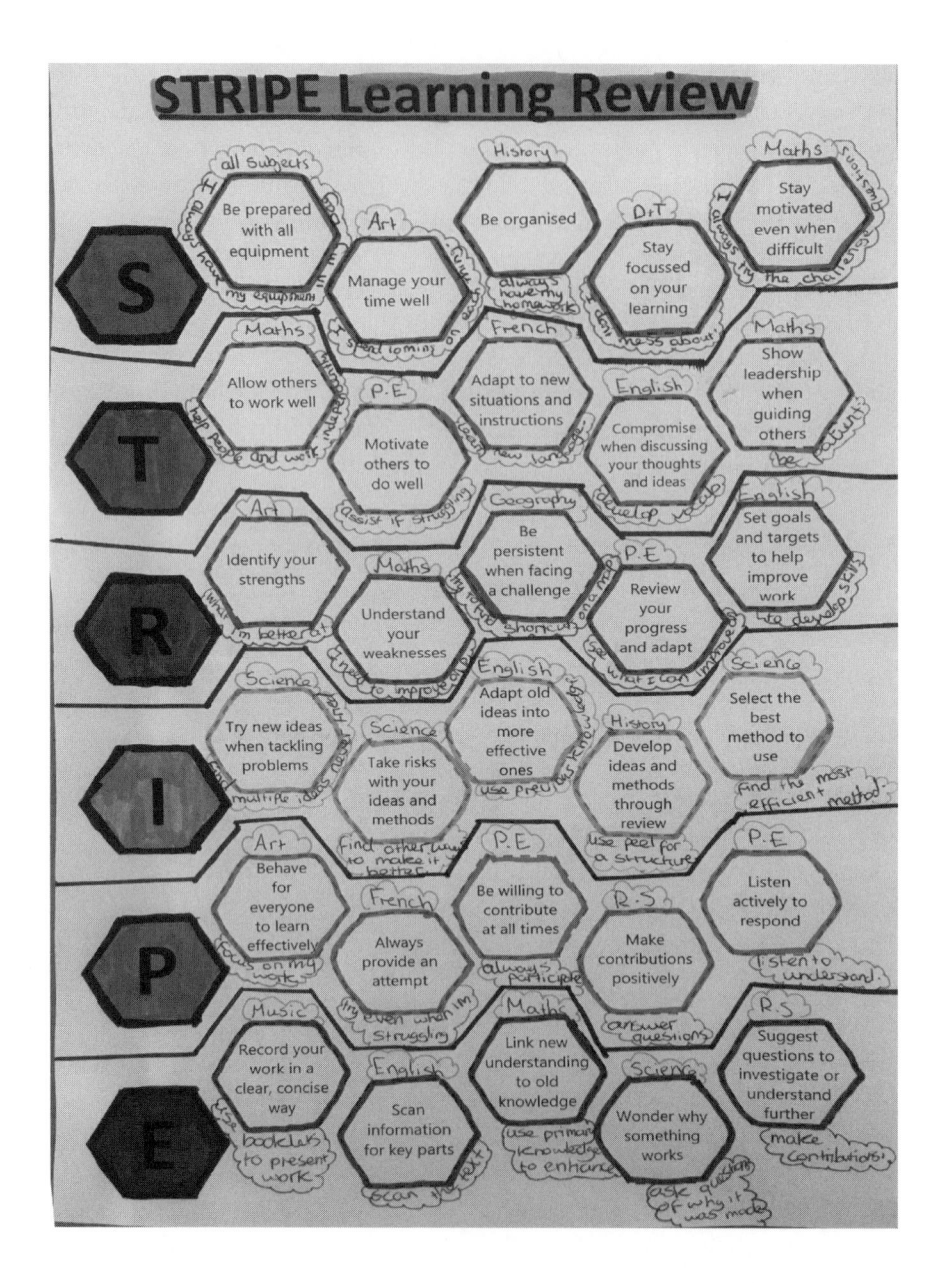

Figure 5.9: STRIPE Student Review

Source: John Taylor Free School, used with kind permission of Sue Plant

The Arthur Terry Learner

The Arthur Terry learner is constantly moving forward, progressing their ability through motivation and a positive attitude to learning. They have a growth mindset: they know with dedication they can improve on their current level of learning.

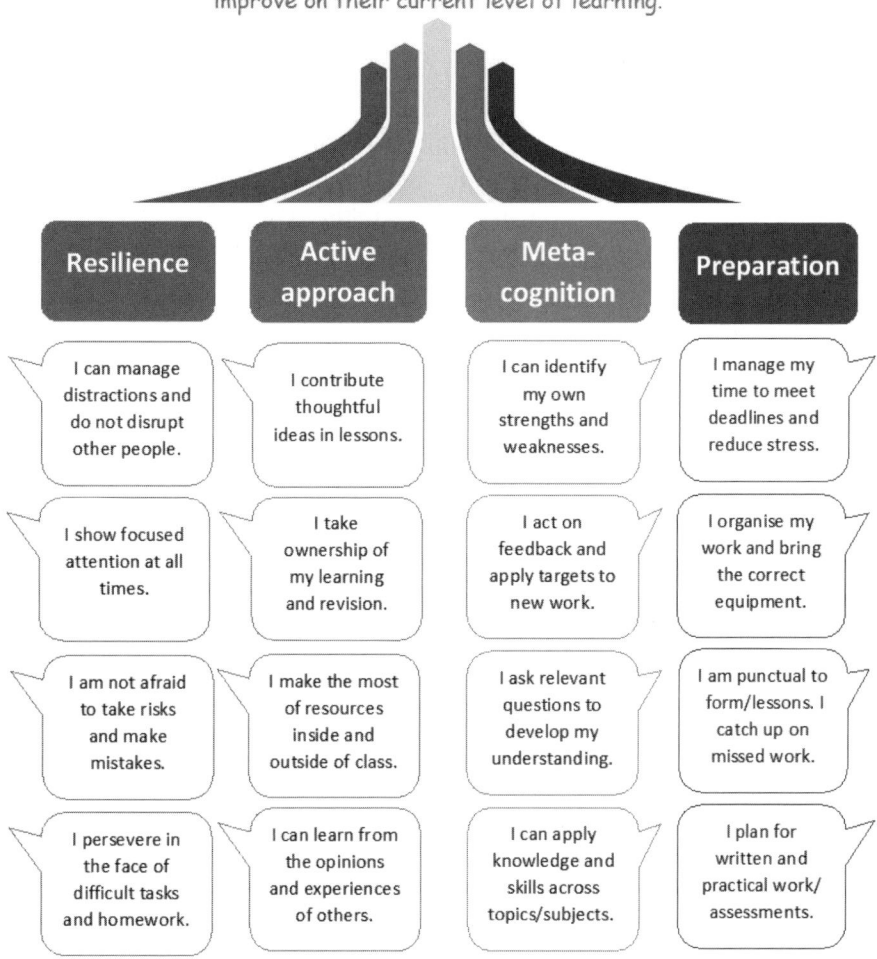

Resilience	Active approach	Meta-cognition	Preparation
I can manage distractions and do not disrupt other people.	I contribute thoughtful ideas in lessons.	I can identify my own strengths and weaknesses.	I manage my time to meet deadlines and reduce stress.
I show focused attention at all times.	I take ownership of my learning and revision.	I act on feedback and apply targets to new work.	I organise my work and bring the correct equipment.
I am not afraid to take risks and make mistakes.	I make the most of resources inside and outside of class.	I ask relevant questions to develop my understanding.	I am punctual to form/lessons. I catch up on missed work.
I persevere in the face of difficult tasks and homework.	I can learn from the opinions and experiences of others.	I can apply knowledge and skills across topics/subjects.	I plan for written and practical work/assessments.

Figure 5.10: The Arthur Terry Learner

Source: Used with kind permission of The Arthur Terry School

How Do You Talk About Learning with Parents?

In an article in *The Guardian*, Suzanne Moore describes her relief at having her last child leave school.[3] She concludes by saying what she really wanted from her children's schools:

> What is a good education? One that makes you feel able to go on learning for the rest of your life, not one that sucks the life out of you by cramming and testing.

And yet many schools continue to talk with parents almost exclusively about grades, effort, and good (or bad) behaviour, while avoiding talking about those vital things that parents really care about – like how their child is developing as a person. In an LPA school, you have to be willing to go beyond the obsession with reading levels, or predicted and target grades, and show parents that you see their child as a developing human being and that you are committed to fostering that development. Think for a moment about how you talk with parents about their children.

Wondering

Are your reports mostly concerned with grades and effort? Is there scope to practise using the language for learning in your reporting procedures?

Do you talk to parents about how their children are as learners?

Do you engage them in conversations about how they can help their children become more resilient, organised, and critical in their thinking, for example?

What part do students themselves play in consultation sessions?

Do your teachers talk to parents about the joy of learning?

---

3   Suzanne Moore, I've had children at school for 27 years. At last I can stop pretending to like it. *The Guardian* (3 June 2019). Available at: https://www.theguardian.com/commentisfree/2019/jun/03/children-school-27-years-parents-evenings-pta?CMP=Share_iOSApp_Other.

Let's look at how a few schools have radically changed the way in which they talk to parents about learning. At Woodbridge School, parents of new students are invited in for "Learning @ Woodbridge" mornings. After a practical workshop that introduces the language for talking about learning, and offers an insight into what learning looks like in classrooms, parents are equipped with a learning wheel – like the ones you saw in Figures 5.4 and 5.5 – for focusing their view of learning and taken into lessons to observe the reality of learning habits for themselves. Accompanied by another teacher, they are helped to see *how* their children are being encouraged to learn. A collective debrief follows that allows parents to share their perceptions and, in some cases, talk with the teachers whose lessons they've observed. On every occasion, this has led to extremely positive outcomes: teachers feel validated and parents feel enthusiastic about what the school offers their children. As one parent remarked to headmaster Neil Tetley:

> Other schools talk about standards, resources, and extracurricular activities – all important, of course – but this is the only school that talks about what really matters to us.

As we mentioned, at John Taylor, principal Sue Plant ensures that students are an integral part of parent consultation sessions. All students take the lead in presenting their learning projects to parents. They don't just talk about what they have achieved but about *how* they have been learning. They use the STRIPE language to articulate the ways in which they have been learning across the curriculum, the ways in which different experiences complement each other, and, most important of all, what they are doing to improve. Parents buy into this and are seeing ways in which they can support the real business of learning at home.

As you will see in Chapter 7, some schools have started reporting to parents using a language that engages and involves them more directly with their children's learning. Whereas parents mostly comply with school reports that – in time-honoured fashion – speak of levels of attainment and effort, when they are given jargon-free language that describes their children's habits as learners, they are better equipped to be partners in their children's education. The portability of learning – out of the classroom and into students' lives at home and beyond school – is an essential part of the LPA.

How Do You Weave Learning Power Language into Everyday Talk?

The adoption of a language to describe learning that is understood by all partners is clearly essential to the LPA. However, subtle shifts in the language of day-to-day discourse can make sure that the culture of the school remains focused on the development of all students' learning capacities.

What is it about the way in which we talk that encourages a learning-oriented mindset? We have discussed this question in much more detail in *Powering Up Children* and *Powering Up Students* – the earlier books in the series. Here, let's just summarise a few of these "modal shifts" in language. As a school leader, you might see it as part of your job to model these shifts in the way you talk to students, staff, and parents.

- Try to use the word "work" less. Work is something you have to get done to a more or less acceptable standard. Instead, talk about the process of *learning*, and convey that this process is interesting and engaging. Balance your concern with the quality of the product with an interest in the details of the process by which that product came to be. So not "Have you finished your work?" but "That looked tricky. How did you go about finding a solution?"

- Don't just put up those growth mindset posters and talk about focusing on *effort* rather than *ability*. Telling someone they "must try harder" is not very helpful: it doesn't tell them what to do. So, again, convey your interest in the strategies and techniques that your students do or could use to help them with their learning challenges. Tell parents that their child can't do something *yet*, rather than imply that they are in the bottom set because they *lack ability*.

- Use less "is" language and more "could be" language. "Is" language presents information as if it were incontrovertible. "There *are* five parts; this *is* how the battle went; this *is* how you solve the equation." Instead, try using softer, more subjunctive expressions like "There *could be* five or more parts; *some* historians have described the battle like this; that *could be* a good way of solving the equation." "Could be" invites imagination and questioning. "Is" demands remembering and understanding. "Could be" encourages deeper learning, so broaden your range to include both. Model thinking aloud – musing, wondering, speculating, and hypothesising.

- Get used to talking about *mistakes* as if they are a normal and inevitable part of learning – steps on the way to competence and comprehension – not shameful evidence of a child's limitations. Encourage teachers to demonstrate to their students the difference between *smart mistakes* (a good guess that didn't quite work out) and *sloppy mistakes* (which happen when you just don't bother to think). Show interest in and appreciation of smart mistakes – made by both students and staff.

In general, encourage teachers and parents to ask learning-related questions. In Figure 5.11 you'll find some sample questions that are used at Isaac Newton Academy. In the information that is given to parents about BRIDGES, the school explains:

> Learning dispositions and character traits are developed most effectively when staff use particular types of language and questions in their dialogue with students.

Bravery

How could you make that more interesting/risky/exciting?

What would you suggest if you were in charge?

If you were to take the initiative, what would you do?

Why not choose a topic that is going to stretch you?

Why not just give it a try?

Resourcefulness

What could you use to help with that?

What are you going to need?

Where else could you make use of that?

Where could you apply what you've just learned?

What do you know that might help?

Integrity

Who did that better than you?

Who could you learn from?

How well did you carry out your role?

How well did you stick to the learning rules?

Discovery

What do you want to find out?

What does that remind you of?

What's odd about that?

What does that make you wonder?

Grit

What are the tricky bits? What's tricky about them?

What could you do when you are stuck on that?

How did you get over your difficulties when you got stuck?

What could you tinker with?

Who managed their distractions well while doing that?

Emotional intelligence

How does that make you feel?

How could you help the group work better?

What are you not so pleased with?

What would have made that easier for you?

Does this way of working play to your strengths?

How could I have taught that better?

> **Self-discipline**
>
> What do you need to practise a bit more?
>
> What would you need to do to improve that?
>
> How could you organise things to help you learn better?
>
> What would "even better" look like?

Figure 5.11: The BRIDGES Questions for Learning

The BRIDGES vocabulary, which is set out in their learning wheel (shown in Figure 9.4), and these ways of drawing students' attention to the learning dispositions are enshrined at Isaac Newton in a formal language for learning policy. Here is what Rachel Macfarlane had to say about how that policy was developed and used, and why she thought it was important to have the linguistic dos and don'ts set out so explicitly:

> I had started to realise the importance of having a common language for talking about learning in my previous headship at Walthamstow School for Girls. There we had adopted BLP and we used the language of learning muscles on our reports, reward certificates, postcards home, and so on. When I had the chance to open a new school, I decided that I wanted to create a policy around the language we use and the language we don't, for the reasons outlined in the policy itself.
>
> This became one of the most influential policies at Isaac Newton. I spent a good half day exploring it with the founding staff before opening, ensuring that everyone understood it, bought into it, had internalised it, and would live it. I revisited it every September with each new cohort of staff (as well as established teachers) to induct and refresh. If anyone joined the school mid-year, it was the responsibility of their line manager to talk the policy through with them. We asked them to sign a form to confirm that they had been inducted in it, which gave accountability and gravitas.
>
> We talked to the parents about the language for learning policy (especially the growth mindset parts and why we never used the word *ability* at Isaac Newton, but instead talked in terms of *attainment*) at workshops and events, and we talked explicitly to students about all aspects of the policy through assemblies, tutor sessions, and other occasions.
>
> Because we all knew the policy and agreed with it, it was not difficult, awkward, or embarrassing to pick people up if they lapsed from it. In the early days, it took some staff a bit of time to eradicate the word "ability" from their vocabulary, but very soon

the reaction that the word elicited on the rare occasions when it was heard was like nails down a blackboard – staff would visibly flinch.

Having the word "recognition" in our praise and recognition policy was also significant. We talked openly with the students about reward being intrinsic, and they understood and appreciated why we gave shout-outs rather than vouchers. But that didn't stop us from giving awards.

Replacing the word "work" with "learning" was also a biggie. We had staff "learning rooms" instead of "work rooms", "independent learning" instead of "homework", "learning walls" instead of "best work", and so on.

I also think that the language of aspiration in our policies was important. We were very careful never to close down opportunities for anyone, regardless of their current performance or visible interests. So we wouldn't assume who would want to apply to go to a science lecture on a Friday night at Imperial College London, or open a trip to the University of Cambridge only to the high attainers (there is no gifted and talented register at our school). And unlike at lots of schools, triple award science GCSE is not reserved for students in the higher sets. If a student enjoyed science, worked hard, and wanted to study it for nine hours per week, they could do so, regardless of their attainment levels in Year 9. Such students very often went on to achieve top grades – they were simply later developers who flourished in Years 10 and 11. And if they didn't get top grades, they had still had a full and thorough grounding in a subject they loved and that would be useful to them in later life.

Wondering

Do you think it is a good idea to be explicit and deliberate, or would you rather adopt a more organic approach?

What would be the pros and cons of each, do you think?

Summary

To sum up this chapter, we have come up with a list of dos and don'ts regarding language. We recognise the irony of telling you to use "could be" language and then telling you what to do, but this is purely to be provocative and stimulate your own thinking. So please, in your own head, feel free to replace our tactical "is" language with some softer alternatives – "You might like to think about trying ..." or "Some people have found it useful to ..."

Do	Don't
Start by just casually mentioning some of the learning muscles in assemblies, staff briefings, training sessions, parental consultations, and when interacting with teachers and students. Train your teachers to plan activities that are targeted (whether they tell students or not) at strengthening particular learning muscles. Note that the point of the LPA is not just to get students *using* certain learning habits, but to be actively *stretching* those habits. It is not just "doing group work", for example. The activity needs to be making collaboration progressively more demanding, so that the *capacity* to be a good collaborator is being expanded. Think about how to introduce the learning powers explicitly to teachers	Keep repeating the same words over and over: teachers and students will quickly get bored and irritated, and just switch off from the whole idea of the LPA, which is the last thing we want to happen. As we have seen, there are a dozen different ways to say "resilient". Just stick up posters listing the key words and hope that it will have a magical effect on how children behave. It won't. Visual displays can help, but only in the context of a wider change to teachers' and leaders' behaviour and the general culture of the school. In the same spirit, don't turn the elements of learning power into something that teachers and students feel they have to learn, or that just get talked about. Becoming knowledgeable

Do	Don't
and students. Get your reasons straight as to whether you are going to introduce them a few at a time, or whether you are going to dive in with the whole framework. You will know what will work best in your school.	about learning power is not the same thing as becoming a more powerful learner. The emphasis should be on changing things that actually affect the way in which students behave in the face of difficulty or uncertainty.
Start using the metaphor of the classroom as a "mind gym": a place where different learning muscles are going to be stretched and strengthened over time. It is a useful way of helping students to see what you are up to and increasing their buy-in.	Let your "learning intentions" for growing students' learning power become tokenistic. Don't allow teachers to just write on the board, "Today we are going to be noticing details and collaborating with each other" – it won't have any effect unless they also offer activities which require students to stretch specific learning muscles.
As all partners in your school become more used to the language of the LPA, and gain deeper understanding of the concepts and why they are important, do start using the concepts as a framework for reviewing learning. Get everyone to start thinking about other situations – both in school and beyond – in which those capacities would be useful.	And finally, don't get too attached to these dos and don'ts. In every school, leading a major culture change is an uncertain journey, and you will have plenty of good ideas that don't work as you had hoped. You will need to get comfortable with regrouping and changing your mind.
Occasionally (certainly not all the time), do take one of the elements of learning power and lead a general discussion about it with the whole staff or with a year group in an assembly. What does it mean? What other ways of saying it might there be? When is it useful? Are there	

Do	Don't
times or situations in which you might *not* want to persist, or collaborate, or use your imagination? Encourage them to think of a time when they used this capacity to learn, or when they would have benefited from it but didn't use it.	

Chapter 6

Targeting Pedagogy: The Design Principles of Learning Power Teaching

Once a clear purpose and vision for the LPA has been shared, and a language for learning has begun to ripple across the school, it's time to purposefully target pedagogy. Learning cannot change until teaching changes, and individual classrooms are the engine rooms of the LPA. One of your key roles will be to let staff know exactly what the LPA expects of them and give them ideas to try, and guide, remind, and cajole until new habits become routine.

> ... individual classrooms are the engine rooms of the LPA.

Small tweaks to existing practice – such as the way in which lessons are planned, how the classroom is organised, and the way in which students are grouped – have the power to shift learning away from dependence on the teacher and towards greater independence and personal responsibility for students. However, this shift cannot be left to chance – we cannot assume that it will occur naturally as the result of "good teaching". There are specific and subtle ways in which this shift can be brought about and, as a school leader, you will need to motivate, guide, and support your teachers in making conscious changes which bring them closer to your learning aims and ethos.

An LPA leader's key role, therefore, is as "head pedagogical coach", organising a system of professional learning in the school which ensures that all staff gradually but relentlessly infuse more and more of the LPA design principles into their routine "ways of being" in the classroom. The main questions that we will be exploring in this chapter are:

- What, exactly, should you ask teachers to do, change, and adapt?

- How do you share practice to support change, without it feeling like a high-stakes monitoring exercise?

- How can you distil your collective experience and pass it on?

You will play a key part in helping staff to gain knowledge and build skills that enable them to carefully orchestrate the design of their lessons and classrooms, maximising opportunities to make students better learners, and therefore better citizens. The visible commitment and participation of school leaders is essential if there is to be a school-wide impact on classroom practice. Your involvement will help to convince colleagues that there is no tug-of-war between content and processes, or between skills and knowledge. By carefully adapting the way in which your current curriculum is delivered, lessons can become dual purpose (what BLP refers to as "split-screen teaching") – targeting both academic content and character development simultaneously without the need for extra hours in the day.

What, Exactly, Should You Ask Teachers to Do, Change, and Adapt?

So what will the LPA actually look like in practice? What are the adjustments that you will be asking staff to make? The LPA depends upon purposeful cultivation of particular habits of mind, attitudes, and dispositions – for example, curiosity, determination, and imagination – which are sometimes referred to as learning strengths or learning muscles. *Powering Up Children* and *Powering Up Students* contain a plethora of detailed information, for primary and high schools respectively, and practical examples of how these learning strengths can be cultivated in the classroom. Here, however, we will give just a brief overview of some of the most vital LPA design principles, and some ideas about how you can help to make them a reality in your school.[1] And, of course, we will offer some questions for your own reflection.

---

1   The full list can be found on page 58.

Design principles 5 and 6: create challenge and make difficulty adjustable

Teachers and students must adjust to the idea that learning something new should feel challenging. It's not true that smart people don't break a sweat. Everyone in the class should be equally challenged, should struggle, should get things wrong – this is how we know that new learning is taking place. These ideas are explained in much greater detail in the work of psychologists, and we'd particularly recommend that of Carol Dweck and Angela Duckworth.[2] There is no shortage of evidence on why cultivating an ethos of challenge is vital for students. But, as a school leader, how can you go about this in practical terms?

> Teachers and students must adjust to the idea that learning something new should feel challenging. It's not true that smart people don't break a sweat.

You will have read about how to cultivate a language for learning in Chapter 5, and much of this advice can be put into use here. The ways in which you conceptualise and talk about challenge is key in shifting attitudes away from seeing mistakes as threatening and towards regarding them as positive learning opportunities. Introducing and modelling words such as *tricky, grapple, resilience* and *determination*, as well as making use of analogies such as *strengthening learning muscles*, and giving your brain a *workout*, will help to create a shared vocabulary to support your ethos of challenge.

If we expect students to become comfortable with being stretched and challenged, staff must demonstrate the same attitude. You have the opportunity to play a key role in modelling these behaviours. Gemma Goldenberg recalls:

> Years before I had even heard about growth mindset, I remember the head teacher of my previous school wanting to encourage the students to be more resilient. She told them that she was going to learn to play the violin, and she talked about the challenges

---

2   For a good introduction, see: Carol S. Dweck, "The power of yet", *TEDxNorrköping* [video] (12 September 2014). Available at: https://www.youtube.com/watch?v=J-swZaKN2Ic; and Angela Duckworth, "Grit: the power of passion and perseverance" [video] (9 May 2013), *TED.com*. Available at: https://www.youtube.com/watch?v=H14bBuluwB8.

that she would face and what she hoped to achieve. Each week that year, she played her violin in assembly. She let the staff and the students see how terrible it sounded when she was first starting out. She talked about the practice she was putting in and her frustration at how slow her early progress was. She positioned herself as a novice, a learner, and let everyone see the vulnerabilities that come with that position. As the months went by, she was able to reflect on her progress with the children. It was a brilliant way to get all of us on board with what it means to model good learning.

It can be helpful to put teachers in the position of learning something new, and to get them to reflect on how it feels to be challenged. We have heard of some schools asking teachers to learn how to count in a new language, or to perform a magic trick during a staff meeting, to stimulate a discussion about their own experiences of being challenged and what they want to model for their students.

We need to encourage teachers to be flexible in their planning so that they are ready to adjust levels of challenge within the lesson. If children are working quickly and easily through the tasks, the teacher should point out that they're not challenged enough and offer an adaptation or extension. Similarly, if a child appears to be overstretched, staff should be on hand to suggest additional scaffolding and support until they have consolidated the learning enough to move on. However, this cannot be achieved if, as a school leader, you expect teachers to stick rigidly to prescriptive lesson plans or schemes of learning. Once the ethos of challenge has been established, rather than allocating tasks, students can be encouraged to select for themselves how much challenge or scaffolding they need. Students will therefore need to be afforded the autonomy to "move up or down" flexibly, within lessons – or from one lesson to the next – selecting more or less challenging work as needed, or selecting additional resources to support their learning. Therefore, as head pedagogical coach, you will need to help teachers become comfortable with designing lessons that afford different degrees of challenge.

A vital part of embedding the LPA in lessons is ensuring that teachers allocate time at the end to reflect on the learning. While this is being established, lessons may need to cover slightly less content, to allow for reflection time. Teachers will need to know how to facilitate conversations between students about what they have learned, how they challenged themselves, how they knew whether the work was too easy or too hard for them, and what they did to resolve that misalignment. This discussion will support those students who are less confident in self-directing and articulating their learning. You, or your LPA champions, may want to model this type of conversation for staff, and offer resources – such as the prompts that follow – to support reflective discussions.

Sentence starters:

- The main thing I learned in this lesson was …
- Something I struggled with today was … I overcame it by …
- Something I need to continue working on is …
- I think my next steps are …

Question prompts:

- How was your focus and attention today? What strategies did you use to stay on task?
- Who worked with someone else today? Did it make your learning easier or harder? In what way?
- Who found today's learning too challenging? What did you do in the face of the challenge? Is there a way in which you would have liked to have been supported?
- Who found today's learning too easy? How could you have stretched yourself?

Visual aids such as the learning pit, the challenge zones, and the blob tree can also be used in class to open up useful discussions with students about the extent to which they are challenged and how this feels for them.

The learning pit (Figure 6.1), created by James Nottingham, is a visual model which helps students to understand how being stuck or challenged can be uncomfortable but is a normal (and actually helpful) part of learning.[3] Students may benefit from discussing how they climbed out of the pit and analysing what helped them after a learning challenge, or from pausing mid-task to plan how they will climb out and to consider which strategies and tools they have at their disposal which could help.

---

3   See https://www.jamesnottingham.co.uk/learning-pit/.

Figure 6.1: The Learning Pit (www.challenginglearning.com) © James Nottingham

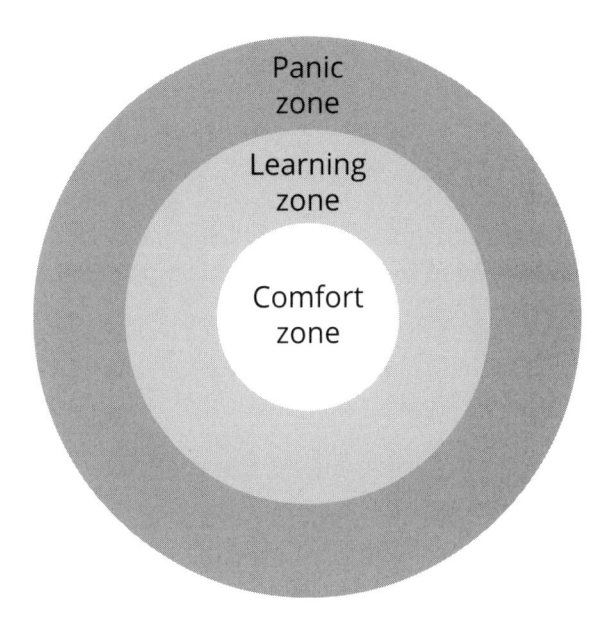

Figure 6.2: Challenge Zones

The challenge zones, Figure 6.2, are a visual aid to help students indicate how challenged they are by the activity in which they are engaged. They too can be used to help students understand the zone of proximal development. Students can be encouraged to talk about how it feels to be in each zone, which zone they spend most of their time in, and where they learn most.

Figure 6.3: The Blob Tree (https://www.blobtree.com/)
© Pip Wilson and Ian Long

There are several variations of the blob tree, Figure 6.3. These are images of cartoon-like, gender-neutral characters at various stages of climbing a tree, which are designed to stimulate discussion about feelings. In the context of challenge, they can be used as a prompt to talk about which blob character students feel represents them in this particular scenario, and how they feel about learning in this area – are they comfortable, scared, bored, frustrated, over-challenged, etc.? Blob trees can also be used to teach various aspects of emotional literacy, such as the concept of empathy.[4]

Consider modelling the use of these visual aids at the end of staff training sessions – reflecting on your own learning and asking colleagues to reflect on theirs by exploring questions such as:

- Who feels that they are in the learning pit right now? Who went into the pit and climbed back out? What helped?

- Which challenge zone were you in today? What would have stretched you further? What would have supported you? How did it feel to be in that zone?

- Which figure on the blob tree represents how you feel about today's learning, and why?

As their coach, allocate time for teachers to reflect on what *they* have learned. What have they tried in the classroom? What worked well and why? Where did things go wrong? How does it feel when that happens and what do they do to overcome their difficulties? The more you embed a culture of honest reflective practice with your staff, the more likely they are to carry out reflective discussions about learning with their students, and to see the purpose of these. In general, you will need to allow teachers the freedom to try things out, to get things wrong, and make adjustments as needed. Your school must have a culture that makes room for fallibility if you want teachers to truly embrace challenge.

---

4   Resources can be found at https://www.blobtree.com/collections/a-blob-schools-visual-curriculum-self-assessment-collection.

> # Wondering
>
> Are you practising a new skill which you could share with staff and students?
>
> Are you willing to make yourself vulnerable as a learner? (For example, to try something outside of your comfort zone, to learn something new in front of others, to get things wrong and admit mistakes, seeing them as opportunities for improvement.)
>
> Do you encourage your staff to be honest about their areas for improvement, to grapple with and reflect on these, rather than "putting on a performance"? Exactly how do you do that? And are you sure that your behaviour is having the desired effect?
>
> What school-wide opportunities are there for celebrating resilience, struggle, and hard work, and for modelling the language around these concepts?
>
> How will you support teachers in making their planning flexible enough to offer different levels of challenge?
>
> How can you, as a leader, demonstrate the importance of reflective conversations about learning – both for staff and children? How will you show that you value these discussions?

Design principles 11 and 12: allow increasing amounts of independence and give students more responsibility

The classroom environment and all routines and protocols should reflect the ethos and learning behaviours that you are trying to cultivate as a school. If you want students to be independent and responsible, they will need opportunities to make their own choices, risk trying things out alone, and reflect on when and how things go wrong. A classroom where students are micromanaged or over-instructed will not cultivate independent learners. So teachers should endeavour to let students make some of their own decisions about how they will work, who they will work with, and how their learning will be presented. It takes confidence and assurance on the part of the teacher to grant these freedoms, and they will need you to support and reassure them that this is the right way!

Consider opening up discussions with your staff about what we tend to take control over, as the adults in the school. For example:

- Ask whether there might be cases when this control could be partially or mostly handed back to the students.

- Explore how much responsibility is currently given to students in terms of the resources and equipment used in class – how and where they are stored and organised and who gets them out or puts them away.

- Discuss how involved students are in organising what happens at break and lunchtimes, and in choosing and designing their own extracurricular activities.

- Ask how much of a say students have in lesson planning and curriculum design.

- Talk about students' role in organising and managing parent meetings, and whether it could be greater.

- And question who decides where students sit in the classroom and whether they have to sit down at all.

Handing over more responsibility to the students can seem daunting, but there are many small shifts that can be made in relinquishing some of the teachers' decision-making power and entrusting students to have more autonomy. As a school leader, you can support your colleagues in making this shift by acknowledging the small steps they take towards it, while letting them know that they are not being judged negatively for any minor slips in performance or behaviour while students readjust to their increased responsibility. For example, you might say something like:

> It was great to pop into Reception today and see that the children were taking responsibility for handing out and tidying away all of the equipment themselves during the carpet session. It was a bit chaotic, as you might expect, because it's their first week of doing it – but I'm sure they'll get the

> hang of it, and well done to our Reception team for taking the leap and trying it out. I also saw a great discussion with the children about why it was important for them to be able to do these things themselves.

Or:

> I was in a Year 8 maths class today and they'd chosen their own groups to work in for the main challenge. It was great to see students making and justifying their choices. For some of the groups, the task may not quite have gone to plan, but we're expecting bumps in the road while students get used to the process. The ones who didn't get along as well were able to start articulating why the group hadn't been successful, so there's already some great learning taking place.

How will you get to see these opportunities for responsibility and independence in action, and assess whether they are having an impact on learning? Consider organising learning walks or informal observations to focus on this, or interview groups of children about their perceptions of responsibility and independence in the classroom. You may want to share this work with other staff members who will act as LPA coaches or champions. It is also worthwhile to bring along less confident members of staff, who will benefit from the opportunity to observe or interview alongside you, especially if they can see you articulate and analyse what you see in terms of these LPA principles. Again, you might like to use some of the following prompts.

Prompts for discussions with teaching staff:

- Tell me about some of the ways in which you enable students to be independent in your lessons.

- How do you scaffold learning so that students who are struggling can still work independently?

- What were some of the decisions that students made for themselves in today's lesson?

- How do you organise furniture and resources to allow for increasing independence and responsibility?

- Are there any examples you can talk me through of when students take responsibility for their own progress and next steps?

- Tell me where you're heading next with this – are there other areas where you could hand more control over to the students?

Prompts for discussions with students:

- What sorts of choices do you get to make about your own learning?

- Tell me about some of the ways in which you take responsibility for equipment and resources in your classroom.

- Do you ever get to decide who you work with in class? Why/why not?

- Do you think it's important to make your own decisions at school? Why/why not?

Again, it is important that you encourage staff to introduce changes like this slowly and gradually, and to give their learners time to get used to a new way of working before adding the next tweak. For example, giving students greater freedom over how they choose to present their work to demonstrate their understanding may need to be introduced gradually so it doesn't feel overwhelming.

Here's an example: let's say that students are learning about the water cycle, and the teacher may previously have instructed them all to draw a diagram to demonstrate their understanding. To gradually give students more responsibility and independence, they may decide to give them just two options at first: either draw a diagram or produce a written description of the water cycle. Over time, as students become more used to making their own choices, more options can be incorporated – for example, create a comic strip, a role play, or a 3D model. Eventually, students may not need to choose from options at all and will come up with their own ideas.

You can provide teachers with examples of how they can incorporate this type of choice into their lessons; there are many more examples in the earlier books in the series. Once you've found pockets of good practice, consider the best ways to share them. You might want to invite students to share examples of when they've been independent and responsible in assemblies or encourage staff to share successes from their lessons during staff meetings or briefings. We saw an example in Chapter 4 of how you could allocate a display in the staffroom to sharing ideas.

Here are a few tips to help you embed these design principles:

- On learning walks, look out for whether resources are labelled and accessible so students can use them independently. Ensure that your school rules and policies allow students to move around the classroom to get the resources they need, as and when they need them.

- Support teachers in creating classroom displays which encourage students to reflect on their learning and monitor their own progress. Find examples for them to look at, encourage them to visit one another's classrooms to see how displays are used, and set aside directed time for teachers to create their displays.

- Review whether staff are affording all students, including the lowest attainers, ample opportunities to work independently.

- Carry out student conferencing across the school to glean students' views on how much responsibility they have for their own learning.

- Create opportunities for staff to research, share, and trial strategies and resources which enable students to take more responsibility for their own learning – for example, introducing a "try three before me" routine whereby students who are stuck must think of – and try out – three ways of getting unstuck, before admitting defeat and approaching the teacher.

- Encourage staff to experiment with giving students choice over when to work independently, in a pair, or in a group, and with whom. Begin by offering either/or options. Allow students to make the wrong choices, then turn it into a learning opportunity by reflecting on what went wrong and why, and thinking about what they'd do differently next time.

- Introduce routines and protocols which reduce teacher "policing" and encourage independence – for example, designating student roles for various aspects of classroom management: room monitors who tidy, distribute and collect resources; peer mentors; class librarians who advise on book choices; etc. Look out for good examples of this, then share and celebrate across the school.

Design principles 7 and 14: talk about and demonstrate the innards of learning and lead by example

Chapter 5 is devoted to the language for learning and described how to introduce and develop a school-wide vocabulary for articulating the LPA, so we won't dwell too much on the language element here. Your job as head pedagogical coach is to ensure that your staff use the language and consistently "talk the talk" of learning power. We need to use our conversations about learning to engage in what's called metacognition – the awareness of our own thinking habits and behaviours. The nuts, bolts, and cogs of learning need to be exposed if students are to understand what good learning looks like and how to go about it. It can help if you demonstrate how true learning is a messy, time-consuming, and often frustrating business. So talk students through the sorts of thoughts that you might have when grappling with something tricky.

> This is hard – harder than I thought. I need to take a break or I'm going to start getting upset. What exactly is it that is confusing me? What could I try? What do I know that might help? Who might be able to help me? Are there any resources to hand that might help? What am I pleased with and what not so much? What could I tinker with to try to make it better?

As a school leader, you need to be openly and publicly engaged in these processes yourself. As much as is appropriate, find opportunities to talk to the students about some of the tricky decisions with which you are grappling, and how you are going about solving the problems you are facing. Here are some further ways in which you could model this attitude:

- When you see a display of beautiful artwork, ask about how students got to that end result. What were the skills they had to learn? How many drafts did they do? How long did it take? What were the tricky bits, and how did they get past them?

- When you praise the school football team for winning a match, focus not so much on the winning score, but on the training they have been doing, the hours put in by them and their coach, and the teamwork and camaraderie which contributed to their success. The same applies when commenting on school shows, musical performances, and so on.

- A focus on the innards of learning will tweak what you focus on when you look at students' books and teachers' planning. Are you looking for perfect handwriting and neat work above all else, or do you want to see notes, edits, and annotations? Mistakes, corrections, and workings may not look as neat and tidy as writing copied from a whiteboard, but it is likely to demonstrate deeper learning.

- Replace certificates, awards, and prizes for outcomes (best essay or story competitions, best musical performance, etc.) with alternatives that celebrate the process which resulted in the outcome – for example, reward dedicated music practice, persevering with a challenge, overcoming fears to perform on stage, etc.

- Put up displays in the corridors and the foyer that show not just finished work but also the learning process: drafts, plans, notes, and mistakes. It might be even better if these are annotated with the students' thoughts and reflections.

- Encourage staff to adopt "thinking out loud" strategies to expose the learning process. For example, in a primary literacy lesson, the teacher could model reading and problem-solving, while narrating their own thought processes. "I'm unsure of what this word means so I am just going to reread that and see if I can figure out the meaning from the rest of the sentence. Hmm, I'm still not sure. I wonder if I can recognise any other words – or parts of words – within it, which might give me a clue."

Design principle 4: make ample time for collaboration and conversation

Learning is frequently a social process and so students need to learn how to learn with and from one another. To allow for this, you must ensure that your teachers give students ample opportunity to work with a range of peers on various tasks, in pairs, trios, and larger groups.

In order to do this, staff will need to have confidence in facilitating quality group work as well as students' individual oracy skills. They may require specific training and it is well worth setting time aside for this. In addition to the guidance in the two preceding books in this series, there are many other sources of inspiration for encouraging collaboration and conversations for learning. These include (but are not limited to) the work of Robin Alexander on dialogic teaching,[5] Neil Mercer's work on oracy and collaboration,[6] and the work of Voice 21,[7] a campaign to raise the status of oracy across schools in the UK.

We recommend that professional learning for staff should itself model effective collaborative strategies and activities. Regardless of the content of the training, giving staff the opportunity to discuss ideas and work together on meaningful projects, as well as reflect on and critique their experiences as team members, will help deepen their understanding of what high-quality collaboration looks and feels like. If teachers recognise that they can work together effectively as professionals, know what it takes to do so, and understand the benefits that this brings, they are more likely to value collaboration for their students too.

The crux of positive collaboration is that it's meaningful and authentic – that is, it actually contributes to the learning, rather than being done for the sake of it. Too often, students are asked to work together on a task which it would have made more sense to carry out alone – or are working under the guise of "group work" but are really just working independently around the same table. So teachers need to orchestrate group work to ensure that this doesn't happen. For example, they may assign roles within the group – or get students to identify useful roles and work it out for themselves. There may be sense in sharing out the workload between group members, especially if there is a knowledge or skills gap between them, whereby one person knows more about a topic. Sometimes students – and teachers – have different strengths, so knowledge and skills can be shared and combined to bring about a better outcome.

For this to work, students need to be aware of one another's strengths and how they can use them, so you need to get teachers used to having reflective conversations with their classes. Students may also need to be taught – or at least given the opportunity to discuss – the different roles that group work might require and how to fulfil

---

5   See https://www.robinalexander.org.uk/dialogic-teaching/.
6   Neil Mercer, *The Guided Construction of Knowledge: Talk Amongst Teachers and Learners* (Clevedon: Multilingual Matters, 1995). Neil also directs Oracy Cambridge, an organisation dedicated to promoting oracy in schools and in wider society, see: https://oracycambridge.org/resources/.
7   See https://www.voice21.org/oracy.

them. There are many resources available such as anchor charts, speaking frames, sentence starters, and lists of group work roles which you can introduce to your staff. As with all learning dispositions, collaboration and conversation are not skills which students either can or can't do well. Everyone's skills in this area can be stretched and improved through carefully designed learning opportunities. Here are some final tips for achieving this:

- Where learning partners are used, ensure that pairings are swapped regularly so that students become comfortable working with a wide range of peers. As ever, teachers should be required to behave in this way too, so ensure that they work with a range of colleagues during professional learning.

- Facilitate discussions about individual strengths in the staff team and how they can be used. This provides a model for teachers to facilitate discussions in the classroom about students' individual strengths:

    - Who has a great vocabulary and can be sought out if someone is unsure of the meaning of a word?

    - Who's an avid reader and would be great at suggesting good books to read?

    - Who explains problems really well in maths and can be our go-to person?

    - Who should others turn to if they're unsure of where equipment is kept?

    You could get students to create a class display which celebrates these strengths and prompts them to learn from and support each other.

Design principle 13: focus on improvement, not achievement

This is perhaps the biggest culture shift that needs to take place in order for the LPA to be successful, and one in which you, as a leader, will play a pivotal role. For too long it has been the received wisdom that schools are primarily about levels of achievement. Rewriting this message, placing equal – if not greater – emphasis on improvement, needs to be a matter of whole-school policy. The whole school will need to adopt a "personal best" approach, with students continually striving to make, and reflect upon, incremental improvements.

But how might you do this? Here are a few ideas:

- Consider the use of assessment data and how it is shared with students. Are they given access to previous data which allows them to track and discuss improvements over time?
- Allow students to redo activities, tasks, and tests to improve their grade or score. Show that you value the process and not just the mark.
- Place emphasis on constructive feedback and consider whether grades/scores are always necessary when marking.
- Think about how you can share the "improvement not just achievement" message with parents and how you can encourage them to support this ethos.

On that final point, parents may find it difficult to accept that achieving well without stretching and challenging oneself is no longer acceptable, and you may have to mount a sustained campaign to get them to change their expectations. Many of our respondents have found that parent workshops which explain what growth mindset is, and how it relates to education, have been hugely beneficial in getting parents on board (there will be more on this in Chapter 10).

As always, what applies to the students regarding learning also applies to the teachers. You may need to look at the way in which your school deals with appraisals, for example. Is there a strong sense that every teacher should be striving to get better, all the time? Or is the idea of improvement tainted by the idea of not being "good enough" to start with? How are teachers encouraged to improve? Do existing systems support continual improvement or encourage staff to "pull a good lesson out of the bag" when they are being observed?

How Do You Share Practice to Support Change, without It Feeling Like a High-Stakes Monitoring Exercise?

In an LPA school, professionals should feel that they want to invite colleagues into their classrooms – and to visit others' lessons themselves – as a natural part of their CPD. In a book that Graham wrote with colleagues several years ago, he suggested that there are three kinds of classroom observation, all of which require a rigorous yet forgiving approach to professional learning about teaching.[8] As Figure 6.4 shows, observation *as* development occurs when a teacher wants to learn from the practices of another colleague; observation *for* development is when a colleague calls in another teacher to help them to look constructively at a challenge; finally, observation *of* development should take place to ensure that the required standards are being maintained. None of these types of observation need to be conducted by a senior or more experienced colleague; they should be part of a collegiate learning culture in which teachers are learning from and with each other.

Low-stakes, informal observation can be highly effective in spreading pockets of excellent practice. However, despite its informality, many leaders have thought that peer observations and observations by LPA champions should still be arranged following a basic code of practice in order to ensure that they are effective. We've condensed some further tips on peer observation dos and don'ts into the table on pages 177–180.

---

8   Graham Powell, Maryl Chambers, and Gillian Baxter, *Pathways to Classroom Observation: A Guide for Team Leaders* (Bristol: TLO Limited, 2001).

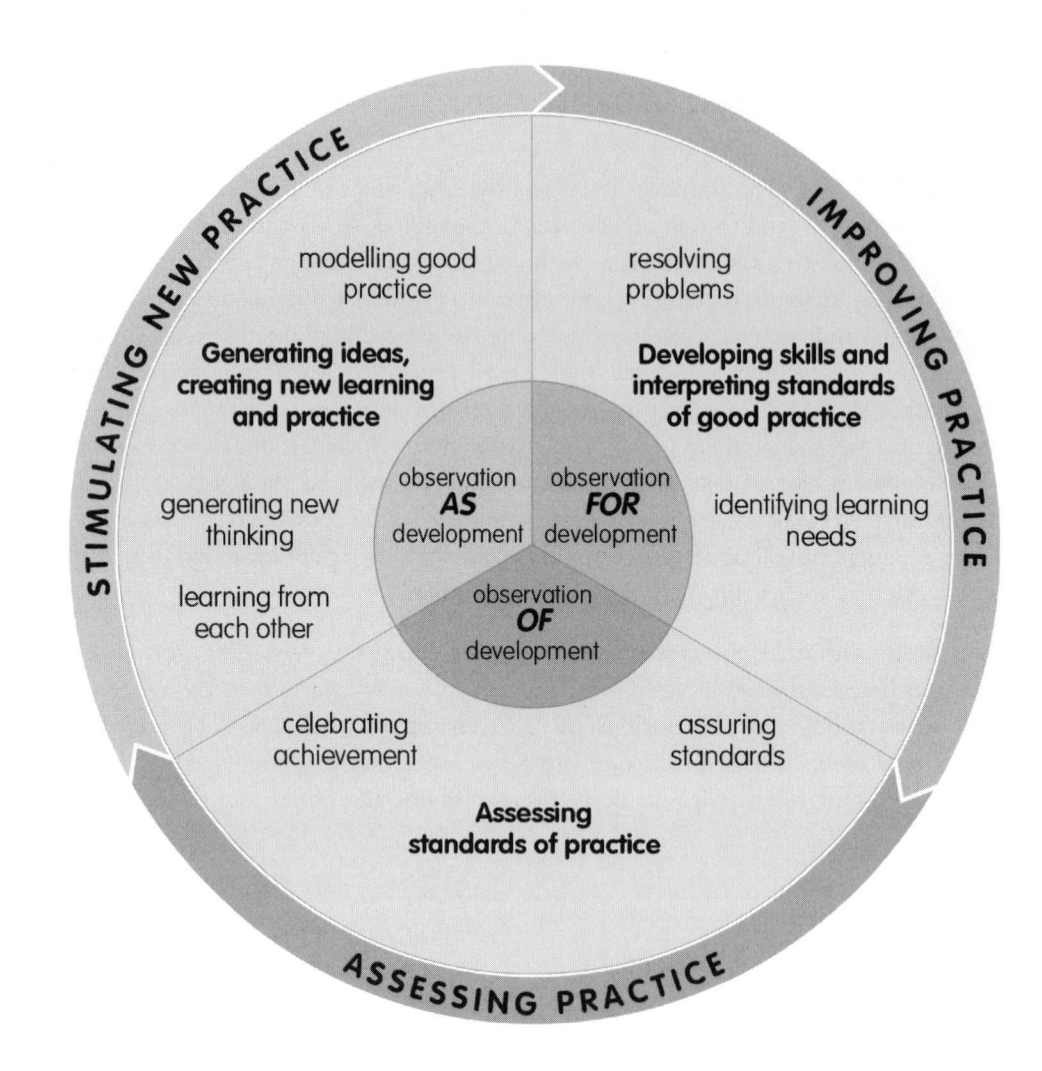

Figure 6.4: Three Purposes of Observation

Source: Powell, Chambers, and Baxter, *Pathways to Classroom Observation*, p. 5 © TLO Limited, Bristol, and used with kind permission

Do	Don't	Why?
Choose one very specific LPA area/skill/strategy as the focus for the observation – for example, use of groupwork during maths, self-directed challenge, use of questioning to encourage curiosity. It should already be familiar to staff and you should identify who you think has been successful.	Set up a very general and non-specific recommendation for an observation – for example, "Go and see Kate, she's great at the LPA."	It's much easier for the teacher to showcase helpful practice if you can be very specific about what you want their observers to get out of the process. The observation can be shorter, which is easier to arrange and puts less pressure on the teacher being observed. The LPA is best implemented using a series of small and gradual changes. Teachers will find it easier to put what they've observed into practice if it's small and specific.
Make sure that you, or another trusted member of the SLT, have seen the teacher use this particular approach/strategy well yourself before recommending that another member of	Assume that someone will be great at implementing the LPA just because you've seen them teach other great lessons in the past.	Time is precious. If a staff member has arranged to see a colleague teach, it's imperative that they see something useful, which will bring them closer to your LPA vision. Peer observations

Do	Don't	Why?
staff goes to observe them.		that are felt to have been a waste of time will soon demoralise staff.
Ask permission of a teacher before you tell others to go and observe them.	Get teachers to directly approach whomever you have recommended.	Teachers can be excellent LPA practitioners but may lack the confidence or willingness to open the door and allow others in. Rather than force the issue and risk losing their enthusiasm and cooperation, press the pause button while you invest more time in building a culture of staff learning and peer observation.
Make it clear that there is a difference between observations to share good practice and observations for performance management.	Allow teachers to feel that they will be judged on their demonstration lesson.	If staff feel judged during observations, it will undermine the culture of staff learning at your school.

Do	Don't	Why?
Make a judgement call on whether your staff need guidance on what is and isn't appropriate for informal observations – for example, do you want to specify the maximum amount of time to stay in a classroom, explain directly that no judgements should be made on one another's teaching, etc.?	Assume that no explanation is needed if peer observations are not already well-established at your school.	Peer observations should be helpful and enjoyable for both the observers and the observed. Clear guidelines can be helpful in ensuring this.
Pair less experienced or less skilled staff with someone who can observe alongside them and point out the key aspects of successful practice.	Assume that observation alone will transform someone who "doesn't get" the LPA into someone who understands the approach and can replicate it in their own teaching.	If someone is new to the LPA, it can be difficult to extract and articulate the specific aspects of the teaching, environment, or lesson which are effective. Great LPA teaching isn't about bells and whistles, so it can often look just like "ordinary teaching". Therefore, it's imperative that the "innards" of the pedagogy are made visible to the observer.

Do	Don't	Why?
		The most effective way of doing this is often for them to discuss the lesson with someone who can guide their observation.
Give staff time to reflect after the observation on what they have seen and how they might use it in their classroom.	Expect them to just "get on with it".	Changes to practice won't happen without time for reflection, consideration, and planning.

At Leigham Primary School, Jane Bellamy started by pairing teachers up – one more "with it", as far as the LPA is concerned, and one less so – to discuss and plan lessons together:

> But we found that just planning and discussing didn't do it. They would happily come up with the same plan – and then go back to their classrooms and teach lessons with quite a different feel to them. And although they might have observed each other teaching as well, even that was not always sufficient to create the shift that we were looking for.

So, says Jane:

> We moved to tag-team teaching, which meant that the two teachers would lead different bits of the same lesson. And we found that when they were together in the classroom, delivering what they had planned jointly, the "learner teacher" would be much more likely to change their practice. Just coaching through discussion didn't have much impact. You have to see it working with real kids, and have a go yourself.

Jane makes the vital point that you have to be able to use the LPA flexibly. You have to understand it well enough that you can spontaneously adapt it to a particular child, a particular moment, or a new topic. She describes a weaker teacher in her school who was paired with an LPA adept. The teacher tried to copy something LPA-ish after an observation – but it misfired badly, because it wasn't appropriate in that context. She was rather aggrieved, and said defiantly, "Well, I did what I saw X doing." But the LPA isn't a piecemeal approach that can be forced to fit. Jane knew she needed to make changes, and organised CPD across all the primary schools in her multi-academy trust (MAT). She told us:

> We got all the science coordinators from the different schools together to plan a really good LPA-style lesson. Then they took it in turns to teach that lesson in their own schools, and to visit and observe each other teaching the lesson. They also involved other teachers in each school as additional observers. After each school visit, the coordinators would get together to talk about the lesson and tweak the format before it was taught in the next school, and so the cycle continued until everyone has taught the lesson. After it had been through all five schools – and subject to four lots of reflection and adjustment – they had a really well-designed lesson, and there had been a lot of thinking and learning done by all concerned. The focus wasn't on asking, "How good was that teacher?" The question was, "How good was the lesson design?" And from all that good, well-grounded thinking, the coordinators were able to extract general principles of lesson design that could be fed back to all the schools.

This method is similar to lesson study, a Japanese model of teacher-led research.[9] In lesson study, teachers work together to choose an area of student learning which they want to improve – for example, students' ability to work collaboratively. They then research the focus area together and use the insights gleaned to plan, teach, and observe a sequence of lessons. Focus students are chosen for teachers to observe. At each stage of the lesson study cycle there are focused and detailed reflections and discussions to review the lessons taught, discuss the learning of the focus students, and plan the next lesson in the sequence. The lesson study protocol dictates that the lesson "belongs" to everybody in the group as it has been planned collaboratively. The teacher who happens to be delivering that lesson is not the person under observation; rather, the focus is on the students and their learning. This distinction can be a useful one when considering whether a lesson observation is for appraisal purposes or not – is the focus on performance or improvement?

Finally, videoing lessons and watching them back is a powerful way of stimulating reflective development. Sandringham have made use of Iris Connect technology, which allows teachers to record and then watch back their own lessons in order to bring about improvements in teaching quality.[10] Some teachers watch their lessons

---

9   For more on this, see Sarah Seleznyov, Improvement Through Lesson Study (2016). Available at: https://www.academia.edu/35010144/Improvement_through_Lesson_Study.
10 See https://www.irisconnect.com/uk/.

alongside a mentor, often with a specific focus in mind for discussion, although staff can also watch their lessons alone, set their own feedback focus and targets, and then discuss their areas for development with a peer or senior member of staff. This has given teachers more autonomy, as well as the space required to take risks, make mistakes, and try things again without feeling like they are being scrutinised by school leaders. There can be some resistance and self-consciousness when you first introduce this idea, but in a culture of continuous improvement, with a supportive focus not on judgement but on learning and experimenting, you should find that teachers settle down and feel intrigued rather than threatened.

The lessons that emerge clearly from these examples are: first, ground all professional development in first-hand experience in real classrooms with real children; and, second, remove the element of judgement from observation and collaborative learning.

Wondering

Consider the use of LPA champions, coaching, team teaching, triads, lesson study, and recording lessons. Which approaches appeal to you most?

What are the advantages and potential challenges of these approaches? What are the logistical issues that you would need to consider? Discuss them with your SLT. Could you trial one of the approaches?

Have you identified any potential LPA champions? Are you in a position to set up some informal observations of these teachers?

How else might you like to use these champions in future?

Do you want teachers to work together from within the same school/department or to work across schools/departments?

How can you enable teachers not just to plan together but to teach together, or to observe one another teaching the same co-planned lesson? How involved should you be in this process?

How Can You Distil Your Collective Experience and Pass It On?

However you choose to support teachers in making pedagogical changes, it will likely be a considerable investment in time, energy, and expertise. You will want to make sure that the fruits of your labours are shared, celebrated, and – most importantly – sustained. The final part of this chapter considers how you can communicate and document the professional development which has taken place in order to ensure that everyone understands the school's pedagogical style.

During the initial stages of embedding LPA principles, staff are likely to be having regular meetings about how it's going so far. Bringing along examples of resources, plans, and student work – or, even better, video clips – to these meetings can help to exemplify good practice and support others. Ensure that you communicate clearly in advance what these meetings are for and what teachers will be expected to discuss and bring along, so that they do not become unstructured "chats" which fail to move teaching forward. You might want to consider allocating facilitator roles so that each group meeting has someone in charge of asking pertinent questions and tying together the main points of discussion.

Heath Mount School created online resources to share due to the difficulty of gathering staff together in one place. Lee Beskeen told us:

> Because our middle and upper school staff are predominantly subject specialists it is more of a challenge to get those teachers together and have oversight of how the LPA is shaping up. So we created an online file, visible to all staff, in which individual teachers could post ideas and initiatives for all to see. This facility also enabled us to monitor how well key aspects of the LPA were being followed. Staff had an initial INSET on the LPA, and we felt that this digital forum was a good way for them to keep their thinking going, and to share ideas and information. This encouraged staff to learn from each other, and it has proved a great success.

Throughout these initial experiments, trials, and demonstrations, it is vital that the reflections made and conclusions drawn lead to a distillation of what works well in your context. Articulating and agreeing upon the strategies, structures, and approaches which serve your school vision for learning is a vital part of the process. What is our version of the LPA? What are our non-negotiables? What does learning look like here, and why have we come to that decision?

Ideally this distillation should become a physical resource which explains and summarises your school's LPA in practical terms for your staff. What do their lessons have to include and why? What is the school's pedagogical style and what is the rationale behind that approach? This physical resource may be in the form of a guide, scheme, poster, or policy. If done well, it will safeguard the school against "losing" the LPA at the expense of competing priorities, staff turnover, and changes in leadership (at both school and governmental level). It should be a document that can be used to hold one another to account: your promise to your students and to one another as professionals.

Summary

However you choose to summarise your school's approach to learning-powered teaching, the process of creating this resource collaboratively will help deepen and clarify your staff's understanding. You should, by now, have a good sense of what the LPA means in terms of classroom practice and how you could go about designing professional learning which enables all staff to align their teaching with the LPA principles. To summarise and reflect on this chapter, and how you will systematically target pedagogy, consider the questions that follow.

Wondering

Which design principles/non-negotiables strike a chord with your aims for the school and your current situation? Which would have the greatest impact on your students?

Do you need to do further reading and research on any of the principles? How about the rest of your SLT? How else can you be well-prepared for leading changes in this area?

Is there one that you want to start with? How will you go about sharing good practice related to this principle?

What professional development will be needed and how can the design of this learning itself exemplify the LPA?

How will you build in time for staff to discuss, reflect on, and refine the LPA?

How will your school's LPA be documented and shared so that it is sustainable and easy to communicate? Who can help in creating this and what is your planned timescale?

Chapter 7

Beyond the Classroom: Changing Structures and Practices on a Wider Scale

We've just seen how the teaching that goes on in individual classrooms is the beating heart of the LPA. Without buy-in and habit change by the majority of teachers, the approach will have limited impact and could end up being marginalised and fragmented. But even with the backing of most – or, ideally, all – teachers, for the LPA to truly take root, a more systemic overhaul will be needed. Indeed, the change in pedagogy is likely to highlight issues that are beyond the control of solitary teachers in their own classrooms. Teachers may begin to feel that school-wide practices – for example, the nature of assessment and reporting, or structural features like the length of lessons or the design of the timetable – are getting in the way of full implementation of the LPA spirit. It is to these wider issues that we turn in this chapter. The questions that we will be addressing are:

+ Which of the school's structural features might leaders need to reconsider?

+ How can you involve students more directly in the leadership of learning?

+ Are your methods of reporting, record-keeping, and nurturing relationships with parents fit for LPA purpose?

+ Can leaders design or modify school buildings to enhance learning opportunities?

> Let's set the scene with head teacher Mark Fenton's reflections on some of these aspects of life at Dr Challoner's Grammar School:
>> As our LPA journey progressed, we began to question wider aspects of the way in which the school operated. I remember one SLT awayday we had, during which I

> challenged the team to think more broadly and deeply. I asked them, "If we were setting up a learning-powered school from scratch, how would it be different to what we have now?" We explored that question in some depth, and then we shifted to, "So what practical steps could we take to move the school in that direction?" We came up with many ideas, some of which we went back and implemented straightaway.
>
> For example:
>
> - We changed the way in which we reported on students to their parents by emphasising their progress with the learning habits.
> - We tried to open up the subject silos so we could have more interesting read-across between different domains.
> - We tried to get students to think more holistically about their learning and development, noticing how their learning in different subjects, as well as in the co-curricular activities, wove together in their development.
> - We got them to plan their personal statement for their university applications around a discussion of their own learning habits, and how those had changed over time.
> - We started to give students greater responsibility by involving them in things like the appointment of new staff.
> - We changed the remit of the student council so they were taking more responsibility – not just for identifying problems, but for proposing well-thought-out solutions – and communicating back to fellow students why, on occasion, their ideas and preferences could not be acted upon by the school.
> - One practical thing that we changed fundamentally was the information we sent out about the school to applicants for teaching vacancies. We put learning power at the centre.

As you read on, you might like to keep a note of any changes that you think might be beneficial in your school. Be on the lookout for ideas that feel both feasible and desirable. Remember that very little in the way in which a school runs is set in stone. You don't need to change the law or wait for the blessing of the school inspectorate. If it is possible to make the kinds of changes that Mark alludes to in a traditional – some might say old-fashioned – high-achieving boys' grammar school in affluent South-East England, it should be possible anywhere. We will show how you can address these issues by looking radically at the structures you have in place at the moment and considering how these can be adapted coherently with the LPA in mind. We will, as usual, draw on a range of examples from many different kinds of schools, so hopefully at least some of what you read will strike you as feasible in your own situation.

Which of the School's Structural Features Might Leaders Need to Reconsider?

Many of our respondents have felt the need to change the length of lessons, for a variety of reasons. In essence, short lessons drastically constrain the amount and quality of active learning that the students can do. Some schools still have thirty-five minute lessons, and by the time the students have settled down, and taken time to pack away and clear up, you might have twenty-five minutes of actual teaching and learning time to play with, which gives little scope for discussing and experimenting with ideas. Many schools have fifty-five-minute or hour-long lessons, but even these may begin to feel as if they are cramping the kinds of learning you really want students to be doing. When they were at Landau Forte College together, principal Elizabeth Coffey and her deputy Sue Plant initiated a discussion with staff and students that led to the introduction of two-hour lessons in which, as one student put it, "You can really get into what you are learning, and not just drive through the content."[1] As you might imagine, it took time to get agreement from staff, and there were many objections that had to be overcome. For some staff, a shift like this requires a major rethink of their teaching style, which is demanding and – sometimes – threatening, so changes of this kind need to be handled delicately, and the ground laid with care.

---

1 Should you want to know more about the college, you can view a film that they made: Landau Forte, "Learning at Landau" [video] (14 October 2014). Available at: https://www.youtube.com/watch?v=_HDL-aH_VFs.

Here is Hugh Bellamy's take on the issue of lesson length during his time at George Pindar School. As we saw earlier, Hugh inherited a seriously underperforming school where examination results were well below the national average, student behaviour was poor, and staff morale was low. From the outset, he knew that the answer was not simply to urge colleagues and students to work harder; more radical action was needed. Hugh recognised that teachers needed longer units of time in which to work and the opportunity to work more flexibly and collaboratively with colleagues if they were to recapture their students' enthusiasm for and engagement with learning. The first step was to move from forty-minute to hour-long lessons and implement a timetable which ensured that departmental teams were teaching the same year group at the same time. This allowed for greater flexibility, with opportunities for classes to come together in bigger groups for launch sessions or for smaller seminar groups to be created to explore challenges. Teachers got into the habit of planning and working together: learning from each other, sharing ideas, and building confidence when things got difficult. In changing the structure, Hugh enabled the teachers to become learners too.

> ... teachers needed longer units of time in which to work and the opportunity to work more flexibly and collaboratively with colleagues ...

But this was only the start. An enquiry-based approach, which meant that lessons focused on an initial driving question and gave students time to really explore the issue, led the school to adopt even longer lessons. Through proper consultation and appropriate training, the school moved to a timetable which allowed for half- and full-day lessons. They could spend a whole day on design technology, or three hours on maths, for example. As we have said, that requires a radical mindset shift for teachers, and also for students. But without doubt, longer lessons certainly fit well not only with traditional subjects but also with a thematic or cross-disciplinary approach to the curriculum. What was the cumulative effect of these and other changes at George Pindar? Can we remind you that after five years, when measured by examination performance, the school was the most improved in the UK? Results had shifted from 23% of students gaining five or more A*–C GCSE grades to 100%.

Some schools, such as Ridgeway Primary School in Croydon, South London, have gone one step further and experimented with not having a fixed timetable at all. They have allowed lessons to run on, provided that the children are engaged and productive, until a natural break or resolution appears. Some head teachers might immediately think of this as an administrative nightmare – but they seemed to be able to make it work![2]

Wondering

What changes could you make to help teachers plan and work together in teaching teams? Could these cross subject boundaries?

Is the lesson length in your school fit for LPA purpose?

Could you enable a more flexible use of time by combining classes together into larger blocks? Would this enable you to explore different learning designs and purposes?

What are the advantages of blocking the curriculum into half- or full-day units? What are the potential pitfalls? Might the benefits outweigh the costs?

How might you start to raise these issues with your colleagues?

At a time of budgetary constraint, are there any efficiencies to be made by adopting these approaches?

---

2   It is some time since we have had contact with this school, so we cannot vouch for whether they have managed to continue with this degree of flexibility.

How Can You Involve Students More Directly in the Leadership of Learning?

Most schools involve students in decision-making to some degree, usually through a school council. Issues related to management and organisation are debated and recommendations made. A few schools have gone further and involved students in exploring the nature and quality of learning. In the next case study, you will see in some detail how Wren Academy has developed the idea of student voice to support the development of an LPA culture across the whole school.

Student voice at Wren Academy

From its inception in 2009, school leaders and teachers at Wren Academy have gone to great lengths to build students' understanding of learning power, and to increase their ability to contribute responsibly to the development of an LPA culture throughout the school. The teacher in charge of student voice at Wren, Will Ponsonby, reflects:

> Schools have always evolved – mostly as a response to government policies or the wishes of senior leaders and governors and at times to suggestions or pressure from the staff. In many schools, there is often a fundamental group that is left outside of the policy- and decision-making process: the students. There may be some attention paid to "student voice", but rarely do students have a significant impact on the core business of the school – teaching and learning. But in a learning-powered school, where teachers are trying to help students understand and take charge of their own learning, it just seems common sense to involve them more centrally. At Wren, we have developed a really powerful approach to student voice, in which they play a major role in thinking and planning for more effective teaching – of both subject matter and learning power itself.

Will describes his role as student voice coordinator as helping students to set the agenda and ensuring that their voice is heard, harnessed, and channelled effectively. There are two key aspects to student voice at Wren. First, there is the curriculum advisor programme. Each department has a link teacher whose role it is to work closely with students in Years 8, 9, and 10 who act as what are called curriculum advisors (CAs). These CAs work with their link teachers to observe lessons and offer constructive comments on the nature of the learning that is going on, and the extent to which teachers are providing opportunities for students to use a wide range of learning habits. Students are explicitly coached to know how to observe lessons precisely and unobtrusively, and to speak with teachers respectfully and effectively.

> Students are explicitly coached to know how to observe lessons precisely and unobtrusively ...

Each term, the agenda for the CAs is set jointly by teachers and students, and together they identify areas to focus on. Sometimes these are whole-school issues, and sometimes they are specific to particular departments. For example, a recent series of CA observations focused on the effectiveness of teachers' written feedback on students' work, across all subjects. They looked at how feedback is presented and how it is responded to by students. Were students making maximum use of the feedback they were getting? And were teachers giving it in such a way that they were also encouraging students to take more responsibility for evaluating and editing their own work? On another occasion, one department asked the CAs to investigate how technology was being used in the classroom – inspired by the academy's commitment to each student having access to a tablet computer in lessons.

As a result of these observations, the CAs – in collaboration with the link teachers – distil valuable questions and suggestions for the staff. Of course the observations yield valuable data, but on top of this, the CAs will often give feedback directly to the teachers about what they have seen in their classrooms. Then the link teacher may present the findings at one of the weekly departmental planning and evaluation meetings. In this way, students not only feed continuously into the search for ever more effective teaching and learning, but they are also learning to think more deeply about

> ... developing into responsible, insightful, and articulate leaders of learning.

the nature of the education they are receiving. They come to understand for themselves how learning can be orchestrated most effectively while developing into responsible, insightful, and articulate leaders of learning.

The second strand to the student voice agenda occurs in weekly one-hour student voice enrichment sessions. A team of about twenty CAs – together with some former CAs who are currently in Year 11 – meet to identify aspects of the school which could be improved and discuss their suggestions for doing so. Will says:

> This is my favourite bit of the week! The students set the agenda at these meetings; I just give them the structure to achieve it. I have been nicknamed "The Map" by the students as my role is only to facilitate and help to coordinate their views and not to push my own, or the academy's, agenda. If I overstep the mark, they are quick to let me know!
>
> This is not just a talking shop; we really get things done. In the last few years we have collaboratively created a prompt sheet to help teachers improve the quality of discussion at parent consultation evenings. This CHIEF sheet [see Figure 7.1] is now placed prominently on every table, so that all those involved can be guided in their contributions to the discussion. Other areas of focus for the enrichment sessions have ranged from home learning timetables to revising the current system of breaks and lunches. Next term, the students will focus on how the school could improve on the content and timing of home learning, and they will present their suggestions at a staff meeting.
>
> I very much enjoy working with the students in this role and it is something I am very passionate about. Not only does it make the students feel empowered, but it makes the school a better place. This could not be achieved without the support that we receive from the whole staff, particularly from the SLT, who are very encouraging and ensure that the changes are implemented.

Here are some of the students' reactions to these innovations at Wren:

> Year 8 student: "With the assistance of our subject link teachers we are able to further improve certain aspects of the curriculum and the way in which we are taught."
>
> Year 9 student: "We chose to look at parents' evenings because we felt it was an awkward and nerve-wracking experience for us."
>
> Year 8 student: "I was so happy at parents' evening when I noticed teachers using my advice, and it was great to see that I had helped make things better."

C.H.I.E.F.

Teacher Tips for Consultation Evening
Written by members of Student Voice

Considerate

"We believe teachers should consider the feedback they give. Parents, carers, and students appreciate constructive feedback."

"A really negative comment could knock our confidence and potentially set us back academically."

"Teachers who give me praise at consultation evening give me the motivation to work hard."

Honest

"We believe it is effective for parents and carers to understand students' strengths and weaknesses. We really appreciate when teachers are frank with how a student is behaving. It is in the teacher's, parent/carer's, and student's best interest that they are all on the same page about how the student is progressing in class."

"If I am not doing well, please tell me!"

"If you teach more than one class, we understand, but please let us know. Sometimes we feel like teachers don't want to see us, even though they actually can't."

"Targets being realistic are very beneficial, because students are working hard to achieve their target grade without being under too much pressure."

Insightful

"Tell our parents/carers the full story. I know we need to speak about grades, but how is my learning and behaviour in lessons?"

"We believe that our parents/carers should have a full understanding of how their child is doing in class."

"Instead of just comparing test results, we also want to be told about the quality of our work in class."

"I would prefer learning about my learning habits as well as my test results."

Empathetic

"We really appreciate that teachers at Wren think about the difficulties we might have in our learning. Some teachers go further by taking into account any difficulties we may have outside of school that hinders our revision and/or academic progress. We, as students, like this, because it shows the teachers understand our situation, which makes us more receptive to criticism."

"Sometimes it feels like teachers don't understand that they could be the sixth teacher we have spoken to that evening! That means it is the sixth time we have heard the question 'How do you think it is going this term?'! Tell us our strengths and areas to improve but also involve us in the conversation."

Fair

"We, as students, want teachers to provide us with open-minded and impartial feedback, without sugar-coating due to the fact our parent/carer is sat right next to us."

"My parent/carer works really late and can't come until after 7pm. Some teachers tell me that they can't do appointments after 7pm or persuade me to make an early appointment. This means I never get to see these teachers!"

Figure 7.1: An Example of the Student Curriculum Advisors' Work at Wren Academy

> Mr Ponsonby showed us the minutes of the staff meeting in which our advice was discussed and accepted by the teachers, and it made me happy to see it. Even though it takes a long time to complete these projects, being able to be part of a big change at the school makes it 100% worth it!"
>
> Year 10 student: "Student voice does exactly as it says in the name: it gives students a voice. This voice allows us to have a real connection between the students and the SLT to ensure that real change takes place. With this link, our community is brought closer together with a strong bond of communication on both parts. Everyone in our school is striving to be the best we can be by using student voice."

Wondering

Are there any aspects of this work at Wren that you find inspiring, challenging, counterproductive, or dangerous?

How could you carry forward a conversation about enriching and deepening the responsibilities that your students have?

Are Your Methods of Reporting, Record-Keeping, and Nurturing Relationships with Parents Fit for LPA Purpose?

Maybe it's time to rethink the ways in which we communicate with parents and start talking with them about the ways in which they can support their children to be more confident, independent learners at home. Jann Robinson reflected on the changes that they made to the reporting procedures at St Luke's:

Within twelve months of introducing L@SL we realised that we needed to make changes to reflect our emphasis on learning. We felt that there was a disconnect between what we said we valued and what we were saying in reports to parents. Prior to L@SL, our learner profile contained generic statements like:

- Completes work and set homework thoroughly and on time.
- Maintains interest and commitment to learning.
- Takes responsibility for his or her own learning.
- Manages classroom behaviour.
- Brings correct equipment to class; is well prepared to work.
- Respects peers and teachers.

These criteria were meant to reflect how students engaged in learning in the classroom. The change we made was to provide a learner profile which specifically used the language of BLP.

On the surface, this reporting seems perfectly fine, but what are the qualities that are being valued and recognised? It is very concerned with process and compliance, rather than with learning. There is no real indication of what parents can do to support their child with their learning at home. How does this compare with the reports that are produced at your school?

The team at St Luke's worked to revise these statements, resulting in this new list:

- Manages distractions and remains focused on learning during class.
- Demonstrates resilience when faced with challenging learning tasks.
- Collaborates effectively in a variety of learning contexts.
- Listens respectfully to teachers and peers during class discussions.
- Effectively selects and uses resources for learning.
- Asks thoughtful questions to clarify understanding.
- Takes responsibility for planning and organising his or her learning.
- Reflects on his/her own strengths and weaknesses as a learner.

Jann continues:

> The level descriptors used the language of work, not of learning. These were changed to reflect the students' development as learners. We knew that what we reported on signalled what we thought was important. The teachers embraced the change because they found it to be a more meaningful way to report.

This shift is shown in the following figures.

Highly developed	Is an independent worker who displays initiative.
Competent	Is able to work with minimal direction.
Developing	Works well with guidance.
Experiencing difficulty	Experiences some difficulties remaining on task.

Figure 7.2: Pre-L@SL Learner Profile Levels

Self-motivated learner	The student regularly displays the capacity for learning at a high level and knows how he/she can strengthen this capacity. He/she regularly reflects on his/her progress as a learner.
Purposeful learner	The student often displays this capacity in the classroom and responds well to guidance on how he/she can improve. He/she looks for ways to grow as a learner using this capacity and is able to reflect on how he/she can strengthen this capacity.
Apprentice learner	The student has started to display this capacity independently in the classroom but requires some

	encouragement to appropriate this disposition on a regular basis to support his/her learning.
Scaffolded learner	The student is able to display this capacity in the classroom with encouragement and support.
Dependent learner	The student requires significant support to demonstrate this learning capacity in the classroom.

Figure 7.3: Post-L@SL Learner Profile Levels

Jann continues:

> The other significant change we found ourselves making was to the awards given at end-of-year presentation day events. In the third year of L@SL, I was speaking at the end-of-year event and suddenly had this realisation that while I was talking about the importance of learning, and how important it was to grow the dispositions of a good learner, all our awards were for academic excellence. I stopped mid-speech and acknowledged the irony of the situation. The next year we introduced new awards.
>
> There has been some trial and error, but the pattern that has evolved is to have awards for outstanding achievement and awards for outstanding learning. Sometimes the same student will receive both, but it has led to greater recognition of those students who are great learners and show all the characteristics that are desired, even if their attainment isn't as high. The learning awards are as valued by the students as the academic ones.
>
> Further to this, the senior school has introduced a termly learning assembly. These celebrate the growth of students' learning dispositions. Teachers nominate students for the awards, and a wider group of students is being acknowledged. Previously in the junior school, a range of social behaviours were recognised, but now we have changed the weekly awards to focus on learning dispositions. The little figure Riley Resilience was developed by the children. There are four other figures: one for each learning muscle.

Mark Fenton, head of Dr Challoner's, was also very clear about his core educational beliefs in the presentations that he made to parents:

> Most Dr Challoner's students can, of course, succeed at the qualifications game. The problem is that, unless you're careful, concentrating on qualifications can direct young people's interest and energy away from the learning itself and put all their attention onto the result. Getting at least two As and a B at A level becomes the goal, and

learning is the chore which you have to do to get there. "Bright" students can develop an instrumental attitude towards their education which leads them to sacrifice their natural curiosity and instead learn for the test. As a result, their knowledge is only skin-deep, and their learning habits and attitudes are tied directly to the specialised job of doing well in exams.

Like many other leaders, Mark was keen to go beyond the rhetoric and build a genuine partnership with parents that made use of a common language for learning and provided them with guidance about how to support learning at home. What do you think of the advice that he gave parents?

- Be a visible learner for your son.
- Involve your son in adult conversations.
- Let him spend time with you while you are doing difficult things.
- Involve him in family decisions.
- Tell your son stories about your learning difficulties.
- Encourage your son to spend time with people who have interesting things to share.
- Don't rush in too quickly to rescue him when he is having difficulties.
- Restrain the impulse to teach.
- Don't praise too much – use interest rather than approval.
- Acknowledge the effort, not the "ability".
- Don't overstimulate – boredom breeds imagination.
- Talk to your son about the process of learning (without offering too much advice).
- Watch and learn from your son's learning.

Can Leaders Design or Modify School Buildings to Enhance Learning Opportunities?

It is clear that the physical look and feel of a school contributes massively to the quality of learning that takes place. In the earlier books in this series, we have shown how teachers can adapt their classrooms to enable the LPA through the rearrangement of furniture, the provision of accessible resources, and the use of display material to support learning. For school leaders who do not have the privilege of helping to design a brand-new school, the challenge is to make circumspect modifications to open up the environment for learning.

Hugh Bellamy recognised the importance of the learning environment in those schools where he was principal. He was prepared to do anything to make space for the kind of learning that he wanted to promote – including moving his office into an alcove in a busy corridor in order to free up valuable space for a seminar room. Some of Hugh's other innovative moves included:

- Removing walls to create bigger learning spaces for large group team teaching.
- Shifting established classroom bases so that complementary curriculum areas could be grouped together.
- Securing funding for sports facilities that could be used by the wider community.
- Equipping inauspicious "temporary" accommodation with real-world vocational facilities so that, for example, catering, childcare, and hairdressing businesses could be run by students within the school.

Wondering

Does your school have flexible spaces available for both large group team teaching and small group sessions? If not, are there any spaces that could be repurposed?

Are resources available to support autonomous learning in a variety of places around the school, as well as within individual classrooms?

What is the key message about learning that a visitor to your school would recognise on entering your building? How is this message complemented on the walls of corridors and classrooms?

Are displays around the school designed to be interactive? Are they changed regularly?

> What words would you like your students to use to describe the appearance of your school? What words do they actually use?
>
> Which classrooms – in terms of layout, display, and resource provision – support the LPA? Which classrooms inhibit the kinds of learning that you would wish to see in your school? Could you take action to ensure a flexible house style for learning across the school?
>
> Have you surveyed staff and student attitudes to the learning environment? Have you gathered any suggestions from them about how things could be improved or changed?

Summary

In this chapter we have shown how school leaders, in a variety of contexts, have addressed the whole-school structures that will provide a firm scaffolding with which to build the kind of teaching and learning that they want for all young people. Some of these ideas will, we hope, have struck you as good ones; others, perhaps not so much. But all of them will require planning and agreement from a variety of stakeholders. So do not underestimate the debates that may need to be had, and the anxieties that they may cause.

For many school leaders, it can feel like there is little room for manoeuvre when it comes to the structures within which they have to work. A prescriptive and overburdened curriculum ties your hands. And yet we have shown you examples of schools – like George Pindar – where structural change was exactly what was needed to liberate learning and allow teachers to improve their students' life opportunities. You don't necessarily need a brand-new, state-of-the-art building to allow for flexible approaches to learning and teaching; there are modifications that can be made to even the most dilapidated of surroundings to change the way in which young people experience school.

Above all else, the examples that we have given show you that the most important factor in making radical structural changes is stakeholder involvement and engagement. Whether it be teachers, parents, or students themselves, there is no substitute for sincere consultation. Look again at what Mark Fenton, Rachel Macfarlane, and Will Ponsonby have done to communicate with and involve others. Remember, it's not just communication and consultation that matter, but involvement and engagement with all partners as changes are introduced and embedded.

But what do you do if the teachers in your school are resistant to change? Try to identify your positive change agents in the staffroom and help them achieve some modest transformations that can act as "proof of concept" for others to observe. Support your pioneers in experimenting with better ways of, for example, managing time or space in their classrooms, and show others that you approve.

What if your students' parents seem to be exclusively focused on examination results? Take courage from the experience of Mark Fenton and keep explaining that your innovations will boost, not jeopardise, their children's grades. Most parents can be persuaded that new ways of working that enable their children to learn how to learn are desirable, especially if they see the evidence in their children's attitude. The more you are prepared to take them into classrooms and hear what they have to say, while arguing your own case persuasively, the more likely they are to say, "Why wasn't it like this when we were at school?"

What if the students themselves are indifferent to student voice initiatives because the school council has not changed anything in the past? Most importantly, keep talking to them about your genuine wish to improve their education and enlist their support. Show them that you are hearing and heeding what they have to say and involve them, as far as you can, in your own thinking as it develops.

Chapter 8

Making It Stick: Sustainability

We've seen how leaders have worked with teachers to change their everyday practices so that the LPA is embedded in all facets of school life. In this chapter, we look at the sustainability of this transformation. The LPA involves culture change and habit change, which takes time – weeks, months, or even longer – to become so embedded as to be second nature. This means that we, as leaders, (a) have to stay on the case, constantly reminding and encouraging people, coaxing and cajoling them along, and (b) have to make sure that they are staying on track and not drifting off into variations that begin to miss the point or blur the framework. To do this, we need systems and standard practices that serve to keep the pressure on and reinforce it with a bit of accountability.

The questions we will explore in this chapter are:

- What might leaders do to ensure that the LPA persists after they leave?
- How do leaders keep the LPA fresh and sustain it over time?
- How can you develop and distribute leadership capacity in other members of staff?
- How can students become the carriers of the LPA culture?

What Might Leaders Do to Ensure That the LPA Persists After They Leave?

This is probably the most challenging part of developing sustainability. The school leaders who have embraced the LPA have done so because they believe that it is important for the next generation to be prepared for a rapidly changing world. All of them face the dilemma of knowing that they will leave their schools sooner or later. Not only that, but others who have championed the LPA and led it with them may well also depart. What might leaders do to secure the future of the LPA in their schools despite a change in personnel? What can we learn from those schools where it has continued to thrive after its champion's departure? What are the lessons we can learn from those whose legacy did not survive under a new regime?

At Walthamstow School for Girls, Rachel Macfarlane introduced BLP in 2005, and even though she left in 2011 it is still going strong. Rachel says:

> In the fourth year of BLP its main champion, Janet Cassford, left to take up a promotion elsewhere, and I appointed a new BLP coordinator, Laura Fearon. I have to admit that I did not give specific thought to future-proofing BLP before I left the school, but I think that was because it was in such good shape and so well-embedded within the school's DNA. Also, Laura was so settled in her post and enthusiastically supported by the deputy head teacher who line managed her that I thought there was nothing to fear. Now, fourteen years after BLP was first introduced at Walthamstow, it still lives on, although it has evolved over time.

At Norwest Christian College in Sydney, the LPA survived the departure of the principal who had introduced the framework in 2016. While the recruitment process was open, the deputy principal, Felicity Marlow, was duly appointed. Felicity had been responsible for the LPA under her predecessor. She shares her story:

> Typically, a newly appointed principal would have difficulty ensuring that a teaching and learning framework strongly linked to the previous principal is sustained. However, because I was responsible for leading professional learning during my tenure as deputy principal, the transition into the role and continuing the work of developing the LPA framework was quite seamless. I was, however, conscious that staff may assume that with the departure of the principal the vision and enthusiasm for the LPA would dissipate. In order to address this, I made it clear in my first address to staff – outlining my vision for the next chapter of the college – that I was deeply committed to the framework. I also spent significant time during this address – and in subsequent professional learning meetings – stimulating staff to again consider the "why" that sits behind the LPA. I have actively and frequently shared my personal "why", and have invited them to think about why aligning their practice with the vision is so vital. It is important that staff see that I haven't merely continued with the initiative; they need to see that it is central to my vision for the college. If the framework is to be sustained, we must continually refresh our understanding of the moral imperatives that underpin it. As a leader, I am aware of the power of culture. Once culture is established, other technical elements begin to develop naturally, and so while techniques come and go, culture is sustainable even when you remove the passionate leader.

At Oaklands Primary School, Tessa Hodgson's approach has been focused not as much on developing champions as on building the LPA into the regular rituals and practices of the school. Tessa feels that the LPA is now so securely embedded that it can survive any change in leadership. The steps they took to achieve this rock-solid foundation include:

- Linking the LPA into their core values and behaviour reward systems.

- Getting parents, governors, staff, and students to sign up to learning this way through the school website.

- Providing workshops for parents to familiarise them with the LPA.

- Stressing the importance of the LPA during every welcome tour for prospective children and parents.

- Making sure that the messages and language of the home–school agreement and all the handbooks are aligned.

The school has evidence that this approach has worked. An Ofsted inspection report described the learning behaviours of the children as "exemplary".[1] SEND and whole-school peer reviews and student voice interviews have consistently given positive feedback. The Fischer Family Trust data shows that the children are significantly more likely to make productive attempts to answer questions in the Key Stage 2 SATs than they are in other comparable schools.[2] Staff now apply to the school because they want to work in this way. The local community chooses to come to the school because of the ethos and the staff's commitment to this way of learning. Tessa comments:

> Working in this way now feels like common sense. Why would we change it?

Sometimes it is not just the principal's departure that can cause the LPA to falter. Robert Cleary at Sandringham Primary School experienced the impact of being

---

1 See Ofsted, Short Inspection of Oaklands Primary School. 11 December 2017. Available at: https://www.oaklands-primary.co.uk/docs/Oaklands_Primary_School_Ofsted_Report_1718.pdf.
2 For more information, see https://fft.org.uk/pupil-tracking/.

without a key member of staff, which provided a chance to think about how to sustain the LPA. He says:

> Gemma has taken two periods of maternity leave during her time at Sandringham. During her first leave of absence the LPA did suffer. The strategies and whole-school approaches that had been established were maintained, but there was little taking place that moved the LPA forward. This was an oversight on the part of our SLT.

As a result, Robert and the SLT have now put much more effort into developing other teachers as LPA leaders, ready to take responsibility for championing it.

A similar challenge faced St Luke's Grammar School when, in 2017, dean of professional development and learning James Pietsch moved on to take up the headship of another school. He was perceived as being so vital to the implementation of the initiative that one staff member said, "What will happen to L@SL now that James has gone?" While Jann didn't think that James's departure was going to be critical, because her own commitment was unswerving, it did make her think about how sustainable L@SL would be if she left. Jann reflects:

> I knew of schools where the LPA had not survived after the head left, and James's exit was a critical moment for me as I realised that my own departure could see all the work that went into building a strong learning culture collapse. It made me think about how to spread the ownership of L@SL so it wasn't just invested in one person. In the first year I appointed four mentors and in the second year appointed two more, as well as a new dean of professional development and learning. I have had them work alongside me to deliver professional development to the whole staff. The new dean of professional development and learning asked for time to focus on learning during heads of department meetings. I am hoping to secure the framework by making it less closely tied to me.

Wondering

Can you identify any potential LPA leaders in your school?

What roles might you create for them?

Can you think of other ways to promote the LPA so that it can withstand the loss of its champions?

The fear that the hard-won LPA culture might be jeopardised by the loss of key personnel is a real one. We have come across several schools where, despite their best intentions, departing principals have seen their legacy diluted or even, in a few cases, deliberately dismantled by incoming leaders who did not understand or value the LPA. This has caused them to think hard about what else they could have done to protect the culture.

Hugh Bellamy, for example, is deeply disappointed by the way in which his efforts at both George Pindar School and South Dartmoor Community College faded away after he left. He concedes:

> Of course, every incoming head of a school wants to make his or her mark.

But it is heartbreaking when a learning culture that has been carefully nurtured over several years, with patently obvious benefits, is allowed to dissipate. After just such a painful experience at George Pindar, Hugh went out of his way to recruit key staff at South Dartmoor who would carry the flag of the LPA after his departure. He deliberately trained up teachers who were respected by the rest of the staff, hoping that their influence would continue. And he had organised for governors – who would be involved in appointing his successor – to have sessions with an LPA consultant to help them get their heads around the approach, and he involved them in visiting classrooms to see the LPA in action. He thought that they had understood it, but perhaps, with hindsight, even those sessions were not enough. Hugh now thinks that he could have immersed his governors and directors in the life of the classroom even more, preparing the group before the learning walks, and debriefing them afterwards, so they could deeply appreciate the difference that the LPA makes to children's lives and behaviour.

Jane Bellamy also worried about the fact that her successor at Leigham Primary School had not worked with BLP before and was keen that the school adopted a growth mindset approach, broadening the focus away from the LPA. As advocates of the LPA are always keen to point out, Carol Dweck's work is foundational to their own practice, but "doing growth mindset" does not mean sticking up inspirational posters and talking about perseverance all the time. It means adjusting your practice so that the classroom becomes a powerful incubator of adventurousness and resilience – whether you talk about it or not. In fact, the staff had so fully embraced the LPA, and it was such a strong part of the teaching culture, that it soon became clear to Jane's successor that a change of focus did not need to happen. The teaching remained strong and the school went on to have national progress scores that were significantly above average. Jane makes a very important distinction between "doing the LPA" and "living it":

> Doing it means following recipes and sticking to the script. It is teaching by numbers. And when you do it by numbers, you lack the sensitivity, flexibility, and creativity to make your approach come alive in the moment.

Both Hugh and Jane eventually became CEOs of multi-academy trusts (MATs) – taking on schools that had not been using the LPA – and they now wonder whether involving the governors of their own schools in inter-school reviews would have helped them to understand what was different about their schools, so that they would want to protect it for the future.

For Jann Robinson, the lessons of other head teachers are very pertinent. She has announced to her staff that she will retire in July 2020. Having read Hugh's and Jane's reflections, she is now keen to work with her governors to secure L@SL. Jann says:

> From the beginning, the school's governors made a significant investment in L@SL. For starters, they committed to funding the appointment of the original dean of professional development and learning. Each year, as part of setting the school's goals with the council, I have included an area of development for L@SL and reported against it in my end-of-year appraisal. In 2017, the SLT and the governors worked on developing the next five-year strategic plan, and they agreed a number of measures designed to deepen and strengthen L@SL. Budgeting allowed for appointing learning mentors, funding research into disposition development, providing ongoing professional development for staff, and running conferences. We invite the governors to these conferences, and I am confident that they have a good understanding of what we are doing. I am also hopeful that because a number of governors have children in the school – and so have seen the impact of the LPA first-hand – they will want to make sure that it continues, and so make a good appointment.

On the optimistic side, even if the whole-school culture is not quite the same, the departing principal's legacy lives on in the teachers who were transformed from deliverers of content into masters of learning, both their own and their students'. These teachers will, one would hope, continue to practise the LPA in their own classrooms. They also leave a powerful and worthwhile legacy in those students who have been stretched to grow and to know themselves as learners, and in those parents who have seen their children learn to achieve beyond the level which they thought possible. Their legacy endures in the lives of all those who have been touched by these leaders' passion and vision.

How Do Leaders Keep the LPA Fresh and Sustain It Over Time?

Leaders sometimes manage to launch the LPA with a degree of enthusiasm and buy-in but find that it quite quickly dries up or fizzles out. In the early days of BLP, for example, teachers would come to Guy and Graham following consultancy work and say, "We've done the 4Rs. We've put up the posters and we've talked to the children about how important these things are … Now what?" All school leaders face the challenge of keeping the momentum going. Once teachers have mastered the language of the LPA, for example, how can they be motivated to keep going deeper?

Jane and Hugh Bellamy are clear that the answer lies not so much in trying to "jazz it up" as in developing the staff culture of learning that we talked about in Chapter 4. As Jane said:

> The question of keeping it fresh only seems to arise in a culture where teachers are *doing* the LPA – adding a few extras onto their normal teaching methods, often "because we have been told to" – rather than living and breathing the values. In a school where all members of staff see themselves as learners – keen to find ever more subtle and effective ways of boosting the children's learning power through discussing, reflecting, and continually experimenting with their own ways of teaching – new questions and possibilities just keep bubbling up.

Guy remembers being picked up from a local train station by an exemplary LPA educator, Andrea Curtis, when she was head of Bushfield School. As they were driving along, Andrea started to apologise as she thought that Guy might be disappointed with what he saw and heard in her school. In fact, he was mightily impressed. Reflecting later on, Andrea said:

> The LPA is like the horizon; the faster you approach it, the more it recedes. I know we have done a lot, but to me now, it feels like we have only achieved a fraction of what we possibly could.

As she watched the children rise to the challenge of taking more responsibility for their learning, her head was constantly full of new ideas about how the staff could help them become ever more independent and powerful learners.

For a number of schools, keeping the model fresh has meant that they have revisited the language and, in some cases, added new practices. At Walthamstow School for Girls there have been regular refreshes and relaunches in the fourteen years in which they've been using BLP. The first was a language review, carried out four years in. This had the advantage of grounding and reuniting the school around its learning-powered approach. Subsequently, the 4Rs and the learning dispositions have been reviewed and updated. The school then adapted BLP and renamed it the GREEN programme – a nod to how it was often referred to by the local community because of its green uniform. This rejig of the language has had the effect of creating greater ownership by the teachers; because they contributed to it, it now feels like theirs.

Growth:	Progress and improvement, applying learning in different ways, open-mindedness, maturity, setting and striving for targets.
Resilience:	Perseverance, practice, redrafting, reinforcing.
Energy:	Enthusiasm, engagement, participation, proactivity.
Empathy:	Kindness, helpfulness, sharing ideas, supporting others in groups or teams, sensitivity.
Newness:	Originality, creativity, independence, mastery.

Figure 8.1: The Walthamstow GREEN Values and Dispositions

Leventhorpe School introduced the LPA in 2010. By 2015 they too were facing the fact that their programme, Learning at Leventhorpe, had lost its initial focus and impetus. There had been significant staff turnover, which meant that few remaining staff had taken part in the initial LPA training. The SLT was forced to look for ways to refresh the learning framework. They discovered the Thinking Schools project (originated by Professor Bob Burden at the University of Exeter), contacted them, and visited other thinking schools.[3] They adopted the "Thinking Tools" devised by psychologist Edward de Bono, and these have given teachers and students practical ways in which to develop and make use of the learning dispositions.[4] They have continued to refresh the learning, recently launching David Hyerle's "Thinking Maps", for example.[5] Through these updates, Learning at Leventhorpe has been renewed, and teaching is once again strongly focused on learning.

Sometimes, changes in the school itself keep the LPA fresh. For Rachel Macfarlane at Isaac Newton Academy, BRIDGES was constantly high on the agenda due to having to induct new staff each year as the school was growing. Rachel reflects:

> The leadership team had to keep thinking about the new teachers who were coming in each year – and, of course, the new cohort of students – and develop increasingly effective ways to help them understand what we were doing. I also needed to change the BRIDGES lead every so often, and this meant a fresh set of eyes looking at the programme. It led to new approaches being taken. The BRIDGES assemblies and the fortnightly newsletters were frequently revamped, and this kept them fresh. Once the school reaches capacity, though, I guess our approach could change.

At St Luke's, the language of BLP has not been changed, but Jann has made other adjustments to maintain the momentum. In the second year, PLGs were introduced, as was a teachers' guide which shared suggestions for practical ways to implement the framework. In the third year, developing the PLGs and adding learning walks provided new energy. Jann recalls:

> At the beginning of the fourth year we were asking what should come next. We decided to add teaching sprints – focused efforts by teachers to change one specific classroom habit – to see if this would help teachers to hone their practice.

However, by the end of that year, the working group could see that some teachers were struggling to see how everything fitted together and that there had been a loss of overall focus on L@SL. At the first professional development session of the next

---

3   Bob Burden, What is a Thinking School? *Creative Teaching and Learning* (2010), 1(2): 22–26. Available at: https://socialsciences.exeter.ac.uk/media/universityofexeter/collegeofsocialsciencesandinternationalstudies/education/research/groupsandnetworks/cedu/downloads/publications/What_is_a_Thinking_School.pdf; and https://socialsciences.exeter.ac.uk/education/thinkingschools.
4   Edward de Bono, *Edward de Bono's Thinking Course* (London: BBC Active, 2006).
5   David Hyerle, *Visual Tools for Transforming Information into Knowledge*, 2nd edn (Thousand Oaks, CA: Corwin, 2009).

academic year, teachers engaged in an exercise which helped to refocus them. They were asked to write down and complete these statements on two separate sticky notes:

I teach because …

L@SL matters because …

These were displayed on a wall in the staffroom and everyone was given time to read them. Jann says:

> It was a small thing, but it turned out to be very powerful as it invited everyone to tap into their own commitment to teaching and to the frameworks and practices of L@SL.

In the same session, the teachers created their own templates for lesson design. Initially, James Pietsch had developed a template based on Guy's lesson design: framing learning intentions, orchestrating the learning activity, understanding the learning, and then planning the learning (see Figure 8.2). Teachers developed a variety of visual tools that they could draw on in designing their lessons (for examples, see Figure 8.3 and Figure 8.4). Teaching sprints were relaunched with a much tighter focus on the development of learning dispositions. The idea was for teachers to make minor changes to their teaching that would see incremental changes in learning. Teachers have found the focus on small steps very helpful for sustaining change. One of the learning mentors commented:

> I think we understood the value of L@SL in terms of improving student outcomes, but the focus on improving our practice was yet to be fully understood. The introduction of teaching sprints helped to bring attention to this. The message of "small steps" has helped to build confidence and engagement.

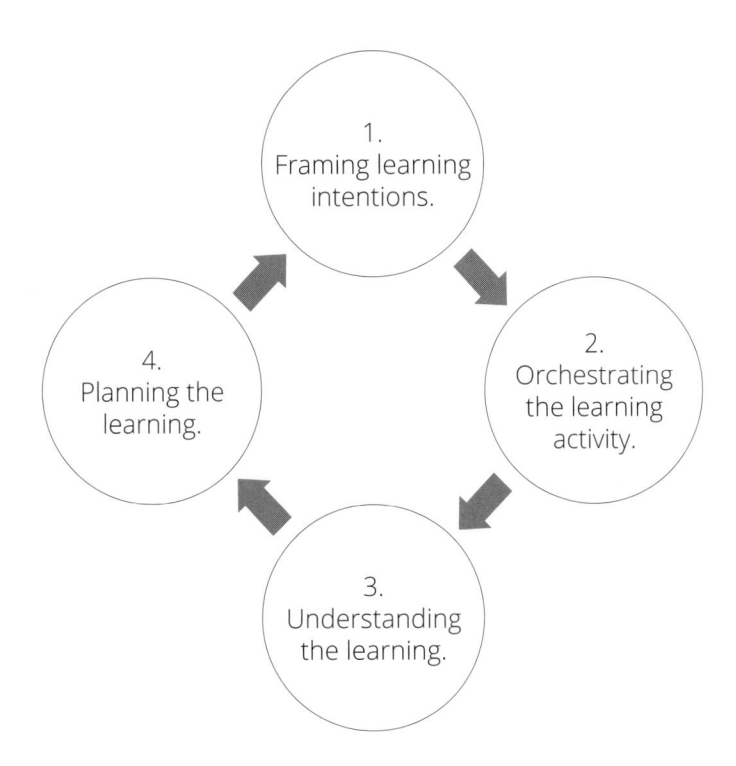

Figure 8.2: Learning Design Cycle

1. Framing learning intentions.
2. Orchestrating the learning activity.
3. Understanding the learning.
4. Planning the learning.

On top of their internal reviews, St Luke's has run three conferences to showcase their progress, which has helped to maintain their momentum. The conferences are open to teachers from other schools, and all staff at St Luke's attend. Guy has been a keynote speaker at each of these, offering new inspiration and strategies. It helps teachers to have a sense that what they are doing fits into a global shift in education and that their work is worthwhile and at the forefront of change. In addition to the keynote address, Jann gets a good many of her teachers to run workshops for the visiting delegates to showcase the LPA work that they have been doing in their classrooms, and this helps them to reflect on and appreciate the changes that they have made – as well as adding a bit of pressure to show the school and its innovations in a positive light!

At Norwest Christian College the model has been kept fresh by the three-year plan: an easy one-page document to which all staff have access. It details their aims clearly

Virtues and character traits
What virtues associated with learning character are promoted by this activity?

Content
What content are we expecting students to grapple with through this learning activity?

Learning dispositions
What learning dispositions are we hoping students will strengthen through this activity?

How does learning this particular content support the development of character?

How does the particular learning disposition relate to the virtue or character trait?

How does the learning activity support the development of learning character and understanding?

How does the learning activity link the content and the learning together?

Learning activity

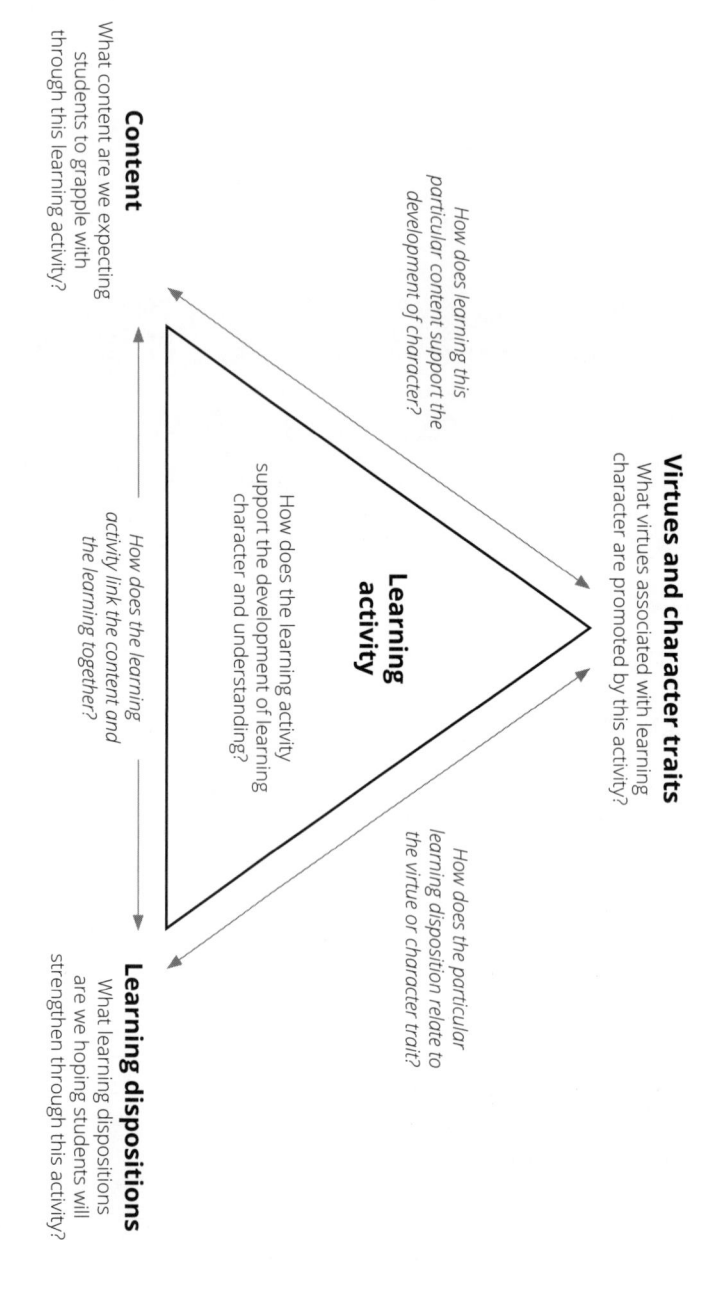

Figure 8.3: Learning Design Triangle

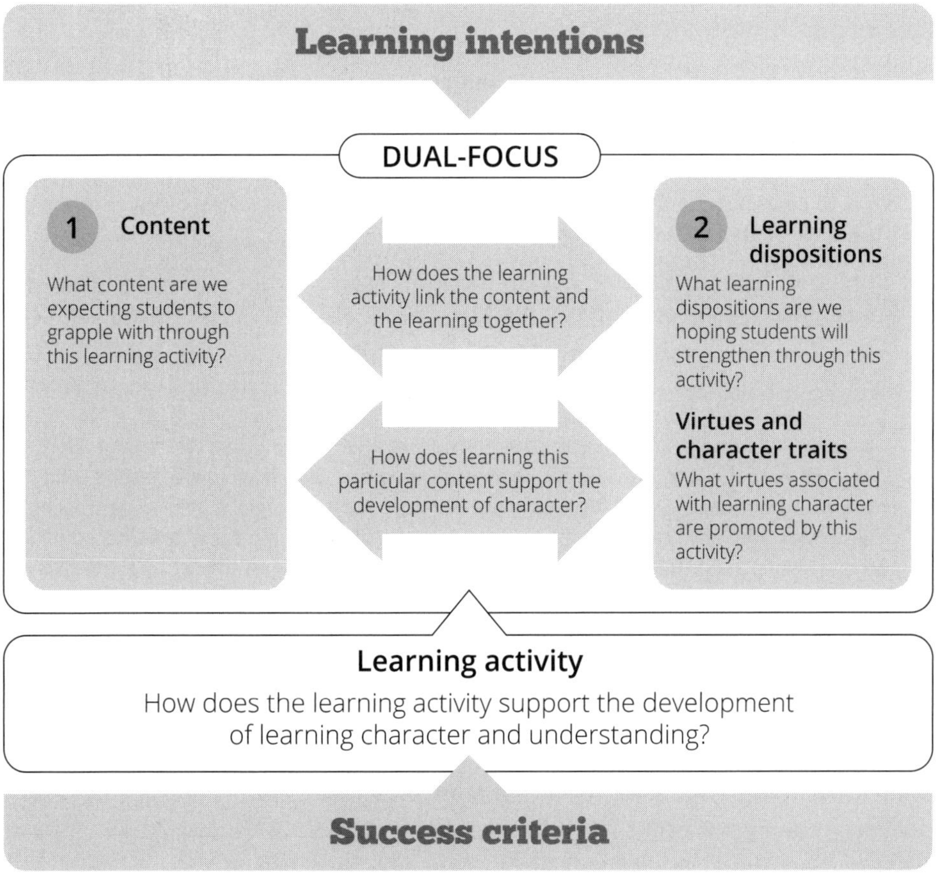

Learning intentions

DUAL-FOCUS

1 Content
What content are we expecting students to grapple with through this learning activity?

How does the learning activity link the content and the learning together?

How does learning this particular content support the development of character?

2 Learning dispositions
What learning dispositions are we hoping students will strengthen through this activity?

Virtues and character traits
What virtues associated with learning character are promoted by this activity?

Learning activity
How does the learning activity support the development of learning character and understanding?

Success criteria

Figure 8.4: Dual-Focus Lesson Design

under the headings: vision, research, review, goal, measure, and plan. It is reviewed and updated each year with input from teachers and students. They check that the stated priorities are still appropriately challenging, and amend them if not. Principal Felicity Marlow realises that it is not enough to merely ensure that targets have been met; she wants a deeper, more thoughtful review of what developing a learning-focused culture really means. She says:

> This shift in focus has reignited the teachers' curiosity around the framework, allowing them to view it from a new perspective. It has released staff from the tyranny of a checklist approach to teaching and learning (i.e. ticking off a range of techniques that align with the framework) and made them think more broadly about what they are doing to contribute to the growth and development of learning-focused students and a learning-focused culture.

Many schools have found that having a critical friend can boost engagement and deepen practice. In Chapter 10 we will look at how Sandringham did this with the contribution of personnel from Whole Education. But here, let's first turn our focus to Mark Fenton's reflections on his experience at Dr Challoner's Grammar School:

> It is generally a challenge to keep an initiative like this growing and deepening. That is why we kept drawing on Graham Powell as our consultant. If we were getting a bit stuck, we would have him in for a day, and he was always very good at helping us see new perspectives and fresh possibilities. He would rally us up a bit and then we could see interesting ways forward. I'd strongly recommend finding a critical and creative friend like that.

At Wren Academy, the SLT could see that after the first two years the initial intensity of the BLP focus was declining. They introduced a tightly prescribed set of activities each week, covering the seventeen different learning habits and the different aspects of what BLP calls the "teacher's palette" – all the little things that teachers can tweak in their behaviour. The move towards a more prescriptive model meant that tightly designed training was needed, and the increased precision of the discussion topics in SLT reviews ensured that more focused discussions were taking place.

Having begun with a founding cohort of just Year 7 students, Rachel Macfarlane and the staff at Isaac Newton had to think about what the BRIDGES concepts should look like as learners get older and progress through the key stages. Rachel reflects:

> As the school launched its new Year 10 in 2015, the SLT reflected on whether the existing model was still fit for purpose as students got older. Following the regular cycle of reflection on what works well and even better ifs, including feedback from all staff,

we modified BRIDGES mentoring for the new Key Stage 4 students, making it more specific to the experiences that they would have: preparing for work experience, GCSE exams and sixth form learning, and thinking about managing their own well-being. As the school prepared for the launch of its sixth form in 2016, a volunteer group of staff again explored what BRIDGES should look like at that stage. As a result, a mentoring programme has been introduced in which students have regular one-to-ones with their form tutor, during which they identify their strengths, targets, and specific areas for development.

Wondering

What are the common ideas for maintaining momentum? Would any of these work in your school?

Who might you use as a critical friend?

What deliberate steps could you take to focus teachers' practice?

How Can You Develop and Distribute Leadership Capacity in Other Members of Staff?

Broadening the group that leads on the LPA is a very common practice. Not only does it help to embed the LPA more deeply, it also helps to build a team of educators who don't just implement it; they own it. While many school leaders have started by recruiting sympathetic members of the SLT, they have often realised the benefit of developing classroom teachers as leaders. This was the case, for example, at Sandringham, Oaklands, and St Luke's. Teachers were identified due to their openness to experimentation and willingness to share what they were doing. The SLT worked with them to grow their capacity to lead.

At St Luke's, the leadership capacity of the working group had to be given some focused attention. The group was assisted by an outside consultant, Simon Breakspear, who helped them understand the complexities of leading change and worked beside them to develop a delivery plan. At each meeting, the plan was reviewed and next steps decided upon. The group is now able to do this work unaided. When the learning mentors were appointed, the same pattern was followed. Simon helped them to appreciate the challenge of leading their peers. Jann comments:

> I wanted to develop the learning mentor role to try to spread the framework further. Initially the role was about inducting new staff, but it soon became clear through listening to them that their role could be broadened. In broadening the mentor role, we have built their capacity to lead and they have appreciated the investment made in their development.

The mentors now lead the PLGs and parts of staff professional development days, trial new protocols for learning walks, and suggest readings for the PLGs. There is a commitment to their ongoing training. They meet regularly with the new dean of professional development and learning, Alma Loreaux, to reflect and plan. To build leadership capacity in the staff, more teachers have been asked to lead PLGs – of course, with the necessary training and support. Building the capacity of such a significant number of teachers has resulted in a greater appreciation of the complexities of leading a school.

There is an obvious downside to capacity building, which is that staff are often then ready and able to seek promotions elsewhere. This has been the case at St Luke's, where three members of the working group have left to take up SLT roles in other schools. This is echoed at Dr Challoner's, where building leadership capacity has also brought with it some instability. Mark Fenton comments:

> I did think about how to make the LPA "future-proof" by developing the leadership capacity of staff members. The problem is, as always, that having done that, they are likely to start applying for other jobs and then leave! It is a real challenge.

Despite this, broadening leadership capacity has the benefit of creating greater, dispersed ownership of the LPA. It helps to embed it into the bone marrow of the school.

How Can Students Become the Carriers of the LPA Culture?

Students can become a powerful resource for sustaining and deepening the culture shifts. They quickly pick up the language for learning and apply it both inside and beyond school. Many schools tap into the student body to help them reflect on how to improve learning. They also have a valuable role to play in mentoring new students and speaking with parents and visitors to the school. Some schools have made use of existing student councils, while in others – as we saw in Wren Academy – groups of students have been convened to review the way in which the LPA is working.

The staff at Isaac Newton Academy take feedback from students regularly. For example, the annual student survey asks about the BRIDGES framework. The SLT has involved high school students in the design and wording of their tools for learning – for example, the Key Stage 3 BRIDGES strength measure (an example of which is in Figure 9.4). When Jann Robinson visited Isaac Newton Academy in 2016, she met with a number of students who shared their understanding of BRIDGES and spoke passionately about why it mattered to them. They also said that their parents had chosen the school because it was about more than knowledge recall: it was about learning for now and for the future.

At Woolenwick Infant and Nursery School, the SLT gathers student feedback and responds to it. This was seen when the children wanted to have a party to celebrate being called "outstanding learners" in the school's 2017 Ofsted inspection report. The children also considered which dispositions are the most important ones for super learners to have, and this evolved into the creation, by the children, of "Super Learning Heroes". They designed a persona for each character and created bespoke capes, which they wore during project learning.

> *Did you know that I have every learning power there is? Actually, I do.*
>
> Alex, aged 4

At Maple Cross Junior Mixed Infant and Nursery School, modelling their ethos of "Reflect, Lead, Aspire", students are given meaningful leadership roles. This has seen them form a range of parliaments, councils, and focus groups, undertaking research that is related to the school improvement plan and sharing their findings with students, teachers, and governors. These activities are supported by Equipping Kids, a learning to learn organisation that aims to give children the skills they need to navigate their out-of-school lives.[6]

---

6   See https://www.equippingkids.org.

Hearing from students has always been an important part of deepening the culture of learning at St Luke's. From the beginning, a student coalition was set up to help teachers understand how they experience the learning. The students were very honest about how awkward the language for learning was at first, but they were also positive about how it was helping them. Each year, senior school students fill in surveys which ask them about their use of dispositions in class – which ones they are finding it easy to develop and which ones are harder. This information helps teachers to know which areas they need to target. They have meaningful suggestions too – for example, they recently asked if the diaries could be changed to make the descriptions of the learning dispositions more user-friendly.

Children in the junior school use the language for learning to describe when they are stuck. In assemblies, they can be asked to sit in the "hot seat" to be quizzed about the learning muscles that they are using. A parent recently shared how when they were getting annoyed with something, they said, "I give up." Then their young child piped up and said, "You mustn't give up; you need to persevere." These students are the carriers of the culture. Giving them a voice to talk about learning and their experiences of it has helped to build, sustain, and embed the culture over time.

> Giving them a voice to talk about learning and their experiences of it has helped to build, sustain, and embed the culture over time.

Summary

Throughout the chapter you have seen how leaders have worked to embed the LPA deeply in their schools. In some cases, this has led to refreshing the language, developing yearly plans for the next stage of development, and using small interventions to redirect the focus. In every school, capacity has been built in other leaders so that they can transmit the culture and the LPA doesn't rest solely on the vision of the principal. They have faced the challenge of a constantly changing school population by establishing induction procedures for students, teachers, and parents.

In each of our examples, students have developed powerful voices which carry the culture forward. Each of our leaders has considered the impact that the departure of the LPA champion (or champions) has had, or would have, and sought to overcome this through distributing ownership of the LPA. What has emerged is that the governors are crucial if the LPA is to survive after the principal whose passion and vision introduced and established it has left.

> **Wondering**
>
> What steps will you take to deepen the LPA in your school?
>
> How will you future-proof the cultural shifts that you have brought about?
>
> How might you work with governors to help them fully understand the LPA?

Chapter 9

Evidencing Progress and Progression

If you have read this far, it will be abundantly clear that schools which commit to the LPA make a significant investment of time and energy. In the preceding chapters you have read stories of leaders prioritising the LPA to the exclusion of all other initiatives for a number of years. So understandably, if you do embark on this journey, you will want to know that the LPA is having the desired effect. You and your governors will seek validation of the strategic direction in which you have chosen to take the school. You and your staff will want to know that your actions are leading towards your envisioned educational goals – producing the kind of learners described in your mission statement. Parents will seek reassurance that the school is developing holistic learners, as promised when they enrolled their children.

But how do you evidence this? There is no point in saying, "We want all our students to become more resilient", but having no idea whether this is happening or not. Or saying, "Our vision is for all our students to leave the school as self-regulating and independent learners", but not taking steps to assess the extent to which this aim has been realised.

So this chapter explores a variety of practical ways in which LPA schools have tracked character development and the acquisition of learning habits and dispositions. It addresses the following questions:

+ What is it appropriate to "assess", and which methods of "measurement" are valid?

+ How can learning power be evidenced in learners?

+ How can you engage the learners themselves in assessing the development of their learning power?

+ How can you measure the impact on staff?

- How can you measure the impact on parents?

- How can you know that your school has a well-embedded LPA culture?

But first, some notes on evidencing culture change. Some people have strong views about how to "evidence" the effectiveness of any proposed change in a school. They may insist that the only valid evidence, following the medical model, involves quantitative measures and sharp, randomised controlled trials, in which an intervention is pitted against a control condition that differs only in one specific way. This, they say, is the only way to tell if your proposed "magic ingredient" actually works. Of course, such tightly controlled studies are useful, but we don't think that they are the gold standard against which all other evidence must be weighed. Classrooms are not simple cause-and-effect places. They are complex systems that are "perturbed" by an innovation, but rarely in a straightforward or predictable way. So, as you will see, we favour and respect a wider range of evidence, and look to see if different indicators are pointing the same way. In that spirit, we offer these rules of thumb for tackling the vexed issue of evidencing:

- **Decide on "What for?"** The "best" kind of evidence depends on the purpose to which it will be put. A useful formative conversation with a student will need quite different "data" from a published article, as will a reflective discussion with governors or trustees about how well the LPA is going. So decide on who and what your evaluation is for and proceed accordingly.

- **Mind your language.** What exactly are you going to do? Measure? Assess? Evaluate? Evidence? Track? Demonstrate? Illustrate? Be careful that you don't slip into using the words at the start of that list by default, because they will trap you into looking for certain kinds of data that don't fit your purpose. We tend to use "evidence" (as a verb) because it is the most neutral, and leaves open the question of what kind of information will fill the bill.

- **Check out the options.** As you will see in this chapter, there are many ways of trying to capture the information that you need. There are questionnaires, observation schedules, digital tools, 360° appraisals, documental analysis, expert visits, video recording, and artefacts. So explore, and don't just assume that the first approach that comes to mind is the best one.

- **Don't forget to fatten the pig.** You do not fatten a pig by constantly weighing it. Some teams get very worried about how they are going to evidence the development of resilience, for example, and become paralysed. Remember that our first job is to find plausible, proactive things to *do* in our schools and classrooms that might help to develop those qualities. Evidencing should support that aim, not distract from it.

- **Ask the audience.** It's useful to know what teachers, parents, and governors think – but your best informants are probably the students themselves. Get them involved in the problem of how best to demonstrate that their learning power is strengthening and spreading into different areas of their lives. Not only will you probably get good ideas, but the activity will help your students to think about their own progress, and to identify areas in which they could improve.

What Is It Appropriate to "Assess" and Which Methods of "Measurement" Are Valid?

Evidencing the impact of the LPA is not as straightforward as measuring other aspects of educational provision. Infant children's reading skills can be assessed through phonics tests and high school students' numerical understanding with a maths exam. But there is no GCSE in resilience, and we wouldn't advise setting a test on self-regulation and awarding students scores out of 10!

Of course, schools which are serious about embedding the LPA keep a close eye on test scores and exam grades. They seek reassurance that conventional academic performance indicators are not suffering as a result of a focus on the LPA. Very often, in fact, schools which have successfully built the learning power of their students see their performance rising – for the reasons well covered in Chapter 2 – as was the case with the impressive exam outcomes at Wren Academy, which adopted BLP from its opening. Similarly, at Isaac Newton Academy, the outcomes at primary and high school level have been well above the national average every year, and the progress made by students over time by age 16 is consistently in the top 1% of all schools nationally (according to Progress 8 measures). Jackie Egan, head teacher of Icknield Infant and Nursery School in Hertfordshire, England, reflects:

> As well as having an impact on each child's approach to learning and character development, this work has had a positive impact on their progress. Since embarking on the BLP journey, our trend data for Early Years Foundation Stage, Year 1 phonics and end of Key Stage 1 SATs is one of steady and significant improvement.

And a similar picture has been seen at St Luke's Grammar School. Jann Robinson says:

> In the league tables, St Luke's has traditionally been ranked, on average, about 57th in the state. Over the five years of the LPA framework being in place, there has been a gradual lift in this ranking. In 2018 it was ranked 34th, and in 2019, 28th. While this was not the intention in introducing the L@SL programme, it demonstrates that a focus on learning has changed how the students approach the examinations and it has flowed through to their results.

However, an improvement in external data alone does not prove conclusively that the desired traits are becoming stronger. We know that cohorts change from year to year, and that the quality of the teaching team fluctuates as colleagues come and go. And, of course, it is perfectly possible to achieve better results through cramming for exams and teaching to the test. So, in addition to measuring the impact of the LPA through academic outcomes, our respondents have looked at a range of other indicators to evidence the effect of their learning-powered approach to education. They include:

- Student behaviours.

- Student attitudes to independent study and revision.

- Students' progression beyond school into adult life.

- The language used by students, members of staff, governors, and parents.

- Teachers' teaching styles and the sorts of activities taking place in the classroom.

- Parenting skills and learning activities that take place within the family.

We'll now dive into looking at how our case study schools have tracked the impact of the LPA. Tools used have included lesson observation; interviews with students, staff, and parents; less formal information-gathering activities to collect feedback and views; external reviews and inspections; and the creation of strength measures and progression trackers. Throughout, you might want to consider which methods you would want to pursue in your own setting.

How Can Learning Power Be Evidenced in Learners?

Student behaviours

Schools which have embedded the LPA over a number of years tell us that they have seen a change in the behaviours of their children. By this, they don't just mean that their learners are better behaved (although this is often the case!) but that they have acquired the behaviours of reflective and successful learners.

Usha Dhorajiwala at Woolenwick Infant and Nursery School offers interesting insights on this. The school serves a tough and disadvantaged catchment area in Stevenage, Hertfordshire. She says:

> In the early days, many children were disengaged from learning; there were a number of behaviour issues, particularly with certain boys. We had poor attendance and a high number of persistent absentees. Children were reticent, used limited language, and had little to say. There has been a gradual shift in culture. Now, children can talk confidently about their learning and show more independence when they become stuck. There are fewer tears. Children are engaged, excited, and enthusiastic about learning, bringing in things from home to complement projects and learning in class. The children embrace challenge and now perceive themselves as learners. This has resulted in improved attendance across the school and has also given our teachers more time to learn alongside the children, guiding them and extending their thinking. Quality classroom interactions have developed, allowing teachers to focus on learning behaviours as opposed to behaviour management.

Notice the link here between children developing the behaviours of effective learners and teachers enriching their pedagogy and involving the students in the learning process. We will return to this relationship later in the chapter.

For many observers, the change in students' attitudes and behaviour is tangible. You don't always need the numbers to tell you what's happening. For example, Mark Fenton, head teacher of Dr Challoner's Grammar School, told us:

> At Dr Challoner's we were actually rather wary, in principle, of trying to "measure" something as subtle and organic as the change of traits and attitudes in the students. But I do remember the many visitors to Dr Challoner's who expressed astonishment at how mature, reflective, articulate, and curious our students were. We would leave the visitors to talk with a group of boys and invariably they would later say, "Your boys are amazing." That was the best yardstick for me.

Similarly, Jann Robinson reflects on her experience at St Luke's:

> We are seeing a clear shift in attitudes in terms of how students approach challenges. Across the school, they are more engaged in class. When walking around, there is sense of deep engagement. This is not through classes being quiet, but through students being actively engaged in learning.

When a group of 8-year-olds were interviewed at Isaac Newton Academy about the impact of BRIDGES on them, it was interesting to note that many of them talked about changes in their character as well as in their learning habits. For example:

"Without BRIDGES I would be a meaner person."

"It encourages us to be more honest, creative, and resourceful."

"It has made me braver and more hard-working."[1]

Time and again, external reviewers have felt the need to note the positive attitude towards learning, and the effective learning behaviours, of students in LPA schools. For example, in the report following the inspection of Woolenwick in 2017, Ofsted reported on how the children encourage, support, and guide one another when they become stuck:

> pupils ... participate confidently and enthusiastically, contributing their answers willingly. They enjoy working with partners to develop their ideas and solve problems.[2]

---

1 The quotes from children here and on page 235 illustrate the kinds of vocabulary that is used in LPA classrooms to sharpen children's ability to reflect on their own learning. As you can see, even quite young children can become impressively proficient at using such terminology.

2 Ofsted, Woolenwick Infant and Nursery School: Inspection Report. Ref: 117323. 12–13 October 2017, p. 6. Available at: http://www.woolenwickinfants.herts.sch.uk/images/Ofsted%20Report%202017.pdf.

In the 2017 Ofsted report on Sandringham Primary School, the inspectors commented on the children's learning behaviours:

> Pupils are keen to work together and consistently show respect and tolerance. [...] They enjoy their learning and are quick to offer support and guidance to others in the class. Pupils are curious learners, who act upon the advice of teachers and show perseverance and resilience when attempting difficult tasks. [...] In particular, pupils work collaboratively, supporting each other as they attempt complex tasks.[3]

At Isaac Newton, the 2014 Ofsted report said:

> Students' behaviour in lessons is exemplary. They have a passion for learning, actively contributing to and supporting their own and each other's learning very well. [...] The unique "BRIDGES" programme and lessons develop students' knowledge, skills and qualities to support them in becoming effective learners, well prepared for the future.[4]

Articulacy about learning, and about their identity as learners, is a common characteristic in students who are well-versed in the LPA. Isaac Newton, for example, won the national Pearson 'Shine a Light' Secondary School of the Year Award in 2018 for the well-developed communication skills of the students.[5] And this verbal articulacy is, of course, needed if adults and children are to engage in productive dialogue about the learning process. Usha Dhorajiwala says of the 4–7-year-olds at Woolenwick:

> At the start of each lesson, children consider which learning behaviours will be most helpful. Throughout the session, children and educators may draw attention to particular learning behaviours in action and, at the end of each lesson, children are asked to reflect on which learning behaviours they used and which were the most supportive.

The infant children are co-planning and co-reviewing the learning process with their teachers.

---

3   Ofsted, Sandringham Primary School: Inspection Report. Ref: 130381. 23–26 May 2017, pp. 1, 5, 7. Available at: http://sandringham.newham.sch.uk/wp-content/uploads/2017/10/Ofsted-Report-2017.pdf.
4   Ofsted, Isaac Newton Academy: Inspection Report. Ref: 138518. 5–6 June 2014, p. 1, p. 6. Available at: https://files.ofsted.gov.uk/v1/file/2400094.
5   See https://schoolsweek.co.uk/winners-of-sixth-annual-shine-a-light-awards-revealed/.

> # Wondering
>
> What behavioural changes would you expect to see in learners once LPA was embedded in your school?
>
> How would you measure this?

Student attitudes to independent study and revision

Learning-powered students should be better able to cope with the pressure of tests, prepare for exams independently, and manage stress levels. But, in the real world, this is not always easy to achieve. Malcolm White is very explicit about the issues that they faced at Leventhorpe School:

> The initial aim was to break the spoon-feeding culture and shift the focus from teaching to the test. In this respect, we have been partially successful. After nine years of working on the LPA, students are more resilient, they are more equipped, and they can manage their learning better than our students could ten years ago. However, they still want staff to cram them with the exam skills and knowledge that will help them to achieve the highest grades. Parents want this as well. Staff are reluctant to let go and will still teach to the test. In some respects, this is inevitable and part of the system in which we operate.

There is a salutary reminder here of the questionable influence of national accountability frameworks on the priorities of many adults and students.

Year 2 children at Woolenwick (like the Year 6s at Oaklands Primary School who we mentioned earlier) now tackle SATs papers with more confidence, attempting more questions and applying their reasoning skills more effectively than they did prior to adopting the LPA.

At St Luke's, the Year 12 students sit a high-stakes examination each year. Jann Robinson says:

> Since we started using the L@SL framework, the most noticeable difference has been in how the students approach this examination. Within two years of the framework being

in place, students have shifted from being focused on the mark to asking what they need to do to improve. The students have taken the initiative to develop study groups, to share notes, to teach each other, and to promote a climate of learning. They have realised that by working together, they all improve their understanding.

Anecdotally, we have seen fewer students being stressed by examinations. Students have been assisted to understand the distinction between "learning mode" – where mistakes, and seeking help to correct them, are to be expected – and "performance mode", where you are on your own and trying as hard as possible to be error-free.[6] They know that they will experience stress in performance mode and that this is normal and not something to get more stressed by. These insights have helped them to recognise and manage the stress of examinations.

Students' progression beyond school

Helping young people to develop learning dispositions and character traits that will support them throughout their lives is, of course, the key priority for LPA leaders. At Isaac Newton the BRIDGES mentoring sessions for older students are used to support them in preparing for their work experience placements and for Key Stage 4 to Key Stage 5 transition (moving into sixth form). Mentors encourage the students to identify the learning habits and behaviours that they will need to utilise to study at this higher level, and to think about what the key learning challenges will be.

It is often hard for schools to maintain contact with students after they have left to join the world of work or to take up higher education or training placements. However, in 2017, staff at St Luke's sent out a survey to former students who, depending on their age, had been in the school for at least one year, and up to four years, while L@SL was in use. They were asked about their level of understanding of the framework, how they grew in their use of the dispositions at school, which dispositions had been easiest to develop, which had been harder, whether the dispositions had proved helpful in their transition from school to the next stage of their lives, and whether they still used the dispositions. The general trend was that the longer students had

---

6   More on learning mode and performance mode can be found in the earlier books in the LPA series.

been exposed to the framework, the more they understood it and the more they were still using it. Jann says:

> We continue to survey students. Each time, the responses are indicating that a consciousness of the dispositions required for being a good learner, and the opportunity to develop them, is linked to greater confidence in transitioning from school.

When students were asked about the extent to which the dispositions have helped them beyond the school gates – and, in particular, in taking their next learning steps – half of those who graduated in 2018 said that they had found the dispositions "helpful" or "extremely helpful". This is a positive start, but, of course, means that half didn't find them as helpful – clearly there is room to investigate how the framework can be tied even more explicitly to helping them develop as lifelong learners.

Wondering

How do you keep in touch with students once they have left your school?

What measures could you use to assess the long-term impact of the LPA on former students?

Have you used former students to assist with conveying messages to current students about the importance of developing great learning habits? If not, how might you do so in future?

Language used by students, members of staff, governors, and parents

Chapter 5 looked in detail at the ways in which LPA schools have worked to establish a learning-powered vocabulary and a common language for learning. But how do they evidence their success?

The head teacher of Icknield Infant and Nursery School, Jackie Egan, says:

> A definite strength of BLP is the common language used across the school. Although there have been the challenges of inducting new staff, children, parents, and governors into "the Icknield way", the underlying theme of a consistent use of language has always persisted. There have been periods of revisiting and re-establishing expectations, but the consistency of language in the past two years has demonstrated how strong BLP and character education has become at Icknield, as with so many new teaching staff, it could quite easily have slipped away – but it didn't! This is partly due to the children keeping it alive. Parents contribute to this too.

In June 2019, a group of 8-year-olds at Isaac Newton Academy were interviewed to gauge how well they understood the learning dispositions and character traits included in the BRIDGES framework, and the extent to which they naturally used the LPA language. The Year 4s reflected articulately on their strengths. Different children said:

> "I'm strongest at self-discipline because I'm very organised and love to learn. I'm very diligent in class and manage distractions and self-regulate."
>
> "I'm most confident with resourcefulness because I like making connections and am always asking questions in class."
>
> "Some people know a lot about it and feel confident with it. Some can do it themselves a bit. Some need a lot of support. Some need a bit of support. I'm most confident with my bravery."

At Sandringham, word cloud software has been used to analyse the language used on the school website and in school policies, staff handbooks, and other key documents. This software creates a visual image of all the words included in each document. The larger the word, the more times it is featured. This is a great way of monitoring whether the LPA has truly infiltrated all organisational aspects of the school. Gemma Goldenberg says:

> The wording used in these documents should mirror the language for learning being promoted among staff and students and should, of course, reflect the school's vision. Measuring the extent to which it does, and how this changes over time, is one way of evidencing progress.

But, of course, these tools only show that the documentation is "talking the talk". To check whether the LPA is making a difference to the way in which students actually go about learning, other methods will need to be used as well.

> **Wondering**
>
> How would you assess the extent to which your school community has established a common LPA language?
>
> Does consistent use of the language for learning prove that the LPA is well-embedded in a school?

How Can You Engage the Learners Themselves in Assessing the Development of Their Learning Power?

Key to determining the extent to which the LPA is impacting on students is collecting feedback from them directly. At Sandringham, staff regularly ask children, "What does good learning look like?" and "What do good learners do?" The words and phrases given in response are collated and then tallied to show how many times children within each year group mentioned the same thing. The resulting lists are then turned into word clouds, depicting what each group believes good learning to be at that moment in time. The word clouds are an easy way to compare views about learning between cohorts, and to monitor the progression and understanding of the same cohort over time. They can also be used as a benchmarking and comparison tool to measure the impact of particular initiatives: i.e. by comparing the results before and after.

The first time that this activity was undertaken at Sandringham, it revealed that some of the younger children had confused good learning with compliant behaviour. The largest words and phrases in the word cloud were "sit quietly", "hands up", and "don't call out"! This enabled the teachers to reflect on the behaviours that they paid most attention to in class, and to adjust what they noticed and praised. Teachers began noticing and acknowledging children for being independent, collaborative, and resilient. Some teachers appointed children as learning mentors to look out for these learning behaviours in the classroom and report back at the end of each lesson. Figure 9.1 shows the word cloud created the following term, demonstrating that these character traits had been assimilated by the children, who by then had a clearer idea of what good learning is and how they could practise it.

Word cloud containing: helpful, respectful, practice, listening, polite, hard-working, teamwork, engaging, share thoughts, positive attitude, reflective, concentrate, curious

Figure 9.1: An Example of a Sandringham Word Cloud

At Isaac Newton, students reflect on how well they are developing the BRIDGES dispositions and character traits in preparation for their twice-yearly mentoring sessions. Adults mentor high school students, who, in turn, mentor their primary counterparts. These mentors can gauge how well these habits are developing in their mentees by comparing their presentations and the subsequent discussion from one session to the next. In the high school phase, they record a comment at the bottom of the mentoring pro forma and a copy goes to their tutor and parents (see Figure 9.2). In the primary phase, teachers support students in filling in their BRIDGES books.

Strength	Evidence
Energy	Since the last BRIDGES session I've started being more energetic, and I've started focusing my energy into different activities - e.g. student librarian (show badge). So now when it comes to enrichments, I'm ready!
Organisation	Now at school I'm completely organised, and at home. This is because I've made an A3 timetable of what independent learning I'll do (show timetable). And because I'm so organised, I've only had one detention!
Experimenting	From the start of the year I've started practising different techniques for independent learning, so now I'm experimenting with different things - e.g. mind maps and revision cards (show example of revision task).

Target	Action: behaviours I need to develop/display
Self-regulation	I feel that I need to improve my self-regulation skills. I think this because when I get distracted by friends I don't always complete work. So I need to improve these skills, and I can complete work at break.
Questioning	I feel like I need to improve my questioning skills because sometimes when it comes to independent learning I don't ask questions about it if I'm curious, so I don't always understand. To improve I will ask more questions.

Listening	I think I need to improve my listening skills because I sometimes interrupt in form. I also need to improve because I don't always listen to people's opinions. To improve I will try to focus on my listening skills and ask myself if what I am going to say is relevant.

Final comment **Mentor name:**	A well-presented, thorough, and thoughtful discussion based around strengths and targets. Mentee sat up straight and explained clearly and concisely and it was a real pleasure to talk.

Figure 9.2: BRIDGES Mentoring Session

Likewise, at Sandringham, the children make a judgement three times a year on how they are performing against the school's desirable attributes for learning. They write about this and their reflections are shared with parents in school reports. The school's monitoring cycle includes a focus on asking the children how they are using the attributes in their learning, including asking them to articulate what they need to do next to develop as learners. We can see how dialogue with the children is built into many feedback processes, in small but powerful ways.

Many schools ask their students to complete questionnaires to gain feedback on the LPA. If the same questions are asked at regular intervals, say annually, the responses can be compared to gauge change over time. Alternatively, students can be asked to reflect on differences in their behaviours and skills as learners. At Walthamstow School for Girls, students were routinely asked to complete questionnaires to help the BLP coordinator and working group to assess the effect of the initiative in the early days. An example of the analysis from one such questionnaire – conducted back in February 2006, relatively soon after the introduction of BLP – follows. You will see that the questions were probing and sought honest and objective feedback, which could be used to assess the current picture and action plan for future improvements.

Findings from Walthamstow's Year 7 BLP questionnaire

The following is an analysis of the responses of 113 students (all Year 7 students who were present on the day that the questionnaire was administered, minus students with SEND who had assistance to complete a simplified version).

Students were asked what the initials BLP stand for. All 113 could answer correctly. The majority, 88 students, could explain clearly and accurately in their own words what BLP is all about.

The students were asked to list and explain the seven learning muscles that they had worked on to date. Seventy-five students listed them all correctly, sixteen got 6 correct, ten identified 5, six students named 4, and four students listed 3. All but nine of the students could confidently describe the learning muscles that they identified.

The students were asked in which lessons BLP skills and dispositions were being addressed. The responses were as follows, the number indicating how many girls listed that subject: English 52, humanities 45, maths 43, drama 30, science 6, Spanish 4, craft, design, and technology 4, PE 2, assembly 2, art 2, music 2, food 2, textiles 1, personal, social, health, and economic (PSHE) education 1, while nine said it was in all subjects and five gave no response. The students gave clear and relevant examples of how BLP was being addressed in a variety of lessons.

The students were asked which of the learning muscles they had got better at as a result of BLP. Perhaps because of the wording of the question, most girls named just one. The results were as follows: managing distractions 28, planning 20, imagining 17, listening 14, questioning 13, empathy 12, reviewing 5. Two girls said none and eight left this question blank.

In response to the question "Has BLP helped you become a better learner?", seventy-four replied yes and twenty-nine replied no. Two were not sure.

The following are examples of the responses given to the question "Has BLP changed you in any other way?"

- It has made me more organised.
- It has changed my attitude towards learning.
- It has increased my confidence.
- It has helped me to understand learning.
- I am better at thinking about how people feel.
- It has made me wiser.
- It has made me more responsible.
- I am a better listener.
- It has made me more aware of how important learning is.
- It's made me think more.
- No, I am still myself.

And lastly, here is a list of their ideas for making BLP better:

- Make it more fun. (30)
- More activities and games. (22)
- Outdoor learning. (8)
- Have the session at a different time – not Friday afternoon. (8)
- Less writing. (7)
- More group work. (1)
- Less frequent sessions. (1)
- More frequent sessions. (1)
- Less chat. (1)

> ## **Wondering**
>
> If you were the BLP coordinator at Walthamstow and you received this feedback, what might your reflections be on the impact of the initiative to date? What actions might you take to further embed it?
>
> What questions would you put in a student questionnaire to elicit honest and objective feedback about the impact of the LPA in your school?

Assessing how well students are embedding and extending certain learning habits can be tricky. Many learning dispositions can't easily be written into a "level ladder", from basic active listening to advanced, for example. With character traits it is even harder: how would you go about measuring levels of humanity or integrity? In fact, it is debatable just how possible it is for anyone other than the learners themselves to assess how their habits of mind are developing – sure, we can observe their external behaviours and appraise what they might be telling us, but we can't know how they are thinking. It is also important to remember that acquiring learning dispositions isn't a tick-box exercise: you don't lack the skill of risk-taking one day and then master it irreversibly the next. Learners need to understand that habits of mind can be developed to varying extents and depths. To this end, several of our schools have designed progress trackers or strength measures to assist learners in monitoring how habitually, instinctively, and independently they are utilising these skills.

Jann Robinson explains how this was done through the design of "learning progressions" at St Luke's:

> Learning progressions were developed by teachers during the first year of L@SL to describe how students' learning would be evidenced. In the senior school, the progressions have been used by teachers and students as a reflective growth tool. Initially, when students undertook self-reflection, we found that they tended to overestimate where they were in the development of the dispositions. By comparing their self-ranking with the teacher's ranking, this has given the students a greater understanding of what each disposition looks like when it is well-developed. Over time, students have become more accurate in estimating where they are at. The learning progressions are listed in their school diaries and at the beginning of each term, in tutor groups, they are asked to set a growth goal which they reassess at the end of term.

An example follows in Figure 9.3.

Absorption	
6	I become absorbed in learning on my own or in groups. When learning, I become unaware of events happening around me and I lose track of time. I can remain focused for a long time even after the lesson has ended and I help others to be absorbed in their learning.
5	I become absorbed in my learning on my own and in groups. I am not easily distracted by events happening around me as my focus is taken up by my learning. When distracted, I am able to focus again quickly.
4	I become absorbed in learning when I can block out distractions with some help from my teacher. I can be distracted by events happening around me and can focus again with assistance.
3	I become absorbed in learning, but have difficulty remaining focused for a long period of time. I am sometimes distracted and find it difficult to regain my focus.
2	I can be absorbed in learning activities, but often lose focus and can be distracted by others or my own thoughts.
1	I can focus on learning for a few minutes.

Figure 9.3: Absorption in the St Luke's Learning Progression Framework

Powering Up Your School

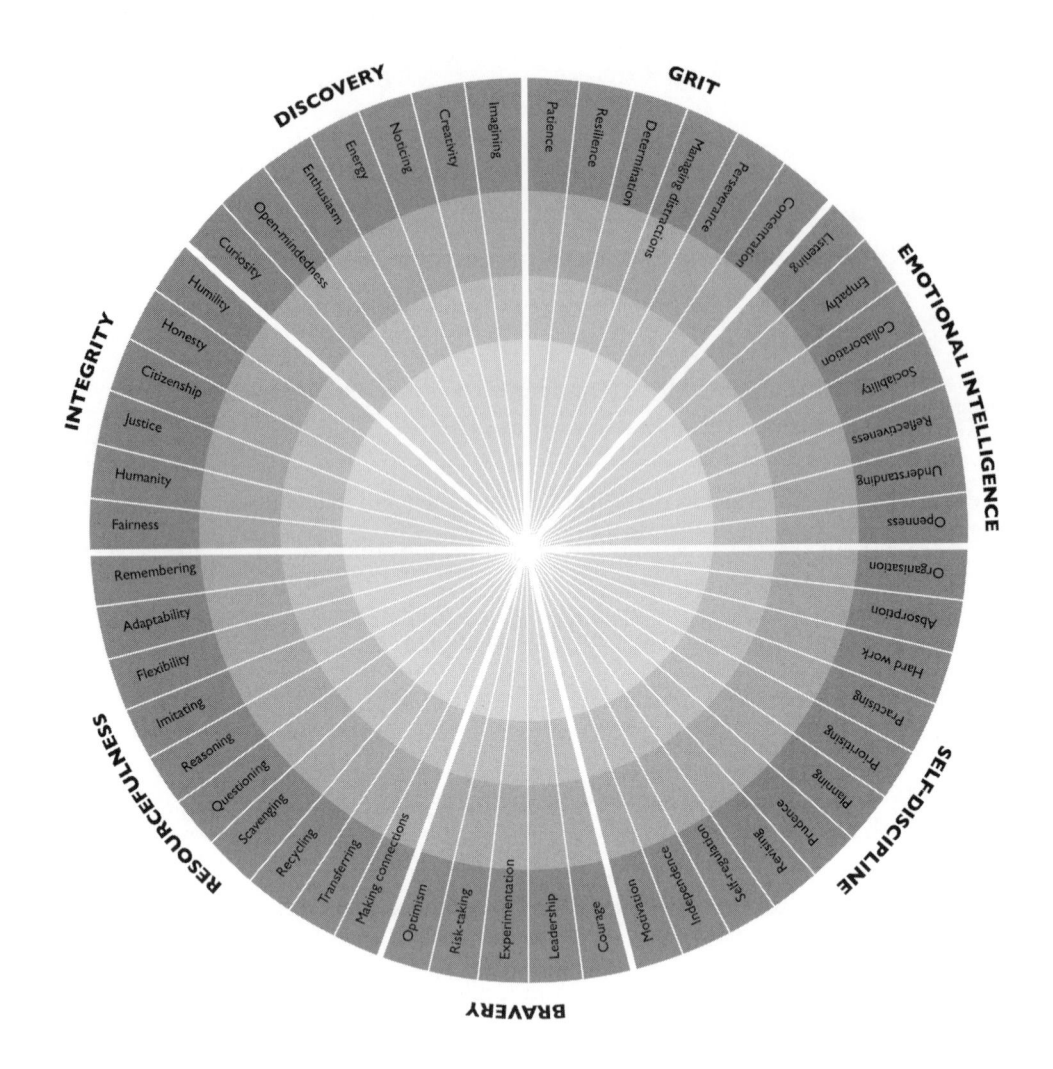

STRENGTH MEASURE

	1	2	3	4	
BREADTH	With adult direction	With adult support and reminders	With few prompts: Self-aware	Independently	**DEPTH**
	Use now and again	Use some of the time		Use habitually	
	In one subject	In several subjects	Widely used in school	Used out of school too	

Figure 9.4: BRIDGES Learning Power Profile and Strength Measure

244

In a similar vein, Jo Spencer, founding vice principal at Isaac Newton Academy, developed a strength measure to support the high school students in tracking how well their BRIDGES dispositions are developing. She says:

> We started work on the Key Stage 3 strength measure about three years into the BRIDGES programme. We wanted to create a tool we could use on a regular basis in BRIDGES lessons and also during mentoring sessions for self-review and as a prompt for discussion. I worked with a group of students from our founding cohort to try to describe different stages of their development of each of the fifty-two dispositions. We then devoted several staff CPD sessions to refining the statements. While the strength measure has evolved quite a lot from the initial idea, it's still imperfect. As it has evolved, we have played around with our descriptions of each stage of development. [See Figure 9.4.]
>
> When the Key Stage 3 BRIDGES strength measure was near completion, we shared it with primary staff and ran some training. They then worked on the wording of a primary strength measure for the seven overarching dispositions, using the early learning goals to support the development of the statements.

Figure 9.5 shows an extract about "noticing", which falls under the "discovery" arch of BRIDGES.

Noticing
Working beyond I am skilled at attentive noticing. I am able to identify significant detail, and perceive underlying patterns of connections and subtle nuances. I watch others carefully, notice how they are learning, and can emulate it. I use my noticing skills independently, at home and at school.
Working at I am learning to be more skilled at noticing and using this as a strategy in my learning. I have shown that I can really pay attention to something and make perceptive observations – for example, noticing patterns in a text or mathematical problem.

> **Working towards**
>
> When I am supported through questioning, I can make good observations which show that I am using my noticing skills, but I do not yet routinely and independently use them, so I still need to develop my noticing skills further.

Figure 9.5: BRIDGES Noticing Example

At the primary stage, there are comparable tracking tools in the students' BRIDGES books (with differentiated books for Years 1–2, 3–4, and 5–6). Rather than having a strength measure for each of the fifty-two dispositions in the BRIDGES wheel (as they do for high school students), there are seven – one for each main group of dispositions. We saw what "bravery" looks like back in Figure 3.1.

In their mentoring sessions, the students are assisted to assess themselves using the strength measure and to record how they use each disposition at school and at home. A Year 4 pupil said:

> You shouldn't just be using the dispositions at school; you should be using them at home as well. If you're not using them at home, you're not doing it as well as you could.

How Can You Measure the Impact on Staff?

There are many ways in which you can test the impact of the LPA on staff behaviours and attitudes. We have seen how the SLT at St Luke's undertook learning walks, asking students about the learning intention for the lesson and what success would look like. Such monitoring doesn't have to be undertaken by members of SLT, of course. At Wren Academy, students act as learning coaches to their teachers.

At Walthamstow School for Girls, Laura Fearon remembers:

> We were always evaluating BLP. I did a lot of evaluations with staff. We developed an online system which helped with this. It was useful for checking which of the habits we needed to go back over and which skills were less developed. You need to know what is working and what isn't.

Rather than creating additional monitoring and accountability systems, evaluation of the LPA can often be incorporated into existing practices. Gemma Goldenberg recalls changing the observation sheet used by staff at Sandringham as part of appraisals and standards monitoring:

> The sheet outlined what observers would be looking for in a successful lesson. After implementing the LPA, we reviewed the sheet because we realised that some of the points weren't really reflective of LPA principles – for example, "Children are on task throughout the lesson." We discussed how children could easily appear "on task" (for instance, by working quietly in their seats) without high-quality learning taking place. So we changed the wording to be more specific about how we want to see children challenging themselves, asking questions, and managing distractions.

Gavin Smith at Wren Academy reflected on the impact that weekly training has had on his staff as well as on the students:

> We are often asked whether we can prove that the training has been effective in developing better learners. To be honest, we have no evidence of the kind that would convince a hard-nosed sceptic. But what is abundantly clear is that colleagues regularly provide positive feedback about what they have learned through our home-grown CPD approach. Each triad has to complete a digital log each week, so we are able to monitor how the groups are doing and can, and do, intervene if they are not productive. And we get everyone to fill in a survey twice a year about how their triad is going – what's working well and any suggestions for improvement.
>
> We are sure that relationships between colleagues from different departments are unusually strong for a high school, partly due to their collaboration in the triads. In general, it is clear that the triads have played a big part in building this whole-school culture of openness and inquisitiveness about teaching and learning, and making sure that departments do not disappear into their own silos. Everyone feels like a full member of the school.

Likewise, Mark Fenton at Dr Challoner's is confident that engaging in learning reviews has had a significant impact on his staff:

> Staff feedback from participation in the learning reviews is consistently positive. Comments ranging from "reinvigorating" to "thought-provoking" are testament to the strength of the process in affording staff time to reflect on their own learning, their teaching practice, and the impact on their students' learning. Learning reviews are completely voluntary but over 90% of staff have signed up. Subject teams have overwhelmingly appreciated having the development time away from school to reflect on schemes of work and integrate the learning habits into the curriculum.

At Icknield Infant and Nursery School, Jackie Egan has seen a significant change in her staff:

> Our staff now seem more like-minded and, due to CPD and staff meetings, have a better understanding of our collective approach to supporting our children to become independent learners. Our most recent review from the local authority, in April 2019, states, "Positive attitudes to learning were seen throughout the school. Intensive work linked to Building Learning Power and Character Education helps to support the development of all students and this is reinforced by all adults."

Wondering

What systems do you currently have for monitoring and evaluating the quality of teachers' planning and lesson delivery? Could they be adapted to assess the impact of the LPA on staff?

What changes in staff behaviour would you be looking for to determine whether the LPA was having the desired impact?

How Can You Evidence the Impact on Parents?

You will have read in Chapter 5 about the ways in which our case study schools talk to parents about the LPA. Some have taken steps to gauge the depth of understanding that parents have and the extent to which that knowledge impacts on dialogue and parenting practice at home. A question or two can be included in the annual parent survey, but to take this one step further, it can be illuminating to interview learners and their parents about whether they use the LPA at home. However, gauging depth of impact is tricky. Chantou, an 8-year-old student at Isaac Newton Academy, is interesting on this point:

> My mum and dad say that I should use my "bravery" a lot. But they don't really understand what it means to me.

This would suggest that, while Chantou's parents know that bravery is part of the BRIDGES framework, more could be done to ensure that they are fully conversant with the ways in which the school is developing this disposition and confident as to how they can assist at home. Weekly top tips in the newsletter, a parent handbook, and regular parent workshops may not be enough, or perhaps they are not the most impactful strategies (although, as the saying goes, "every little helps").

Farhana Ali, a founding member of Isaac Newton staff, feels that the learners play an important role in increasing parental understanding:

> The majority of parents understand the LPA, yes. They've learned it from their children. And they have seen their child teaching their younger siblings. The children are the greatest teachers.

Chantou's testimony would support this:

> If my family go on a bike ride, I will say to my sister to use her perseverance because her bike doesn't have gears!

At Dr Challoner's, staff are starting to prioritise parental learning around the LPA. Mark Fenton says:

> Parental learning has been an important development, with many parents requesting to read our research. Feedback is extremely positive about the messages we send. Parenting courses and parental engagement are integral to further improvement in the school.

How Can You Know That Your School Has a Well-Embedded LPA Culture?

It is hard to put your finger on culture change. As we have seen, it is not something you can easily measure, or ever complete. However, the questions "Is it happening?", "How do we know that what we are doing is working?", and "Is everyone on board?" are important ones to keep in mind. One way in which to effect change – possibly the best way – is to build a culture of cumulative small acts of experimentation, coupled with continual honest reflection and discussion.

Here is what Hugh Bellamy has to say about his days at South Dartmoor Community College:

> At all the schools in the South Dartmoor MAT, we were continually reviewing teaching and learning, both within each school and, crucially, between them. We grew a culture in which it was just accepted that people were in and out of each other's lessons. Members of the SLTs especially were constantly dropping into lessons and having formative conversations with teachers about their practice. It happened, and people just got used to it. So we were continually getting a sense of how teaching was developing, and where the spots of real strength were, so we could nudge team leaders or heads of department in that direction. We also regularly had more formal reviews across the whole MAT, in which a team of SLT members from all the schools, plus some governors or directors and maybe some community members as well, would visit all the schools and compare notes.

The most honest and objective feedback can sometimes come from external reviewers. Confident school leaders regularly invite external experts in to examine practice, take soundings, and feed back a "warts and all" account of what they have experienced. Sandringham uses an external consultant who comes into the school to complete what is known as a "blink" – an in-depth look at one area of practice. Tessa Hodgson and her fellow heads in Ealing have set up cross-school peer review triads. Following this model, staff at Oaklands are also embracing peer review. Several of our case study schools have booked Guy or Graham to spend the occasional day with staff and students, to feed back on where the LPA culture is relative to other schools that they have observed. The advantage is that contacts between LPA schools can be fostered and follow up peer-to-peer visits arranged.

Establishing a well-embedded LPA culture takes time. Malcolm White at Leventhorpe School reflects:

> Ten years on, the school has a much stronger emphasis on learning and a love of learning. This is evident in lessons and in staff conversations. The culture and climate of the school is different. Lessons promote engagement and challenge, and this is a healthy development with positive outcomes. We never forced all staff to demonstrate X or Y in their day-to-day teaching. We provided core input, sold the strategy, trained champions, and raised the profile of positive practice. The soft sell worked for us as a school, but it meant that the pace of change at times was slow. However, teaching and learning are now prioritised as the most important issues and have been given significant CPD time.

Head teacher Hannah Trickett's reflections of change at Maple Cross Junior Mixed Infant and Nursery School similarly acknowledge the need to slow down the pace at times:

> There have definitely been pinch points when it has been necessary to ease back. Being a new head has also impacted on how much I can drive change and where my focus needs to be. With the staff recruitment crisis, it has also been vital to develop our teachers and ensure that there is not undue workload or pressure. One of my personal ongoing battles (I have not yet found the perfect balance) is between my aspirational high standards and not wanting to dictate my agenda without "allowing" teachers to flourish as individuals. With any new development there can be easy early buy-in, but continued support is the challenge. Returning to the LPA every few weeks in CPD sessions has ensured that there is a constant focus.

This is an important point. In some cases, establishing an LPA culture can be a relatively quick process, but maintaining it over time – inducting new staff, students, and parents, and keeping it top of the agenda among a plethora of other priorities – is much more challenging.

Malcolm White says of his experience at Leventhorpe:

> It has felt necessary to update and refine the strategy to stop some things going a bit stale. Yet innovation brings its own risks and not everything works. There is a distinction between innovating because there is a need for change and innovating to keep the culture vibrant. It was important for us to find fresh ways to enthuse staff and students.

At Isaac Newton Academy, Jo Spencer, founding vice principal, reflects:

> The LPA is an integral part of the school's culture. It's how we talk to students when they get things wrong or make errors of judgement, and how we support them to get things

right. It's how adults and students talk about how they learn. It's in the language we use when interviewing prospective staff. It was evident in the UCAS applications that our sixth formers (our founding cohort) wrote this year. It's how we behave towards each other and our cohesiveness as a community. But we haven't cracked it yet and our next challenge is to think about how to make the LPA fresh and relevant to our primary students as they move up into Year 5.

Guy and Graham's former colleague at TLO Limited, Maryl Chambers, has developed the Learning Quality Framework (LQF) as a rigorous tool for school self-evaluation that many leaders have adopted. This is designed as a formative tool to guide the strategic development of learning-powered approaches over a period of years. It embodies a progression through levels labelled Bronze, Silver, Gold, and Platinum. The process of audit, diagnosis, action, and review leads to an external assessment relating to the appropriate level, with recommendations for improvement towards the next level.

Whether schools have just embarked on the LPA or are well on the way and want to have their suppositions rigorously tested, they all seem to benefit from this way of looking at existing structures. And schools are reporting the benefit of the framework. A deputy head teacher at a high school in Solihull, near Birmingham, England, said:

> It made sense of my random thoughts. We had been struggling to think about what we needed to do next. We had lots of ideas, but they were random and disorganised. The framework has drawn these all together. It's the school's plan for the future.

As one primary school head teacher said:

> We have been working with learning to learn for a little while now, but it had started to fizzle out because we were unsure what to do next – how to grow it. This framework showed us what we need to do.

The LQF is divided into four dimensions comprising twelve principles that set the standard for a learning-powered school.

The LQF describes these principles in more detail in terms of thirty-three indicators, each presented at the four LQF levels to aid schools' self-evaluation and planning.[7]

---

7   For more on which, see: www.learningqualityframework.com.

Evidencing Progress and Progression

Principles	Indicator		
	Bronze	Silver	Gold
Commitment			
1. Vision for learning			
2. Framework for learning			
3. Language for learning			
Plans/strategy			
4. Leading innovation in learning			
5. CPD policy and strategy			
Action			
6. Curriculum design			
7. Teaching for a learning culture			
8. Learning from a learning culture			
9. Learner engagement			
10. Parents, governors, and community			
Evaluation			
11. Evaluating the impact			
12. Evaluating the learning organisation			

Figure 9.6: The Principles of the Learning Quality Framework

Source: www.learningqualityframework.com © TLO Limited, Bristol, and used with kind permission

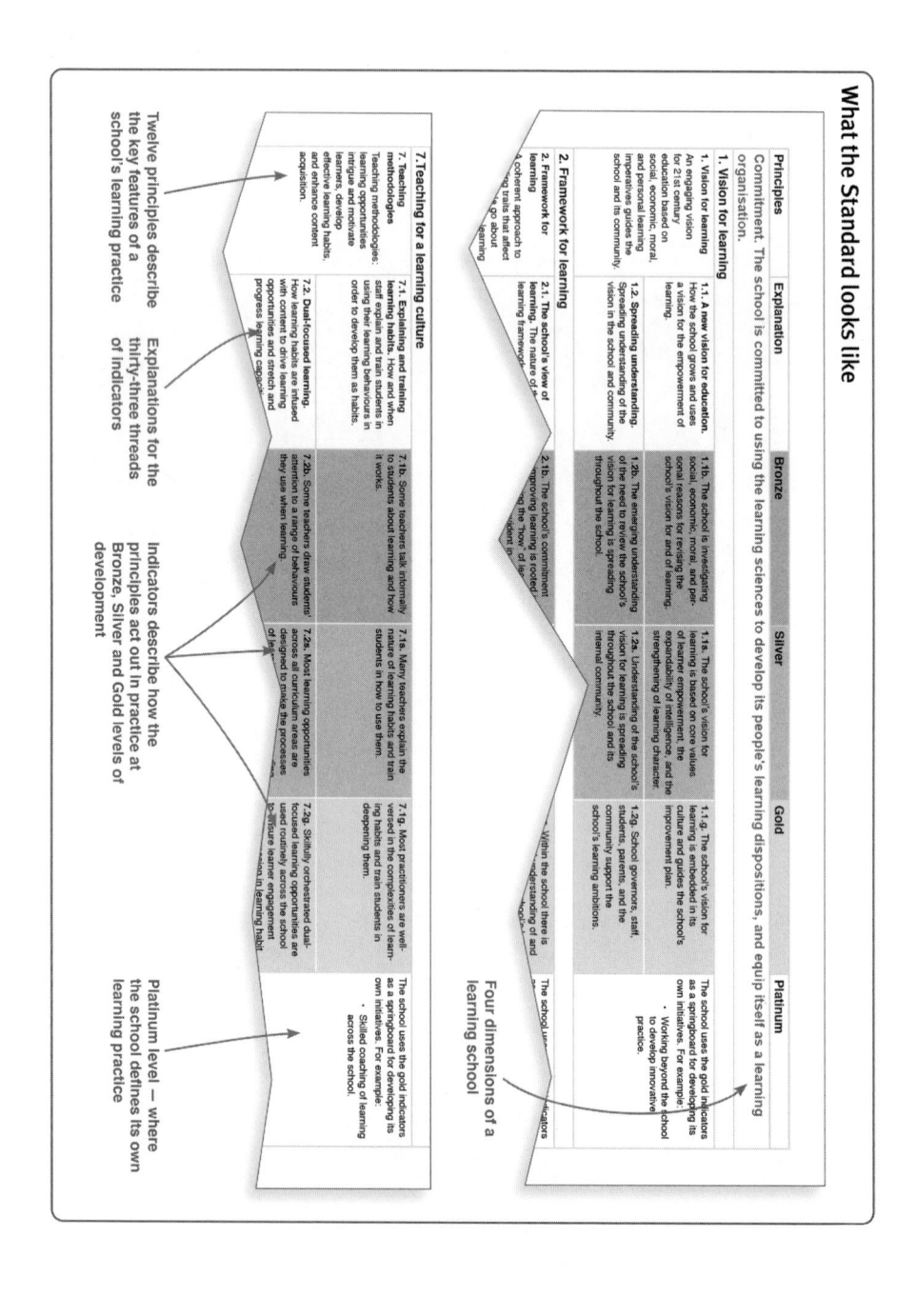

Figure 9.7: Extract from the Learning Quality Framework Standards

Source: www.learningqualityframework.com © TLO Limited, Bristol, and used with kind permission

Schools using LQF are provided with tools for auditing and surveying the attitudes of all their partners. The rigorous approach works well as a way of ensuring that the school asks itself hard questions about all those features that contribute to building learning capacity in young people. You might like to take a moment for a final reflection on your own procedures.

Wondering

What are your current procedures for school self-evaluation? Do they take as their starting point the quality of student learning and achievement?

Would all partners be able to give a simple explanation of your school's learning philosophy?

Would they be able to explain to a lay person what this looks like in practice?

Who conducts your school's internal evaluations: is it a top-down responsibility for senior leaders or are more partners – teachers, students, and parents, for example – involved in some way?

Would colleagues view your current approach as monitorial or developmental?

In what ways do you use your self-evaluation to assure improvement in the quality of learning?

Summary

We are very aware that demonstrating the impact of educational initiatives (the LPA included) over time, in a scientifically robust and valid way, can be problematic. There are so many variables in schools that it is hard to isolate individual factors and determine specific cause-and-effect relationships. For example, an improved attendance rate may indicate that students are enjoying lessons more as they become more engaged in their learning. But it could also be attributed to changing demographics in the catchment area, improvements in local transport routes, or more determined efforts on the part of attendance officers.

Added to that, many schools do not take stock of the state of affairs prior to implementing the LPA, so there is not a full and accurate picture of the starting point with which to make comparisons. Indeed, at Wren Academy and Isaac Newton Academy – both brand-new establishments – there was no existing practice with which to compare! We can only speculate as to how their learners might have turned out had the LPA not been part of the schools' DNA.

A lot of the evidence provided in this chapter has been qualitative. Those who are committed to the LPA will inevitably, you might say, point to the benefits and see only a positive impact. But we hope that you will agree that the schools have been robust and determined in their attempts to measure progress objectively, fairly, and thoroughly. In general, we think that seeking a mix of quantitative and qualitative indicators is most effective, and that evidence-gathering is most impactful when done formatively, so that tweaks and changes can be implemented speedily. Indeed, we'd argue that you've never really "finished" the LPA, in which case a summative judgement is neither helpful nor appropriate. The best approaches of all, we think, have students themselves involved in self-monitoring and at the centre of the tracking process. Once their voice is heard and respected – provided that they have the insight to give robust, honest, and accurate assessments – the data collected is invaluable for evidencing impact and determining next steps.

Chapter 10

Connecting with the Wider World

So far in this book we have focused largely on what is going on within the school. In this chapter we turn our attention outwards and look at the relationships that the school has – or could have – beyond the school gates, and how they can help to foster the development of a successful learning-powered culture. You don't want that gate to remain locked; you need to encourage people to get out and see what is happening elsewhere, and to welcome in people who might have different experiences or fresh eyes, even if the scrutiny may feel uncomfortable at first.

One of the main barriers to embedding a new culture is the invisibility of the existing one. Once you have been in a school for a year or two, the prevailing routines, attitudes, and habits just seem natural – or even inevitable. Culture is "the way we do things around here", and it's easy to lose sight of the many choices that have made it that way, and the many alternate possibilities that have therefore been excluded. So a major benefit of having relationships beyond the school is that it makes your own culture more visible to you, and thus you are more capable of questioning and developing it. New intakes of teachers – and, indeed, students – are also sources of fresh perceptions, waiting to be tapped. There may also be untapped sources of information and ideas from regular visitors to and friends of the school, such as governors.

When you become more conscious of the existing culture – the habits and practices that are typically taken for granted – you can see how bitty they are. Schools often become the way they are not as a result of a deliberate plan, but just as an accretion of separate initiatives, scattered among the traces of past personalities and earlier ideas. Unpicking this, and really thinking clearly about its own values and identity, enables a school that is embarking on its own heartfelt culture change process to be more discerning

> Schools often become the way they are not as a result of a deliberate plan, but just as an accretion of separate initiatives, scattered among the traces of past personalities and earlier ideas.

about what new initiatives – from government or from professional learning providers – to adopt, and which to ignore.

Being able to articulate, with clarity, your own cultural vision also makes it easier to identify like-minded schools and other organisations with which to collaborate, which is another massive benefit of reaching out beyond the confines of your own school. Here are some ideas to consider:

- For high schools, smooth transitions by sharing your philosophy and practices with your feeder schools or nurseries.

- For primaries, talk to the schools that your students will go on to, so that they are aware of the capacities for independent learning that your students will bring with them. Lack of awareness of the powerful learning that has gone on in feeder primary schools sometimes means that new Year 7 students are effectively "infantilised" by their high school teachers, meaning that their learning power goes unacknowledged and untapped. South Dartmoor Community College, for example, worked with its feeder primary schools to develop a kind of passport that children could work on in Year 6 – showcasing their learning strengths, passions, and achievements – which was then used in tutor time as a way for the new Year 7 classes to get to know each other and, more importantly, for teachers to discover just how mature and responsible these learners are capable of being – given the chance.

- Identify like-minded LPA schools and make exploratory visits. Having your imagination fired by hearing – and, even more potently, seeing with your own eyes – what teachers in schools like yours have been able to achieve is a powerful thing.

- Host reciprocal visits during which you can showcase your tried-and-tested LPA strategies and invite visitors to run CPD sessions about their own practices. Talking to visitors about your own LPA journey, and the successful tweaks that your school has discovered or developed, is a good way of crystallising your own understanding and commitment, and of building confidence, fluency, and a sense of pride in your staff.

- Join existing clusters, networks, and professional learning organisations which offer LPA-focused support, courses, and resources. All of these relationships tend to build courage and provide reassurance that you are on the right track.

- Keep your eyes peeled for good grapevine information about other mentors, trainers, consultants, and researchers who can provide high-quality LPA input, support, and critical friendship.

- Form your own clusters and "soft federations" to share good LPA practice and resources.

- Contact local initial teacher training providers to explore hosting school-based training, thus ensuring a regular supply of new teachers who are already schooled in the ways of the LPA.

- Attend conferences and workshops, and workshop the ideas gleaned with colleagues back at school.

- Scour the Internet for blogs and websites that could provide useful resources.

- If the situation warrants it, consider calling on regulatory bodies (such as Ofsted in England) to provide perceptive advice and guidance. (You may remember that Paul Jensen did just that when he arrived at Sunnydown School and found a big disparity between the unsatisfactory culture that he had inherited and the last rating given by Ofsted.)

With these potential benefits in mind, let us look at some detailed illustrations of these wider relationships, and so seek to answer three questions:

- How can you make best use of LPA-minded professional development organisations?

- How should you go about building your own LPA-focused network?

- How can you build an LPA alliance with parents?

How Can You Make Best Use of LPA-Minded Professional Development Organisations?

To begin answering this question, we're going to take an extended look at a case study of Sandringham Primary School.

Sandringham's search for supportive partners began with an itch that the SLT knew they needed to scratch. Gemma Goldenberg sets the scene:

> For a while, we had been feeling that we had been quite "piecemeal" in our approach to the development of teaching and learning. We'd taken inspiration from lots of different places and there were some great things going on across school. All staff had been trained in philosophy for children (P4C) and we'd also introduced Singapore maths after the head teacher had visited the country and been impressed with what he'd seen. I'd introduced a thematic skills-based curriculum, and the English lead was rolling out reciprocal reading. It was all exciting, and it felt right, but I struggled to articulate why we had chosen these ideas above others and what it said about our approach. It was all "good stuff", but we didn't have a coherent sense of "who we are" or where we are heading as a school.
>
> Before we opened the pre-school, the team put together a set of "pre-school principles" which outlined their shared beliefs about what pre-school education should be and why. These principles were to guide the design and creation of the new pre-school and ensure that new recruits would be on board with the ethos and values. It was at this point that it became clear that we needed the same thing for the primary school. It didn't matter that the school already existed or that we would be working retrospectively; it was about defining what mattered most to us and articulating the underlying vision and values that tied together all the different things we had put into place over the years.
>
> A member of the governing board, David Hall, offered to support the leadership to write, share, and agree the purpose, vision, values, and strategies (PVVS) for the primary school. David works in organisational development at a large financial services company and has a wealth of experience handling these kinds of discussions. He was adamant that this process should not change what the school was already doing but, rather, should capture the essence of the school in a way that could be shared both internally and externally.

To scaffold their thinking, David – together with the head teacher and the school business leader – signed up for an eighteen-month course with a London-based organisation called Whole Education.[1] The course was designed to support schools in creating their distinctive culture and ethos, with the emphasis on going beyond exam results and striving to develop knowledge, skills, and the qualities needed to thrive in life, learning, and work. Sandringham asked Whole Education to organise a review focused around two questions: "Are we delivering a broad and balanced curriculum?" and "To what extent are the children leaders of their own learning?"[2] After observing lessons, conducting learning walks, and speaking to staff, parents, and children, the review team then fed back their observations to the SLT. Gemma Goldenberg was leading on curriculum design and the LPA at the time. She recalls:

> The feedback was really helpful; a fresh pair of eyes and an outsider's perspective helped shed light on things which we might have overlooked. The conclusion was that there were many fantastic things happening across the school, but that, at times, it felt like this was due to chance rather than design. It made me realise that I needed to develop a more cohesive narrative around our curriculum. I realised that it wasn't just a case of me knowing why the curriculum was designed in the way it was, why we valued certain attributes, and so on: rather, each and every member of staff needed to be able to articulate our approach. We set to work on this as a school and it ended up being recognised as a real strength during the Ofsted inspection which took place later that year.

Guided by coaches from Whole Education, the school set about clarifying its purpose (a simple yet motivational high-level statement), vision (an inspirational statement that sets the bar high for what they want to achieve), values (timeless in their relevance, easy to recall, and useful for holding everyone in the school to account), and strategies (clearly set out high-level priorities which help the school to bring the purpose to life, achieve the vision, and stay true to the values). The PVVS process was a collaborative effort, involving everyone with a stake in the school, and it was important that everybody felt they had a voice. Head teacher Robert Cleary was struck by how powerful the PVVS could be with all stakeholders involved. He

---

1　See https://www.wholeeducation.org/.
2　For more on this theme, you might be interested in Ron Berger, Leah Rugen, and Libby Woodfin, *Leaders of Their Own Learning: Transforming Schools Through Student-Engaged Assessment* (San Francisco, CA: Jossey-Bass, 2014).

also learned how important it is that the vision reflects the needs of both the school and its community. Sandringham's PVVS ended up (after many revisions!) as shown in Figure 10.1. However, Robert cautions against casting these outcomes in tablets of stone. He believes that it is good to review and ponder at regular intervals, both when things are going well and when the school is struggling. As we have seen in other examples, it is good practice for all stakeholders – including parents and students – to be a part of the reflection on whether the school's PVVS still holds true and whether it is meeting its stated aims.

Our purpose:

To inspire and empower the next generation.

Our vision:

To be an outstanding, dynamic, and vibrant learning community.

Our values:

Children first.

Inquiring minds.

Agile to change.

Research-driven.

Nurturing well-being.

Our strategies:

Provide and deliver a holistic education.

Apply the pedagogy and research behind shared approaches.

Understand and provide for the needs of our children.

Seek out and deepen partnerships across our wider educational landscape.

Immerse our children in a mastery curriculum.

Purposeful professional development.

Figure 10.1: The Sandringham PVVS

Wondering

Are you happy with your existing vision and values, or is it an area which needs to be reviewed?

Could you have a go at writing your own PVVS following the process that we have outlined? Consider asking others in the school to do the same – perhaps a selection of support staff, teachers, and members of the SLT. How similar or different are their PVVSs to yours and to one another's? How can you use this information to evaluate the extent to which you have a shared understanding of your school's ethos and culture?

Are you able to use your school's vision and values to make decisions about which projects, initiatives, and opportunities to take on or continue with, and which to discard as not fitting with your purpose and aims?

Sandringham consulted with parents to elicit their opinions on what should be included in the PVVS; however, this did not generate the level of discussion that they had hoped for, and the SLT reflected on a number of possible reasons why. They concluded that they needed some external support to find more effective ways of engaging with parents and other community members. Because many of the Sandringham children are from Muslim families, they decided to team up with Maslaha, "an organisation that works to change and challenge conditions that lead to inequalities for particular (especially Muslim) communities".[3] Maslaha is now working with the school to help them to develop engagement strategies to encourage parents to play an active role in school life. Ideas have included gardening and cooking projects; inviting parents to planning meetings; discovering more about parents' skills and strengths; and designing, with the community, practical ways in which such initiatives can be used to connect the curriculum more strongly with the lives of the children and their families.

---

3 See www.maslaha.org.

Robert reflected that:

> One small but very significant change that has come out of the collaboration with Maslaha is that the school has stopped talking about "difficult to reach" parents and replaced this phrase with "easy to ignore" parents. The hope is that this will put the onus on the school to make and retain the links with these parents, rather than blaming the parents themselves.

A third organisation that Sandringham has involved itself profitably with is the London East Teacher Training Alliance (LETTA). It is always hard to recruit staff who have the skills, attributes, and attitudes to match the purpose, vision, and values of the school – especially when these are as ambitious as the LPA. It can be problematic when new appointments turn out not to fit, so if you can become involved with a school-based initial teacher training provider who shares your outlook, you may well be able to tap into a steady supply of teachers who already subscribe to the LPA. LETTA, under the direction of CEO Jo Franklin and supported by professional tutor Brigitte Boylan, fits the bill perfectly.

Sandringham has been involved in shaping the LETTA curriculum from the start, and takes a number of their trainees every year. LETTA trains more than forty teachers annually and has a good reputation in East London. The training includes sessions on the LPA – including evaluating the trainees' use of it – and school-based mentors will have received the same training, or might even have been LETTA trainees themselves. Sandringham always has a good pot to pick from when the time comes to recruit next year's intake of NQTs. In addition, school leaders can offer graduate teaching assistant placements, with support on offer if the graduates are then interested in applying for a LETTA School Direct place. Therefore, these heads avoid the last-minute scramble to fill positions that many other schools complain about. Through the partnership with LETTA, schools in East London are being proactive in attracting, recruiting, training, and employing teachers as part of a supportive network of like-minded organisations. In a period in which recruitment is becoming more problematic for school leaders, networks like this are important.

As you will see, Sandringham benefited significantly from reaching out to kindred organisations – in this case, Whole Education, Maslaha, and LETTA – but there are many others and we'd encourage you to explore what might be a good fit for your school. The next case study describes two such learning organisations that Guy and Graham have been involved with (and which we hope you will glean further insights from): the Expansive Education Network and TLO Limited.

> The Expansive Education Network is a professional learning network coordinated by the University of Winchester, with a number of university partners across England.[4] Expansive Education focuses on how to help schools and teachers to develop positive learning dispositions in their students – much like the LPA does.
>
> The network also provides practical training and mentoring support for teachers who want to undertake their own action research. This involves teachers planning a change to their practice, enacting the change, observing it carefully, and reflecting on the process. Changes are deliberately small and manageable. Results are shared with colleagues in the form of posters, presentations, and short reports. These are then uploaded to the website as useful materials for others to use. Teachers are invited to frame their enquiries in the format: "If I do X, will Y happen?" For example, "If we stop directly answering students' requests for help, will they become more resourceful?" or "If I devise a game to challenge students to ignore distractions, will their powers of concentration improve?"
>
> Professor Bill Lucas (who set up the network with Guy and has now taken over the running of it) has some further pointers for leaders of LPA schools:
>
> - Explicitly articulate a vision of expansive, powerful learning.
> - Put curiosity at the heart of all that the school does.
> - Identify and reward teams of teacher researchers and create time and space for them to work together.
> - Integrate the sharing of teachers' findings into the school's professional development programme.
>
> ---
>
> 4   See www.expansiveeducation.net.

Undertaking enquiry	Using evidence
Evidence-informed and research-engaged culture	
School-to-school professional learning communities	Annually updated research strategy
Embedded researcher	Research centre	Kitemark
	School-published research journal
	School-based programme of action research
	Research lead as member of SLT
Annual research conference	Active in researchEd
Teachers at master's level	Research bursaries
Instructional rounds	Small tests of change
Learning walks	Lesson observations	TeachMeet hosts
CPD on action research	Evidence digests	Toolkits
Book groups	Journal club
'Membership'	Termly seminar	CPD on using evidence

Figure 10.2: LPA Culture Change Strategies

Source: Expansive Education Network, used with kind permission of Bill Lucas

> - Make a long-term commitment to monitor and research aspects of the school's LPA culture change strategy and don't treat it as a short-term fad. Imagine moving from relatively straightforward changes, shown at the bottom left of Figure 10.2, to the deeper cultural shifts shown at the top right over the course of a few years.

Learning power reviews

Many LPA schools have benefited from external help in the form of learning power reviews. You will have read about the role that such reviews have played in schools such as Dr Challoner's Grammar School and Wren Academy. Here, let us say a little more about how they work.

Learning power reviews are designed to help schools identify two features of teaching and learning: first, examples of LPA-style teaching that already exist but which may have gone unnoticed or unidentified as examples of good practice; second, opportunities that teachers may currently be missing to improve the range and quality of their students' learning habits. The review helps schools to see what kinds of learning are going well, where they are happening, and how they might be extended and deepened, so that teachers can gain a more objective overview.

> Graham Powell, who has conducted many learning reviews at the invitation of schools as a principle consultant for TLO Limited, stresses that it is important to make sure – before the review begins – that teachers understand that this is not another form of appraisal. In any feedback, no teacher will be identified and anonymity is guaranteed. The focus is on how the *students* are behaving as learners in lessons, not (directly, at least) on the performance of the teacher.
>
> Reviews usually take place over a couple of days and involve a range of stakeholders. At Dr Challoner's, a team of four teachers and four students worked with Graham to develop a lesson observation schedule that focused on students' existing learning habits. By way of an example, here are a few questions that zoom

in on the extent to which students show evidence of being socially sophisticated learners, which illustrate the sorts of things that observers were looking for:

- Do students know when it is best to work alone or with others?
- Are they able to use a range of roles in collaborative group work?
- Do they listen to others carefully and try to understand how they are thinking?
- Do they know how to disagree respectfully in group discussions?
- Do they show sensitivity to group dynamics?
- Do they share useful learning habits and adopt them from each other?
- Do they give and take feedback well from each other?

In the Dr Challoner's review, they decided to focus on learning across just two school years – Years 10 and 12 – and observe a range of lessons across different subjects. Some of the teachers who took part were well-established while others were at the start of their careers. After an hour or so spent practising observing and noting what they were going to be looking for, observers made an initial visit to a classroom to make their observations, and then withdrew to discuss what they had noticed and sharpen their attention. Once their observation skills were secure, the team visited classrooms – usually in pairs – to gather further data about the use of learning habits.

At the end of the first day, observation sheets and rating wheels (see the examples in Figures 10.3 and 10.4) were examined for any emergent patterns about the learning in different subjects and in different key stages. These informed and refined the focus for the second day of the learning review, at the end of which a report was written that highlighted the patchwork of places where students are functioning as powerful and independent learners and where opportunities may have been missed. This then shaped the SLT's discussions about pedagogy.

Figure 10.3: A Rating Wheel

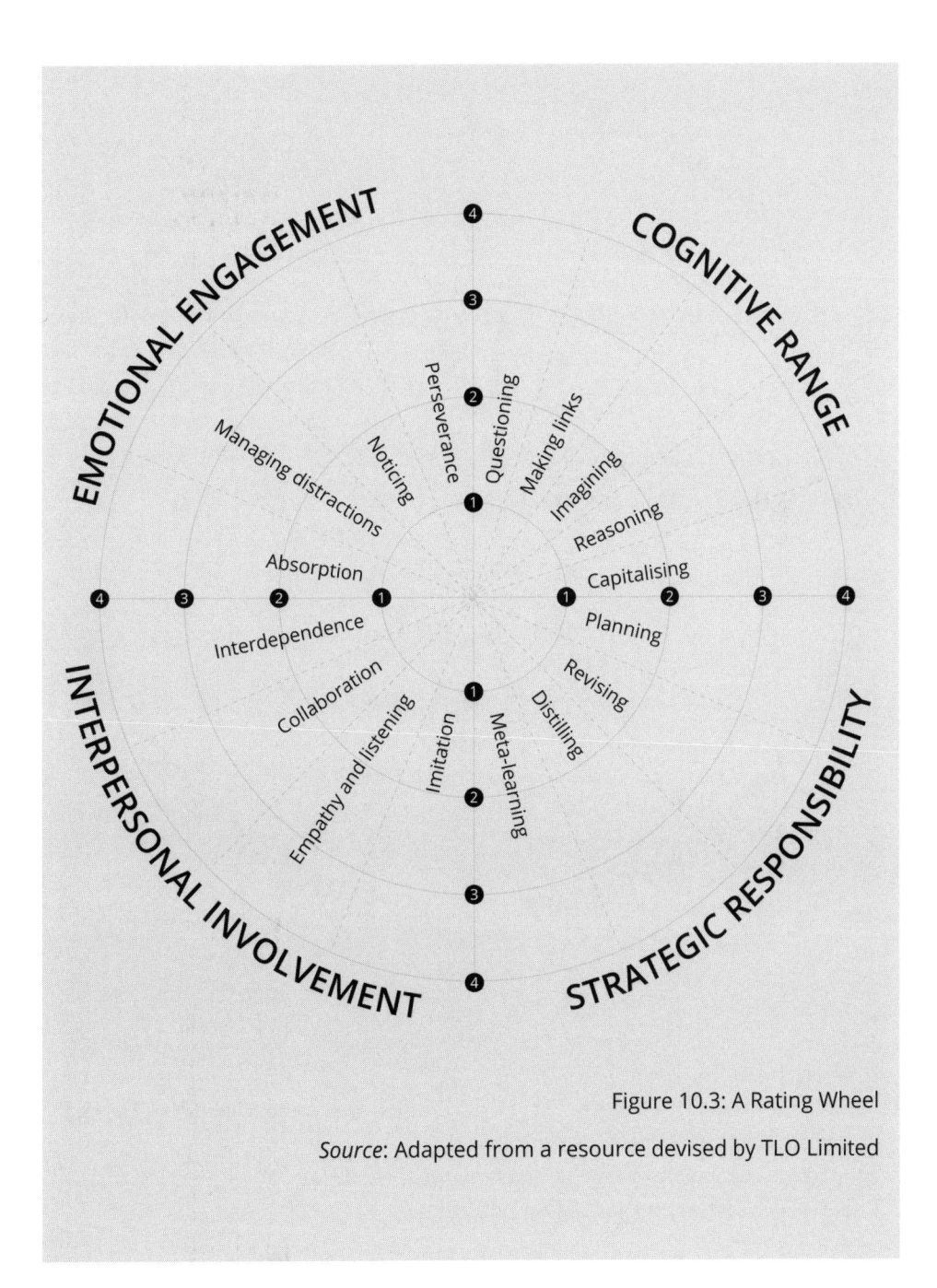

Source: Adapted from a resource devised by TLO Limited

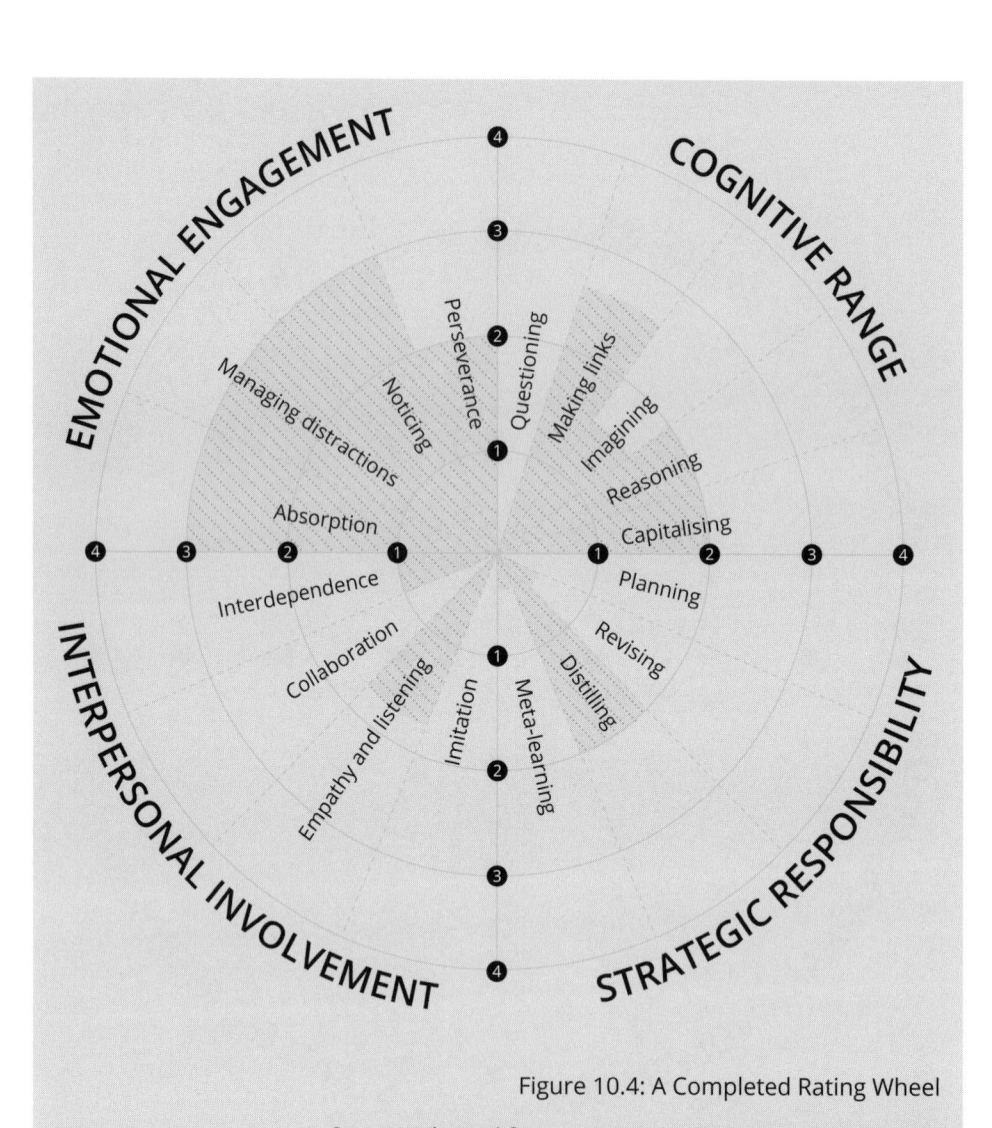

Figure 10.4: A Completed Rating Wheel

Source: Adapted from a resource devised by TLO Limited

What follows is an illustrative list of recommendations that came at the end of one such report, written by Graham, about a different high school. We have annotated the report to show (in brackets) which learning habits, assessed on the rating wheel, each recommendation relates to.

Although there is much to admire about the quality of learning and the development of greater independence and collaboration in students – particularly at Key Stage 3 – there are some areas on which it would be useful to focus to support the next phase of what has been a most impressive development:

- It would be useful to review attitudes to learning in male students in Year 10 so that they can benefit more widely from the approaches used by the most engaging teachers. There are marked differences in the same students' motivation, commitment, and willingness to think for themselves in different subjects. (Managing distractions, absorption)

- Make the generation of curiosity and the development of students' questioning, which is already a part of some teachers' practice, an integral part of learning across the school. (Questioning)

- Build in reflective moments in lessons so that students become used to planning ahead, anticipating difficulties and resource needs, reviewing work in progress, and adapting and changing their learning approach as they go along. (Planning, revising)

- Revisit the work that has been introduced to the learning champions on visible thinking routines that are designed to get students into the habit of thinking more independently. Visit the following websites to support these developments: http://www.visiblethinkingpz.org and http://www.ronritchhart.com. (Reasoning)

- Ensure that lessons end constructively with effective plenaries (that can sometimes be led by students) so that it is clear *what* learning has taken place, *where* individuals and the class need to progress in the next lesson, and *how* they have been and will need to be as learners. (Distilling, revising)

- Draw attention more frequently and systematically to learning habits in lessons and across the school as a whole so that students become increasingly aware of *how* they are learning and are able to make informed decisions about the best ways to operate. (Meta-learning)

- Develop progression routes for learning so that teachers and students understand how students can become better at, for example, posing more searching questions, collaborating more effectively, and using their imaginations more intelligently to explore possibilities. (Questioning, collaborating, imagining)

- Make greater use of classroom displays that show, for example, work in progress and offer hints and reminders as to how best to operate in respect of specific learning habits. (Revising)

- Review the layout of furniture in classrooms to better support flexible approaches to learning. The history classroom we visited provides an excellent example of a layout that enables individual, paired, and collaborative activities while giving the teacher ease of access to coach individual students. Some classrooms still adopt a standard layout with desks in rows facing the front, but since behaviour management issues rarely arise, more imaginative use could be made of the spaces available. (Empathy and listening, interdependence)

- In many of the lessons seen, teachers were using and trialling approaches that have been discussed over the last year. The school needs to ensure that this is becoming standard practice and not something that happens occasionally when the focus is explicitly placed on the LPA. In some lessons we observed, techniques that had been discussed in learning groups seemed to have been adopted without much understanding of their purpose and intended impact. All teachers need to be aware of the end goal of all this work: to develop students who are able to take greater responsibility for their own learning, operate independently, and make assured progress in learning and achievement. (Interdependence, planning, revising)

> A key function of a learning review is to build the capacity of staff (and students) to keep the nature of teaching and learning under their consideration. The consultant works with the group of observers so that they can, in future, take over the running of the reviews themselves.

How Should You Go About Building Your Own LPA-Focused Network?

As well as joining ready-made, like-minded groups, it can be very valuable to think about setting up your own. In East London, a group of schools has formed the Newham North Learning Partnership. The impetus for this began when a group of eight primary heads decided to get together every so often for coffee and cake (the cake was very important!) to share common problems, and for mutual support. Though a head's prime responsibility is their own school – which can lead to competitiveness with nearby schools – in this case, there was general concern for the well-being of the Newham North community as a whole. As trust grew, so the heads decided that they would form a self-organising "soft federation" to support each other in the development of the LPA across their schools. Robert Cleary at Sandringham was one of the leaders of this initiative. The other schools involved and their principals – at that time – were Anne Kibuuka at Kay Rowe Nursery School, Natasha Ttoffali at Park Primary School, Shirleyann Jones at St James' Church of England Primary School, Clare Barber at Odessa Infant School, Sarah Soyler at Woodgrange Infant School, Sally Norris at William Davies Primary School, and Sine Brown at Godwin Junior School.

The development of this partnership was organic and pragmatic. There was no master plan. The first time the governors of the eight different schools met they needed to be reassured about the purpose of the partnership. (This was a time when many schools in England were, as a matter of government policy, being forced into

> The development of this partnership was organic and pragmatic. There was no master plan. The first time the governors of the eight different schools met they needed to be reassured about the purpose of the partnership.

unwanted partnerships.) The head teachers had to reassure their governors that this was their own voluntary initiative to support the development of teaching expertise for the good of the whole community.

Once the heads had the blessing of their governors, there were a number of issues to be worked through. They included:

- Do all our PVVSs match sufficiently closely?
- How will we make sure there is equality and equity in the partnership?
- What actions will make this partnership long-lasting?
- What one action are we going to make sure is taken in all our schools?
- How are the governing boards going to be kept informed of our progress?
- Which governors and leaders in the partnerships can be relied on to be our advocates?

To get the partnerships working actively, they agreed to make time for teachers to visit each other across the schools, compare practice, and explore areas where they might share expertise with their neighbours. Here are some practical suggestions that they found useful:

- If it is not practically possible to release teachers for a whole day's visit, consider using INSET days to free up staff.
- If possible, tie in school visits with regular CPD time. This way, staff can visit lessons at the host school in the afternoon and then stay on after school to join in with CPD.
- Once a relationship is established with other schools, consider taking students along on the visits, as well as hosting students from other schools. Students can reflect on what the LPA looks like elsewhere and whether there is anything they'd like to adopt in their own school. They can then feed this information back to their peers or the staff.

- Collaborating with other schools to deliver shared CPD sessions can be a great way to pool resources and share expertise. Invite other schools to your LPA training sessions or to take part in journal clubs and study groups.

- After-school open evenings or table sharing sessions – a kind of focused TeachMeet – can also be a practical way of sharing ideas and resources. Set up tables with each one hosting a different LPA theme – such as encouraging independence or providing opportunities for collaboration. Invite schools to come and share their ideas, resources, and children's work on the theme. Once staff members have chosen their table, ask each person to present for three to four minutes on what this theme looks like at their school, allowing for a few minutes of questions and answers at the end before moving onto the next person. This same structure can be used to share good practice within a larger school, so staff can hear about what other year groups and departments have been doing.

The early stages of the project involved the leaders of the eight schools reading *The Learning Power Approach* and *Powering Up Children*. Each school then identified three learning power champions. Jessica Hyde, the deputy head teacher at William Davies, recalls the importance of identifying a clear role and purpose for the champions, which would support them in taking the lead in promoting and disseminating the LPA in their school. It was agreed that the LPA champions' network had to be a supportive space in which strategies could be tried and shared without judgement. The twenty-four learning champions from the eight schools agreed the following aim (if you think back to Chapter 2, you will recognise where it came from):

> The aim of the LPA champions is to support other educationalists to develop all students as confident and capable learners – ready, willing, and able to choose, design, research, pursue, troubleshoot, and evaluate learning for themselves, alone and with others, in school and out.

Towards the middle of 2018, the school leaders agreed to host an annual LPA conference for all teaching, support, and administrative staff, which the LPA champions would take the lead in designing. The first conference, which took place at the commencement of the 2019/20 academic year, had a very important role to play in the future of the Newham North community. Guy Claxton was the keynote speaker and he introduced the LPA and why it was important. It ensured that all

400 members of staff (teachers, teaching assistants, and non-teaching staff) had a common understanding which would act as a foundation for the work to follow. It was also an opportunity to bring all eight schools together and promote the benefits of working collaboratively, explaining the collective power that the schools had. At the conference, Robert explained:

> Newham North is a very successful place to be educated. The nursery, infant, primary, and high schools are all very successful. In our schools, over 3,000 children are educated. Collectively, our schools receive a budget of more than £20 million with which to educate the next generation. The schools have the resources to make a significant difference to the life chances of our children and families. The LPA has the potential to change the lives of our children and families. And collectively, the school leaders and champions understand that the Newham North Learning Partnership will allow us all to achieve more than our individual schools could on their own. The whole is going to be greater than the sum of its parts.

The conference also heard a clear message from Natasha Ttoffali, the head teacher at Park Primary School. She said that:

> The LPA gives opportunities to all our children to "find themselves" as learners – to discover their passions and learn how they learn best.

That can only be achieved if all the schools understand how we learn and discover the strategies that professional educators use to support students to be curious, inquisitive, and risk-taking. All in all, the Newham North Learning Partnership looks set to be a very positive and productive step forward for all concerned. There was certainly a powerful buzz in the room at the end of the day.

St Luke's Grammar School has also created its own community of enquiry. The school has made links with a number of others that are at different stages of implementing the LPA, and they too have discovered the power of putting on conferences and showcase days to share pedagogical tweaks and innovations. Jann Robinson recalls:

> The first conference was held on a school day. The teachers had a session with Guy at 7.30 a.m. prior to teaching their normal classes. A number of teachers volunteered to open their classrooms to the delegates, who came from schools that were already implementing a version of the LPA framework as well as those who were thinking about implementing one. These sessions were designed to allow for interaction between the teacher and the observers. At the end of the lesson, once the students had left, there was time for the teacher to answer questions and speak about their own experience with the framework. One delegate, who had a leadership role across a group of schools, commented: "These conferences are game changers. They show a school being

vulnerable and being prepared to open itself up, a school saying it hasn't got it all sorted but that it's prepared to open up a conversation with others."

It was a good experience for the audience, but also for the teachers as it helped them to take greater ownership of the framework. It gave a real boost to how our teachers felt about their work. It affirmed their ability to share good practice. Often teachers feel that their work is not meaningful beyond the students they teach. But our teachers felt trusted, valued, and proud, and it helped to shift practice across the school.

Beyond these conferences, St Luke's teachers have also presented their classroom innovations at networking events in the Sydney area, and Jann Robinson has shared her experiences with heads who are implementing similar frameworks. These opportunities have opened up conversations and ongoing partnerships, which have been invaluable in enhancing the commitment to the approach. Every external interaction has helped to clarify the school's vision of equipping students to make a difference in the world.

How Can You Build an LPA Alliance with Parents?

When a school commences its LPA work, the children might feel the air of excitement, but the parents can be overlooked. LPA leaders understand that the partnership between school and home needs to be nurtured. Parental support is vital. How the school shares its educational philosophy and ethos is important. So what works well to get parents on board with the LPA?

Children as LPA ambassadors

At William Davies Primary School, head teacher Sally Norris decided that it would be easier for parents if they were introduced to particular learning powers to start with, rather than the whole philosophy at once. She asked staff to look at the learning powers and create their own list of the ones which needed promoting most urgently for their community of children. They decided to focus on being collaborative, resilient, enthusiastic, adventurous, curious, and reflective. The first thing Sally did was to send a letter to parents explaining what these learning habits entailed, and why they were important for the children, both in school and beyond. Then, during that first year of implementing the LPA, the school drip-fed more information about the learning powers to parents in a number of ways. They included a detailed description of each, one by one, in monthly newsletters and they discussed them in termly parents' meetings. The initiative which got most parents curious, however, was the learning power champions of the week reward scheme. Sally explained:

> Individual teachers choose a child from their class who has demonstrated the target learning power for that week. During assembly, the children are told who the learning power champions are that week, and those children get to have lunch with me in my office, complete with a tablecloth, flowers, glasses of juice, and biscuits! We talk about what learning involves, and how it is possible to get better at it in the ways that they have just demonstrated. There is an expectation that the children proudly share this experience with their parent or caregiver.

During assembly, the children are also told what the target learning power is for the following week and are offered examples of how they can demonstrate it. Sally gives an example of being collaborative:

> This week, really listen to your group and take their ideas on board – don't just make them do what you want.

She was really pleased that by the end of the first half term parents were asking when their child was going to have lunch with the head teacher and staff were having animated conversations with parents about the LPA.

This is a good example of drip-feeding the message to parents through the children. The children are fundamentally teaching their parents about the LPA through their own excitement. Who could be better at changing parents' attitudes to learning than an extremely motivated and engaged child who can explain to their loved ones that because of the LPA they now know how to work collaboratively, or how to go about something they are struggling with calmly?

At Sandringham Pre-school, Amy Fisher, one of the nursery teachers, regularly encourages the parents to help their children become more independent. Independence for 2- and 3-year-olds means that they should endeavour to get dressed, feed themselves, and walk to school, rather than being pushed in a buggy. For older children it might mean packing their own schoolbag the night before. Children can be heard leaving the nursery telling their parents that they were independent today. Amy enjoys hearing parents asking their children: "When were you independent today?" This is a deliberate strategy designed to involve the family in using the language of the school's key learning attributes in their everyday discussions.

Parents are invited to "stay and learn" with their children at the pre-school. Spending time with their child in the school setting helps them to see how staff encourage and scaffold independence. They will see that the children can put on their own puddle suits and wellington boots, even if this takes a long time! They'll witness that this is considered a vital part of the day's learning: that staff may offer words of support and encouragement, but they won't swoop in and do it for them. In this way, staff model and demonstrate that independence and resilience can be taught from a young age and that all adults can play a key role in nurturing these qualities. The staff of Sandringham Pre-school, in a very friendly and positive way, encourage even the youngest children to take responsibility for themselves at an age-appropriate level, and parents are often surprised to see how much their children can do for themselves. When they comment that "They don't do that at home", teachers reply, "Well they can now!"

At Icknield Infant and Nursery School, to aid parental understanding, staff organised an assembly led by the children to demonstrate what was meant by BLP and the language that supported it. Under their teacher's guidance, the children created and performed a BLP rap. The language is modelled for parents in all assemblies, reports, workshops, and shared learning sessions. Jackie Egan, the head teacher, says:

> We now hear parents using the language all the time – particularly around resilience.

Workshops and performances

A more strategic approach was used to inform and engage parents at Walthamstow School for Girls. Local school leaders – including heads of all the feeder primary schools, governors, and key local authority personnel – were invited to the official BLP launch day in the autumn of 2005. (Walthamstow, you might recall, began by introducing the LPA, in the form of BLP, just to their Year 7s.) At a Year 7 parents' evening, Rachel Macfarlane explained what the school was up to, and parents were supplied with a leaflet explaining the concept of BLP, the reasons why the school was introducing it, and how it would be delivered. Parent workshops were then offered from time to time by the BLP coordinator and one of the deputy head teachers. Parents of Year 7 girls were asked to complete a questionnaire towards the end of the first year to glean evidence of the impact that BLP was having on their children's learning, as well as their level of understanding and involvement.

The outcomes of the parental questionnaire showed both a good understanding of the approach and the beneficial outcomes it was having on their children. Over 83% thought that the approach had helped their daughter with her learning. A number of the replies spoke about their daughters using their learning muscles and discussing how best to learn with them and with siblings. Interestingly, there were a few comments made about how the approach had supported the girls to manage distractions both at home and in school. Overwhelmingly, parents spoke about how the approach had supported their children's academic attainment.

At Isaac Newton Academy, the foundations of the LPA were laid through home visits to each family during the summer prior to the opening of the school. During these visits, students and families were introduced to the BRIDGES framework, the learning characteristics, the rationale behind them, and the importance placed on them by the academy. This was followed up with BRIDGES parent workshops once the academy opened. Rachel Macfarlane says:

> Though they take a lot of time, the practice of home visits has now become enshrined in "the way we do things at Isaac Newton". It has an enormous impact in communicating the key drivers and priorities that make up the Isaac Newton vision and getting each family to buy into the dream.

The school continues to hold annual BRIDGES parent workshops (now at both primary and senior level) open to all parents and carers each September, but especially targeting the new intake (Reception and Year 7). At the primary workshops, 6–7-year-old students will explain what the BRIDGES dispositions are to the parents of the new cohort of 4-year-olds; in the senior school, Year 8s will induct the new Year 7s and their parents.

Newsletters and parents' handbooks

Furthermore, at Isaac Newton, the BRIDGES dispositions that students will be targeting are publicised in the school newsletter: there is a different weekly focus at primary level and a fortnightly one in the senior school. Staff routinely generated top tips documents for parents and, once they had a sufficient number, these were compiled into a high school BRIDGES parent handbook and a primary equivalent.

> BRIDGES is a framework for character education to help fulfil our aim: "To equip every student with the knowledge, learning power, and character necessary for success at university and beyond." BRIDGES has been designed to summarise the main character traits and learning dispositions that are fundamental to being an effective learner and to achieving success and fulfilment in life. They underpin the curriculum at the academy and its policies and ethos.
>
> We know that the development of students' BRIDGES dispositions can't and doesn't just happen at school. This guide is designed to introduce parents to each of the character traits and includes some top tips for students and their parents so that together we can support our students in developing learning power and building character.

Figure 10.5: Extract from the Isaac Newton Academy High School BRIDGES Parent Handbook

Pardeep Chaggar, mother of Avneet in Year 4, says:

> Each week we look as a family at the BRIDGES section of the newsletter. We read it and discuss it. We pull bits out and use it as a family. It unites home and school.

Experiencing LPA teaching

At South Dartmoor Community College, Hugh Bellamy worked to get buy-in from parents by instituting a weekly morning session in which they could come into the school and experience the kinds of teaching their children were receiving. He says:

> We might pose them a maths problem, or show them a confusing picture and ask them to try to figure out what is going on. We might use a thinking routine such as "See-Think-Wonder" [which we described in Chapter 1] or Think-Pair-Share [described in Chapter 2]. We would explain our pedagogy, and then take them into a lesson where they could see how their child was reacting to that kind of teaching. And after that, they would meet with a member of the SLT to reflect on what they had seen and ask questions. They were often astonished at how engaged and thoughtful the children were, and at how different the classroom atmosphere was from when they were at school. To finish, we might give them a few top tips about how to engage with their children at home – for example, how to support them with their homework without jumping in and doing it for them. We might suggest question prompts, such as "What do you know already that might help you to figure that out?" or "What could you try to see if it works?" This was a really effective use of time in terms of building parents' understanding of the LPA.

Talking to parents

Jann Robinson knew that she needed to get the parents at St Luke's to buy into the case for change. The main challenge was to reassure them that the students' results wouldn't suffer. She held parent information nights and asked parents to write down the characteristics that they looked for in their employees and colleagues. These mirrored many of the dispositions in the LPA. This led to discussions about the challenges of the 21st century, rapid changes in technology, the impact on the employment market, and research about skills for the future. L@SL was framed within a bigger picture of the changing world and the demands which it would make on their children as they grew up. This brought parents on board.

Similarly, Mark Fenton at Dr Challoner's reflects:

> We were fortunate that a good many of our parents work in quite high-powered occupations, so they saw learning power as the kind of thing that they were talking about in their own workplaces. They were quick to see that if the idea of a "learning

organisation" was good enough for a successful company, it was equally applicable to the education of their sons. The ideas behind BLP weren't that new or strange to them. They wanted good grades, obviously, but they were comfortable with the idea that other outcomes such as resilience and resourcefulness were just as important – if not more so. The majority thought that it was great that the school was paying attention to these kinds of things. Their reaction helped to encourage the staff to take it seriously. There were no objections along the lines of "Yes, but what are the parents going to say?"

Mark never missed an opportunity to share BLP with parents. He says:

It was my job to take every opportunity to make clear to parents that learning power is important. As just one small example, before BLP, at the end of a school concert I might have stood up and congratulated the orchestra on how talented they were. But later I would comment on how fantastically hard they had all worked and how skilfully they had practised. In many little ways, I was trying to put learning power at the centre of the school's philosophy.

Summary

There are many compelling reasons to connect with the wider world. To make the most of opportunities to network and share practice, a school needs to be comfortable with itself. Success is not a destination; it is a journey. All schools are on a journey, but if they are happy to take risks, try something different, make mistakes, and acknowledge that there might be some false starts, then connecting with the wider world will be enjoyable and inspiring, and it will support the whole community of learners.

At the start of the journey, it can be difficult to get your bearings and understand the direction you are heading in, but making friends, having learning conversations, and deciding who you want to work with will all clarify your vision. The friends you make share your values and principles, those will be the relationships that last. LPA schools have considered their direction and that clarity enables them to hold firm to their beliefs. And together, through good times and bad, they retain their focus on enabling all children, teachers, and parents to be successful.

Wondering

Are there any like-minded schools in your area with which you could collaborate? What would be your first steps in creating a grassroots network?

Is there the potential to collaborate on LPA training or CPD? Or to recruit LPA champions to work together across several schools?

Would a learning review be a helpful process for you? Would you prefer for this to be carried out by an external organisation or another school?

Chapter 11
Some Tentative Conclusions

Let's conclude by summarising what we can distil from our experience that might be of use to anyone who may be thinking of pushing on down the LPA path.

The job of creating culture change is demanding, and can seem daunting. It involves winning hearts and minds, and getting people to examine their beliefs and adjust their habits, some of which might be deeply engrained. We have to persuade them that to "get on board" is in their own best interests in two ways. First, it will enable them to prepare young people better for life beyond school, and so to feel a deeper pride in a job well done. And, second, it will make their lives as teachers more enjoyable, because learners who possess strong, positive learning habits are easier and more satisfying to teach.

It also requires us as school leaders to value – and, where necessary, develop – our own learning muscles. We too will need reserves of resilience and determination, good communication, imagination, and flexibility. We will meet opposition and incomprehension, and have to hold to the spirit and values of the LPA even while we are having to be patient and change tack. We need to keep ourselves well-informed, so that we can speak with clarity and conviction about the "desirable outcomes" that we are after, and about the demands and timescales of the journey we are asking people to undertake. We have seen that culture change is subtle, slow and strategic: leaders need tenacity and guile.

We have to know – or get to know – our schools, our staff, our students, and their parents well, so that we can "speak their language": anticipating their misgivings and tailoring our messages accordingly. We have to judge when, where, and with whom we can push on faster, and, conversely, tell when we may need to hold back, sowing seeds and allowing time for them to germinate and for resistances to soften. And we have seen how important it is to keep seeking – and adjusting – that elusive, shifting balance between "tight" and "loose": between using our authority as principals to set the direction and require conformity, yet also avoiding alienating people by appearing too draconian and inflexible, thereby risking losing their goodwill and support. We have to hold the course, and identify the pedagogical design principles that are emerging as essential – and therefore "non-negotiable" – while also creating the leeway and autonomy that will allow every member of staff to find their own way of engaging with and adopting the LPA. We won't always get it right – certainly not for everyone – and will sometimes have to be ready to rethink and redesign the path.

We have demonstrated abundantly that, when it comes to culture change, there is no one size that fits all. George Pindar School, Isaac Newton Academy, and St Luke's Grammar School are very different high schools; Heath Mount School and Sandringham Primary School are very different primaries. But, by telling our different stories, we have – we hope – shown you some of the various means that can lead, eventually, to similar valued outcomes. We have unearthed a few general rules of thumb or top tips – for example, do work to build an open and supportive learning community among staff, and do make sure that governors or boards of trustees really *understand and experience* the value of the LPA for themselves – but we have also illustrated a variety of options that are available to you, and identified a few of the pitfalls that it would be good to avoid.

We hope that, as you have been reading, many of our examples will have rung bells with you, and that our suggestions will have struck you as valuable, plausible, and practical things to try out in your own school. We hope that the frequent invitations to stop and "wonder" about what we have been saying will have helped you to plan your own route and to know how to recognise where you are on the journey, what progress you have made, and what your next steps might be. The appendix offers you a self-evaluation tool that sums up a lot of our thinking. We hope that you will find that useful too.

Because we wanted to give you enough detail to be useful – rather than some vague exhortations and frameworks – we have had to describe a few schools in some detail. We hope our sample has been varied enough to reassure you that the LPA is suitable, and effective, in any kind of school you could imagine. Whether your school be high or low achieving, new or old, large or small, urban or rural, northern or southern hemisphere, or a primary, high or special school, we believe that your students and your teachers would feel the benefit of the LPA.

And there are, of course, many more schools, and groups of schools, around the world that have made great strides in the same direction. Some groups we know of: the New

Pedagogies for Deep Learning schools in Canada and elsewhere, the EL Education schools in the United States, the Whole Education schools in the UK, the Project for the Enhancement of Effective Learning (PEEL) schools in Australia, the English Speaking Scholastic Association of the River Plate (ESSARP) in Argentina, for example. But we also know of many individual schools that have developed their own versions of the LPA to good effect: kindergartens in New Zealand; primary schools in Poland and Spain; high-achieving international schools in China, Thailand, Brazil, Dubai, and Iceland; inner-city state schools in the United States and Ireland; and many more.

What we find most exciting is that all these innovators, including ourselves, seem to be heading in the same direction, aiming to achieve the development of both epistemic character and useful knowledge. A new vision of education is being born. It contains a joined-up philosophy and pedagogy. It has a model of the learning mind derived from good cognitive science to underpin the approach. There is data to show that it really is possible to get good grades by building students' capacities and appetites for independent learning. There are implications for how you assess their progress. And there are ideas about what you need to do, as a school leader, to create a culture that supports everyone in the school to work towards those ends. Wow! What a creative, hands-on project to be a part of. We hope that you share our excitement as you continue on your journey.

Appendix

A Self-Assessment Grid for School Leaders

In this final tool, Gemma Goldenberg has distilled our key lessons into a reflective tool for school leaders to use as they embark upon the LPA journey. We hope that you will find it a useful guide as you set out and as you make progress along the way. You could use the question prompts to begin planning your LPA journey, either on your own or with your SLT. Once you have begun to introduce the LPA, you can use the grid to discuss where you are currently and what your next steps could be. Revisiting the self-assessment grid from time to time could help you to keep track of your progress and maintain the momentum.

Where Am I Heading?

	Questions to prompt the planning process	Self-assessment levels		
		Developing	Embedding	Innovating
Getting buy-in	What is it about LPA which has captured me? How am I going to share this with staff? How will I persuade others of the importance of developing learning dispositions? Do I want a strategic plan/mandate for introducing the LPA, or will I let it grow more organically?	I have clarity about what the LPA involves, why it's important to me, and why it's the right approach for the school. I've introduced the key concepts to staff. Staff are aware of the importance of developing students' learning dispositions.	I've shared my LPA vision with all stakeholders including students, governors, and parents. New staff are inducted into the LPA. I have begun to identify teachers who are using the LPA effectively and use them as models.	Stakeholders and students have been part of shaping and refining our school vision for learning. We have adopted or adapted a version of the LPA which works for us as a school and reflects our purpose, vision, and values. CPD enables staff to develop their understanding of "learnable intelligence" and the

		How will I deal with cynics, sceptics, and blockers?		research supporting the LPA. LPA leaders support peers and newer staff to use the approach effectively.
Creating a staff culture of learning		How will I stimulate discussion and enquiry around the LPA among staff? How can I encourage staff to take the lead in their own CPD? Is there a way of engaging staff in research-based approaches? Could I make use of mentoring, peer observations, and/or lesson study?	Staff have engaged with some key reading around the LPA. Staff are able to articulate what the LPA is and why it's relevant to their role.	Staff share and reflect on their strategies, successes, and difficulties in using the LPA. I am taking steps to develop a sense of learning community among the staff (e.g. by introducing study groups, small scale research projects, and journal clubs).	Staff see themselves as facilitators of learning rather than teachers of subjects/ dispensers of knowledge. Staff are comfortable teaching in front of one another and willingly participate in team teaching, peer observation, and/or lesson study. There is a climate of enquiry around teaching and learning.

	Questions to prompt the planning process	Self-assessment levels		
		Developing	Embedding	Innovating
A language for learning	What terminology do I need to introduce? Do I want to do this in a structured way or let it develop more naturally? Will this language be adapted for different age groups or be the same across the school? How will I introduce and promote the use of this language? How will I know whether it has been successfully adopted and what its impact has been?	Some key words and terms have been introduced across the school. Staff model the use of this language and wall displays act as reminders for the students.	We have developed a common language for learning which is used throughout the school. Students have a secure understanding of what the terminology actually means and how it relates to their learning. New staff are inducted in the language and know why it's important.	I have evaluated the extent to which the language is being used (e.g. through student conferencing, use of word clouds, etc.). Staff and students are able to reflect on the language used and its impact on learning. The language for learning is used naturally and with variations and adaptations rather than being tokenistic/parroted back.

Appendix

| Targeting pedagogy | Do we have a clear set of pedagogical approaches and do I understand the research base behind them?

Who are my strongest champions of LPA pedagogy and how can I use them to enable others?

Do our current systems and structures around teaching practice (e.g. appraisals, | Staff understand some of the pedagogical implications of the LPA (e.g. the importance of challenge).

Leaders are aware of the pedagogy used in classrooms across the school.

Staff are given helpful feedback and time to reflect on their pedagogy. | Good practice is shared and disseminated widely.

The school's approach to pedagogy is clear. Structures and systems support the monitoring and development of this approach.

Staff know who to approach if they need support with the LPA or want to see examples of good practice. | Students use the language in a range of settings and scenarios, both inside and outside of the classroom.

Teachers continually reflect on their own practice and feel comfortable discussing successes, challenges, and changes they want to make.

All teachers are able to articulate the pedagogical strategies and approaches that they use, and why.

Teachers share a common research- and values-based |

Questions to prompt the planning process	Self-assessment levels		
	Developing	Embedding	Innovating
lesson observations, feedback, CPD) support the development of the LPA? Do I want to use external trainers and consultants to support changing pedagogy or keep it in-house?		Staff have had the opportunity to see someone else using the LPA in their teaching.	approach but are able to teach in their own individual style. Pedagogy is not dictated but developed and refined collaboratively. Good practice spreads quickly due to ample opportunities to share, observe, and reflect with others.

How Are Things Going So Far?

	Questions to prompt reflection	Self-assessment		
		Developing	Embedding	Innovating
Beyond the classroom	If I was setting up an LPA school from scratch, what would be different to the way my school is now? Are there school-wide practices (e.g. assessment and reporting procedures, timetabling issues, etc.) that could get in the way of the implementation of the LPA?	I have begun to notice the policies and structures which no longer fit our approach. I have discussed with colleagues the features of an LPA school and the school-wide practices that would best support this.	We have begun to reconsider some of our structures, policies, and practices in light of the LPA (e.g. timetabling/lesson structure, use of assemblies, grouping of children, systems for assessment, and reporting to parents). Students play an active role in the assessment of their own learning.	Staff are involved in reviewing, rewriting, and adapting policies, procedures, and practices so that they are well-aligned with the LPA. Students are leaders of their own learning – involved in parent consultations, end-of-term reports, assessments, and planning.

	Questions to prompt reflection	Self-assessment		
		Developing	Embedding	Innovating
	To what extent do our current policies and systems reflect the LPA ethos? What opportunities do I have to discuss these questions with colleagues and students?			
Making it stick	How will I keep this momentum? How can I build leadership capacity in other members of staff? How can I ensure that the LPA doesn't become sidelined when other pressures and	There is a plan of CPD which enables teachers to learn more about the LPA, trial things, and reflect. I have thought about who might be a suitable LPA champion (or champions).	There is a designated LPA lead/group of champions who are taking increasing responsibility for pushing the LPA forward. Parents have had opportunities to learn about the	We have approached relevant schools (feeder schools in the case of high schools; the high schools that students will go onto in the case of primaries) to work on transition projects using the LPA.

Appendix

	time constraints arise?		LPA and how they can support it at home.	We have approached relevant schools (feeder schools in the case of high schools; the high schools that students will go onto in the case of primaries) to work on transition projects using the LPA.
Evidencing progress and progression	How will I know whether the implementation of the LPA has been successful? Is there a way of measuring impact on learning? Have I taken a baseline measure, so that I can compare outcomes later?	We have discussed and noted our aims for the LPA, when we will revisit these aims, and how we will decide whether we've been successful in meeting them. Staff have engaged in discussions about how the LPA is	Leaders track the development of the LPA – what has been implemented so far, what the impact has been, and what the next steps are.	Students, staff, and governors are involved in the evaluation of the LPA. We have carried out a peer review of the LPA at our school (e.g. in collaboration with another school or with another organisation, as we

Questions to prompt reflection	Self-assessment		
	Developing	Embedding	Innovating
How will I know whether the implementation of the LPA has been successful? Is there a way of measuring impact on learning? Have I taken a baseline measure, so that I can compare outcomes later?	going so far and what our next steps should be.		saw with Sandringham and Whole Education.)
Connecting with the wider world Are there other like-minded schools with whom I could collaborate on the LPA? Do I know of another school that is further along in	We have begun to share our successes (e.g. via social media or with neighbouring schools).	We have visited other schools, or invited other schools to visit us, in order to share our progress.	We routinely work in collaboration with other schools to refine and improve our use of the LPA (e.g. LPA leads working together in

Appendix

	their LPA journey, which I could visit? Which organisations might help me implement and enrich the LPA at my school? What are the opportunities to work with feeder schools/high schools on LPA-related transition work?			networks, shared CPD across schools, peer reviews and observations, cross-school visits, and sharing best practice).
My personal journey	Have I changed as a leader over the course of this journey? Do I feel that I am now leading a school that's closer to my own vision	I have started to reflect on my values as a leader. I've considered what I believe to be the purpose of education.	I've met like-minded leaders who I can learn with and from as we implement the LPA.	I am able to reflect on my LPA journey and the impact it's had on students and staff. I can use this to help other individuals and schools implement the LPA and can

Questions to prompt reflection	Self-assessment		
	Developing	Embedding	Innovating
and values than it was when I first became head? How has this approach affected my wider motivations and ambitions?			see how the approach can be tweaked to fit different contexts and circumstances.

Further Reading

Berger, Ron (2003). *An Ethic of Excellence: Building a Culture of Craftsmanship with Students* (Portsmouth, NH: Heinemann).

Berger, Ron, Rugen, Leah, and Woodfin, Libby (2014). *Leaders of Their Own Learning: Transforming Schools Through Student-Engaged Assessment* (San Francisco, CA: Jossey-Bass).

Berger, Ron, Woodfin, Libby, and Vilen, Anne (2016). *Learning That Lasts: Challenging, Engaging, and Empowering Students with Deeper Instruction* (San Francisco, CA: Jossey-Bass).

Berliner, Wendy, and Eyre, Deborah (2018). *Great Minds and How to Grow Them* (Abingdon and New York: Routledge).

Binet, Alfred (1909). *Les Idées Modernes sur les Enfants* (Paris: Flammarion).

Blatchford, Peter, Bassett, Paul, Brown, Penelope, Martin, Clare, Russell, Anthony, and Webster, Rob (2009). *Deployment and Impact of Support Staff in Schools: Report on Findings from the Second National Questionnaire Survey of Schools, Support Staff and Teachers (Strand 1, Wave 2 – 2006)*. Research Report DCSF-RR005 (London: Institute of Education and Department for Children, Schools and Families).

Boaler, Jo (2019). *Limitless Mind: Learn, Lead and Live without Barriers* (London: Thorsons).

Bodrova, Elena, and Leong, Deborah J. (1995). *Tools of the Mind: A Vygotskian Approach to Early Childhood Education* (New York: Pearson).

Bowman, Bob, with Butler, Charles (2016). *The Golden Rules: 10 Steps to World-Class Excellence in Your Life and Work* (New York: St Martin's Press).

Briceño, Eduardo (2016). "How to get better at the things you care about", *TED.com* [video]. Available at: https://www.ted.com/talks/eduardo_briceno_how_to_get_better_at_the_things_you_care_about.

Burden, Bob (2010). What is a Thinking School? *Creative Teaching and Learning*, 1(2): 22–26. Available at: https://socialsciences.exeter.ac.uk/media/universityofexeter/collegeofsocialsciencesandinternationalstudies/education/research/groupsandnetworks/cedu/downloads/publications/What_is_a_Thinking_School.pdf.

Burge, Bethan, Lenkeit, Jenny, and Sizmur, Juliet (2015). *PISA in Practice: Cognitive Activation in Maths* (Slough: National Foundation for Educational Research).

City, Elizabeth A., Elmore, Richard F., Fiarman, Sarah E., and Teitel, Lee (2009). *Instructional Rounds in Education: A Network Approach to Improving Teaching and Learning* (Cambridge, MA: Harvard Education Press).

Claro, Susana, Paunesku, David, and Dweck, Carol (2016). Growth mindset tempers the effect of poverty on academic achievement. *Proceedings of the National Academy of Sciences*, 113(31): 8664–8668.

Claxton, Guy (1990). *Teaching to Learn: A Direction for Education* (London: Cassell).

Claxton, Guy (1999). *Wise Up: The Challenge of Lifelong Learning* (London and New York: Bloomsbury).

Claxton, Guy (2002). *Building Learning Power: Helping Young People Become Better Learners* (Bristol: TLO Limited).

Claxton, Guy (2006). *Learning to Learn: The Fourth Generation* (Bristol: TLO Limited).

Claxton, Guy (2008). *What's the Point of School? Rediscovering the Heart of Education* (London: Oneworld).

Claxton, Guy (2017). *The Learning Power Approach: Teaching Learners to Teach Themselves* [US edn] (Thousand Oaks, CA: Corwin).

Claxton, Guy (2018). *The Learning Power Approach: Teaching Learners to Teach Themselves* [UK edn] (Carmarthen: Crown House Publishing).

Claxton, Guy, and Carlzon, Becky (2018). *Powering Up Children: The Learning Power Approach to Primary Teaching* (Carmarthen: Crown House Publishing).

Claxton, Guy, Chambers, Maryl, Powell, Graham, and Lucas, Bill (2011). *The Learning Powered School: Pioneering 21st Century Education* (Bristol: TLO Limited).

Claxton, Guy, and Lucas, Bill (2007). *The Creative Thinking Plan: How to Generate Ideas and Solve Problems in Your Work and Life* (London: BBC Books).

Claxton, Guy, and Lucas, Bill (2015). *Educating Ruby: What Our Children Really Need to Learn* (Carmarthen: Crown House Publishing).

Claxton, Guy, and Powell, Graham (2019). *Powering Up Students: The Learning Power Approach to High School Teaching* (Carmarthen: Crown House Publishing).

Costa, Arthur L., and Kallick, Bena (2000). *Activating and Engaging Habits of Mind* (Alexandria, VA: Association for Supervision and Curriculum Development).

Costa, Arthur L., and Kallick, Bena (2000). *Assessing and Reporting on Habits of Mind* (Alexandria, VA: Association for Supervision and Curriculum Development).

Costa, Arthur L., and Kallick, Bena (2000). *Discovering and Exploring Habits of Mind* (Alexandria, VA: Association for Supervision and Curriculum Development).

Costa, Arthur L., and Kallick, Bena (2000). *Integrating and Sustaining Habits of Mind* (Alexandria, VA: Association for Supervision and Curriculum Development).

Costa, Arthur L., and Kallick, Bena (2013). *Dispositions: Reframing Teaching and Learning* (Thousand Oaks, CA: Corwin).

de Bono, Edward (1990). *I Am Right, You Are Wrong* (London: Viking).

de Bono, Edward (2006). *Edward de Bono's Thinking Course* (London: BBC Active).

Duckworth, Angela (2013). "Grit: the power of passion and perseverance" [video] (9 May), TED.com. Available at: https://www.youtube.com/watch?v=H14bBuluwB8.

Duckworth, Angela (2017). *Grit: Why Passion and Resilience Are the Secrets of Success* (London: Vermilion).

Duhigg, Charles (2013). *The Power of Habit: Why We Do What We Do and How to Change* (London: Random House Books).

Dweck, Carol S. (2007). *Mindset: The New Psychology of Success* (New York: Ballantine Books).

Dweck, Carol S. (2014). "The power of yet", *TEDxNorrköping* [video] (12 September). Available at: https://www.youtube.com/watch?v=J-swZaKN2Ic.

EL Education (2016). "Austin's butterfly: models, critique, and descriptive feedback" [video] (4 October). Available at: https://www.youtube.com/watch?v=E_6PskE3zfQ.

Entwistle, Noel, and Kozéki, Béla (1985). Relationships between school motivation, approaches to studying, and attainment among British and Hungarian adolescents. *British Journal of Educational Psychology*, 55(2): 124–137.

Flink, Cheryl, Boggiano, Ann, and Barrett, Marty (1990). Controlling teaching strategies: undermining children's self-determination and performance. *Journal of Personality and Social Psychology*, 59(5): 916–924.

Fullan, Michael (2001). *Leading in a Culture of Change* (San Francisco, CA: Jossey-Bass).

Fullan, Michael (2005). *Leadership and Sustainability: System Thinkers in Action* (Thousand Oaks, CA: Corwin Press).

Fullan, Michael (2014). *The Principal: Three Keys to Maximizing Impact* (San Francisco, CA: Jossey-Bass).

Gardner, Howard (1993). *Multiple Intelligences* (New York: Basic Books).

Gardner, Howard (2006). *Five Minds for the Future* (Cambridge, MA: Harvard University Press).

Gardner, Howard, and Davis, Katie (2014). *The App Generation: How Today's Youth Navigate Identity, Intimacy, and Imagination in a Digital World* (New Haven, CT: Yale University Press).

Ginnis, Paul (2002). *The Teacher's Toolkit: Raise Classroom Achievement with Strategies for Every Learner* (Carmarthen: Crown House Publishing).

Hattie, John (2009). *Visible Learning: A Synthesis of Over 800 Meta-Analyses Relating to Achievement* (Abingdon and New York: Routledge).

Hattie, John (2012). *Visible Learning for Teachers: Maximizing Impact on Learning* (Abingdon and New York: Routledge).

Haynes, Joanna (2008). *Children as Philosophers: Learning Through Enquiry and Dialogue in the Primary Classroom*, 2nd edn (Abingdon: Routledge).

Hayward, Susan (1987). *Begin It Now: You Have a Purpose* (Sydney: In-Tune Books).

Heyes, Cecilia (2018). *Cognitive Gadgets: The Cultural Evolution of Thinking* (Cambridge, MA: Harvard University Press).

Hyerle, David (2009). *Visual Tools for Transforming Information into Knowledge*, 2nd edn (Thousand Oaks, CA: Corwin).

Kegan, Robert (1995). *In Over Our Heads: The Mental Demands of Modern Life* (Cambridge, MA: Harvard University Press).

Kirtman, Lyle, and Fullan, Michael (2016). *Leadership: Key Competencies for Whole-System Change* (Bloomington, IN: Solution Tree Press).

Landau Forte (2014). "Learning at Landau" [video] (14 October). Available at: https://www.youtube.com/watch?v=_HDL-aH_VFs.

Leahy, Siobhan, and Wiliam, Dylan (2012). From teachers to schools: scaling up professional development for formative assessment. In John Gardner (ed.), *Assessment and Learning*, 2nd edn (London: Sage), pp. 49–71.

Lewis, Catherine, and Hurd, Jacqueline (2011). *Lesson Study Step by Step: How Teacher Learning Communities Improve Instruction* (London: Heinemann Education).

Lucas, Bill, and Claxton, Guy (2010). *New Kinds of Smart: How the Science of Learnable Intelligence Is Changing Education* (Maidenhead: Open University Press).

Lucas, Bill, Claxton, Guy, and Spencer, Ellen (2013). *Expansive Education: Teaching Learners for the Real World* (Maidenhead: Open University Press).

Machiavelli, Niccolò (1995 [1532]). *The Prince*, tr. George Bull (London: Penguin).

McGough, Roger (1983). "The Leader", in *Sky in the Pie* (Harmondsworth: Kestrel Books).

Mannion, James, and Mercer, Neil (2016). Learning to learn: improving attainment, closing the gap at Key Stage 3. *The Curriculum Journal*, 27(2): 246–271. Available at: http://dx.doi.org/10.1080/09585176.2015.1137778.

Mansell, Warwick (2010). "Spoonfed" students lack confidence at Oxbridge, *TES* (10 December). Available at: https://www.tes.com/news/spoonfed-students-lack-confidence-oxbridge.

Mercer, Neil (1995). *The Guided Construction of Knowledge: Talk Amongst Teachers and Learners* (Clevedon: Multilingual Matters).

Mitchell, David (2008). *What Really Works in Special and Inclusive Education: Using Evidence-Based Teaching Strategies* (Abingdon and New York: Routledge).

Mitra, Sugata (2019). *The School in the Cloud: The Emergent Future of Learning* (Thousand Oaks, CA: Corwin).

Moore, Suzanne (2019). I've had children at school for 27 years. At last I can stop pretending to like it. *The Guardian* (3 June). Available at: https://www.theguardian.com/commentisfree/2019/jun/03/children-school-27-years-parents-evenings-pta?CMP=Share_iOSApp_Other.

Murdoch, Kath (2015). *The Power of Inquiry: Teaching and Learning with Curiosity, Creativity and Purpose in the Contemporary Classroom* (Northcote, VIC: Seastar Education).

Murray, William Hutchison (1951). *The Scottish Himalayan Expedition* (London: JM Dent & Sons).

Newell, Allen, and Simon, Herbert A. (1972). *Human Problem Solving* (Englewood Cliffs, NJ: Prentice-Hall).

Nottingham, James (2016). *Challenging Learning: Theory, Effective Practice and Lesson Ideas to Create Optimal Learning in the Classroom*, 2nd edn (Abingdon and New York: Routledge).

Ofsted (2014). Isaac Newton Academy: Inspection Report. Ref: 138518. 5–6 June. Available at: https://files.ofsted.gov.uk/v1/file/2400094.

Ofsted (2017). Sandringham Primary School: Inspection Report. Ref: 130381. 23–26 May. Available at: http://sandringham.newham.sch.uk/wp-content/uploads/2017/10/Ofsted-Report-2017.pdf.

Ofsted (2017). Short Inspection of Oaklands Primary School. 11 December. Available at: https://www.oaklands-primary.co.uk/docs/Oaklands_Primary_School_Ofsted_Report_1718.pdf.

Ofsted (2017). Woolenwick Infant and Nursery School: Inspection Report. Ref: 117323. 12–13 October. Available at: http://www.woolenwickinfants.herts.sch.uk/images/Ofsted%20Report%202017.pdf.

Perkins, David (1995). *Outsmarting IQ: The Emerging Science of Learnable Intelligence* (New York: The Free Press).

Perkins, David (2009). *Making Learning Whole: How Seven Principles of Teaching Can Transform Education* (San Francisco, CA: Jossey-Bass).

Postman, Neil (1996). *The End of Education: Redefining the Value of School* (London: Vintage).

Powell, Graham, Chambers, Maryl, and Baxter, Gillian (2001). *Pathways to Classroom Observation: A Guide for Team Leaders* (Bristol: TLO Limited).

Price, David (2013). *Open: How We'll Work, Live and Learn in the Future* (Crux Publishing Ltd).

Radcliffe, Steve (2012). *Leadership Plain and Simple*, 2nd edn (Harlow: Pearson).

Ratcliffe, Rebecca (2017). Teacher knows best? Not any longer as parents muscle in on the classroom. *The Guardian* (30 April). Available at: https://www.theguardian.com/education/2017/apr/29/schools-parents-pupils-education-teachers.

Resnick, Lauren B. (1999). Making America smarter. *Education Week*, 18(40): 38–40. Available at: http://www.edweek.org/ew/articles/1999/06/16/40resnick.h18.html.

Richardson, Ken (2017). *Genes, Brains and Human Potential: The Science and Ideology of Intelligence* (New York: Columbia University Press).

Ritchhart, Ron (2002). *Intellectual Character: What It Is, Why It Matters, and How to Get It* (San Francisco, CA: Jossey-Bass).

Ritchhart, Ron (2015). *Creating Cultures of Thinking: The 8 Forces We Must Master to Truly Transform Our Schools* (San Francisco, CA: Jossey-Bass).

Ritchhart, Ron, Church, Mark, and Morrison, Karin (2011). *Making Thinking Visible: How to Promote Engagement, Understanding and Independence for All Learners* (San Francisco, CA: Jossey-Bass).

Roberts, Hywel, and Kidd, Debra (2018). *Uncharted Territories: Adventures in Learning* (Carmarthen: Independent Thinking Press).

Robson, David (2019). *The Intelligence Trap: Why Smart People Do Stupid Things and How to Make Wiser Decisions* (London: Hodder and Stoughton).

Sandringham Primary School (2016). "Introducing Sandringham Primary School" [video] (19 January). Available at: https://www.youtube.com/watch?v=Ah0JRQikKhQ.

Seleznyov, Sarah (2016). Improvement Through Lesson Study. Available at: https://www.academia.edu/35010144/Improvement_through_Lesson_Study.

Seligman, Martin (2011). *Flourish: A New Understanding of Happiness and Well-Being – and How to Achieve Them* (London: Nicholas Brealey Publishing).

Smith, Alistair, with Lovatt, Mark, and Turner, John (2009). *Learning to Learn in Practice: The L2 Approach* (Carmarthen: Crown House Publishing).

Stobart, Gordon (2014). *The Expert Learner: Challenging the Myth of Ability* (Maidenhead: Open University Press).

Sutcliffe, Roger, Bigglestone, Tom, and Buckley, Jason (2019). *Thinking Moves A-Z: Metacognition Made Simple* (London: One Slice Books).

Thomas, Douglas, and Seely Brown, John (2011). *A New Culture of Learning: Cultivating the Imagination for a World of Constant Change* (Createspace).

Thompson, Marnie, and Wiliam, Dylan (2008). Tight but loose: a conceptual framework for scaling up school reforms. In E. Caroline Wylie (ed.), *Tight but Loose: Scaling Up Teacher Professional Development in Diverse Contexts*. Educational Testing Service Research Report. Ref: ETS RR-08-29, pp. 1–44. Available at: https://www.ets.org/Media/Research/pdf/RR-08-29.pdf.

Tough, Paul (2012). *How Children Succeed: Grit, Curiosity and the Hidden Power of Character* (Boston, MA: Houghton Mifflin Harcourt).

Watkins, Chris (2001). Learning about learning enhances performance. *National School Improvement Network Research Matters*, No. 13 (Spring).

Wiliam, Dylan (2016). *Leadership for Teacher Learning: Creating a Culture Where All Teachers Improve So That All Students Succeed* (Palm Beach, FL: Learning Sciences International).

About the Authors

Guy Claxton is a cognitive scientist with a special interest in education: how schools can expand young people's real-world intelligence. He is the author, co-author, or editor of around thirty books on learning, creativity, and intelligence, including *The Creative Thinking Plan* (with Bill Lucas), *What's the Point of School?*, *Building Learning Power*, and *The Wayward Mind*. His work on Building Learning Power (BLP) and the Learning Power Approach (LPA) has influenced schools across the world, from Buenos Aires to Sydney and Poland to Vietnam. He has been professor of the learning sciences at the University of Bristol, research director of the Centre for Real-World Learning at Winchester University, and is currently visiting professor of education at King's College London.

Jann Robinson taught modern history in both state and independent schools in New South Wales, Australia. In 2005 she was appointed as principal of St Luke's Grammar School in Dee Why, Sydney, and now serves as principal of St Luke's Dee Why and Bayview campuses. She holds a master's degree in educational leadership, a bachelor's degree majoring in English and history, and a diploma of education. Jann is a member of the Australian College of Educational Leaders (ACEL), and former chair of Heads of Independent Co-Educational Schools (HICES), and of the New South Wales/Australian Capital Territory branch of the Association of Heads of Independent Schools of Australia (AHISA).

Rachel Macfarlane is the director of education services at Herts for Learning. From 2007 until 2018 she was a national leader of education (NLE), serving as head teacher of three contrasting schools over a sixteen-year period. In 2011 Rachel joined Ark Schools to set up a new co-educational, all-through academy for 4–18-year-olds in Ilford, East London. This was judged to be outstanding in all areas by Ofsted in 2014 and again in 2018. The school won the Pearson Shine a Light Secondary School of the Year Award in 2018 and, in the same year, was shortlisted for the *TES* Secondary School of the Year Award. Rachel is a senior lecturer at the Institute of Education's London Centre for Leadership in Learning (LCLL).

Graham Powell has held posts at many levels within the education system in England, with roles including head of a large comprehensive school, Ofsted inspector, senior secondary advisor for a local authority, and principal consultant on BLP with TLO Limited. Throughout his career, he has maintained a passionate concern for students' learning that has been focused by his twenty-year professional relationship with Guy Claxton. He has worked with many schools throughout the UK, Ireland, and Spain. With Guy, he is the co-author of *Powering Up Students*, the LPA volume for high school teachers, as well as being co-author of other books, including *The Learning Powered School*, *Pathways to Classroom Observation*, and *Pathways to Coaching*.

Gemma Goldenberg worked in London primary schools for sixteen years, most recently as an assistant head teacher at Sandringham Primary School in Newham, where she led on curriculum design and CPD. Gemma has an MSc in psychology and is currently researching for her PhD, which focuses on the effect of learning environments on children's cognition, wellbeing, and behaviour. She lives on the borders of Essex and East London with her husband and three sons.

Robert Cleary is head teacher of Sandringham Primary School in Newham, East London. He has, so far, committed his career to the children and families of Forest Gate. He is one of the founding head teachers of Newham North Learning Partnership, which aims to facilitate a group of geographically close schools in collaborating and supporting each other. He has a deep interest in training the next generation of teachers. He is a board member of the London East Teacher Training Alliance (LETTA), which trains teachers for the London Boroughs of Tower Hamlets and Newham.